BIOGRAPHIES OF ALASKA-YUKON PIONEERS
1850-1950

Compiled and Edited

by

Ed Ferrell
Juneau, Alaska
1994

Heritage Books, Inc.

Copyright 1994 by

Ed Ferrell

Published 1994 by

HERITAGE BOOKS, INC.
1540-E Pointer Ridge Place,
Bowie, Maryland 20716
(301) 390-7709

ISBN 0-7884-0087-8

A Complete Catalog Listing Hundreds of Titles
on Genealogy, History, and Americana
Available Free on Request

Dedication

These biographies are dedicated to the pioneers of Alaska and the Yukon Territory.

Acknowledgments

I would like to express my appreciation to the staff of the Alaska State Historical Library for their help and suggestions.

Thanks are also due to Dee Longenbaugh, Observatory Books, and to Richard Wood, Alaska Heritage Book Shop, for allowing me to make copies of biographies found in their Alaskana collection.

I am especially grateful to my wife, Nancy Ferrell, for all the hours of typing she put into this project, and for formatting the manuscript into "camera ready" form.

C. Ed Ferrell
Juneau, Alaska 1994

Acknowledgments

I would like to express my appreciation to the following for providing me with biographical material:

Sheldon Jackson College, Sitka
Juneau Public Library, Juneau
Alaska State Historical Collections, Juneau
Alaska State Library, Juneau
Catholic Diocese of Juneau
Episcopal Diocese of Juneau
Alaskan Heritage Bookshop, Juneau
The Observatory, Juneau
THE INDEPENDENT, Middlebury, Vt.
ANCHORAGE DAILY TIMES, Anchorage
CORDOVA DAILY TIMES, Cordova
JUNEAU EMPIRE, Juneau
FAIRBANKS NEWS-MINER, Fairbanks
SITKA SENTINEL, Sitka
WRANGELL SENTINEL, Wrangell
WHITEHORSE STAR (Formerly WEEKLY STAR),
    Whitehorse, Yukon Territory, Canada

I am indebted to early-day Alaskan, Washington, and Canadian publications that are no longer active.

Thanks also to my wife, Nancy Ferrell, for her help.

Ed Ferrell
Juneau, Alaska 1994

A. J. ADAMS

Mr. Adams was born on a farm near Cedar Rapids, Iowa, in 1866. After going through the high school he took a technical course in civil engineering at Drake University, Des Moines, Iowa, teaching school during vacations to earn the money with which to complete his technical education after which he came west and engaged in the practice of civil engineering and surveying in the states of California, Oregon and Washington, which profession he is still practicing. He was for several years city engineer of Port Angeles, Washington, after which he had charge of the hydrographic work of the united States Geological Survey in western Washington which position he resigned to come to Alaska. With the commission as United States Mineral Surveyor he established headquarters in Valdez in the spring of 1901 and has made numerous official surveys around the prince William Sound country and the Copper River country. In the spring of 1908 he made a topographical survey of the townsite and afterwards platted and laid out the town of Cordova.

Mr. Adams is city engineer of Cordova and is the owner of the Adams Block, corner First Street and "C" Avenue.

ALASKA-YUKON MAGAZINE, December 1910

CAPTAIN CHARLES S. ALDRICH

He was born at Tipton, Iowa, September 7, 1872. His father was a farmer and stock raiser, and one of the pioneers of the state, and a member of a family that came to the United States in an early day. Capt. Aldrich's boyhood days were spent in Tipton, where he was graduated from the high school. Subsequently he took a literary and a law course at the State University of Iowa, and he graduated in 1896 with the degree of LL. B.

He was practicing law in Marshaltown, Iowa, at the beginning of the Spanish-American war. He assisted in recruiting the 49th Iowa Volunteers, and was selected as captain in this regiment, serving under General Fitzhugh Lee until after the conclusion of the war. His company was mustered out in Savannah, Ga., May 13, 1899, and Captain Aldrich returned to Iowa, and resumed the practice of law at Marshaltown. The stories of the new gold fields discovered in Northern Alaska induced him to go to Nome. He arrived in the camp in the spring of 1900, and opened a law office. He practiced law until the spring of 1903, when Judge Moore appointed him to the office of United States Commissioner of the Fairhaven District. He took charge of the office July 20, 1903, and resigned the following summer upon receipt of the news of his father's death and returned home.

NOME AND SEWARD PENINSULA, 1905

ANDREW ANDERSON

Mr. Anderson was born in Norway, August 2, 1861, moving to San Francisco first and then to Seattle in 1873, where he had since maintained his home. He went to Skagway in 1897, returned to Seattle, but again went north, going to Dawson, Y.T., in 1898. His family followed him there in 1899. After mining on 37A Gold Run for some time, he became a member of the firm of Anderson Bros. & Nerland, handling painting, decorating, hardware and furnishings, with stores in Dawson, Fairbanks, Iditarod, and Ruby.

Mr. Anderson disposed of his business in the Northland and returned to Seattle in 1913.

Andrew Anderson died July 22, 1929 in Seattle, Washington. He is survived by his widow, Mrs. Amanda Anderson; his daughter, Mrs. N.W. Schoning; two sons, Andrew W. and Myron W. Anderson; and two grandsons, all of Seattle. In addition, he leaves three brothers, Herman, Emil and Antone Anderson, and two sisters, Mrs. Mathea Larsen and Mrs. Mary Jones, all of Seattle.

ALASKA WEEKLY, July 26, 1929

CARL ANDERSON

Carl Anderson was born on a farm near

Kalmar, Sweden. When sixteen years old he went to Stockholm, and learned the trade of painting and apaper hanging. In 1891 he immigrated to the United States, and lived in Chicago until 1898. In the latter part of this period he learne the trade of a tailor's cutter.

In February, 1898, he started for the Klondike. He sailed on the Argo to to St. Michael, and the vessel continued the journey up the Yukon to Rampart. Mr. Anderson spent two winters in Rampart. The first winter he prospected and mined on Little Minook. In the summer of 1899 he worked in the woods cutting logs for Fort Gibbon. This work furnished him a "grub-stake" for the following winter. During the winter he mined on Little Minook, Jr., and he and his partner found the best pay ever discovered on this stream.

In the spring of 1900 he came to Nome. He was employed by the Pioneer Mining Company, and in the following winter he and John Johnson went to the Kougarok District. Mr. Anderson remained on the Kougarok prospecting, while Mr. Johnson went to the Arctic slope. Returning to Nome in February, he and his partner nearly perished. They were two weeks on the trail, and one night were compelled to sleep in a snowdrift. The heat of their bodies melted snow, and next morning when they started on their journey their clothes were wet. As soon as they encountered the open air their clothes froze. When they finally arrived at Sliscovich's road-house Mr. Sepola, his partner, was badly frozen.

September 15, 1901, he and John Johnson started for Candle Creek. They spent the following winter in unsuccessful prospecting on Candle, Chicago and Willow Creeks, living in a tent. In the following summer he worked for Mr. Sundquist, and had charge of a shift on No. 18 Candle. In the latter part of the season he, John Johnson and John Roberg went to the Kobuk region. He mined on the Shungnak in 1903, and near the close of the season returned to Candle. His attempt to return to the Shungnak diggings that fall was frustrated by the misfortune that befell the steamer Riley, which got caught by the ice at the delta near the mouth of the Kobuk. He, with the other passengers, took a part of their supplies to the first timber and built cabins, where they spent the winter. Before the close of the year Mr. Anderson took a trip to the Shungnak and did some assessment work. In the summer of 1904 he worked on Dall Creek and extracted $2,000 in dust.

In the fall of 1904 Mr. Anderson returned to Nome and accepted John Johnson's offer to go in partnership with him on a lease of the Portland Bench. Taking Nels Peterson as another partner, these three men began the work of sinking holes on this claim in November. Pay had not been found, and they were discouraged, however they had enough coal to sink another shaft, which was to be their final effort. Mr. Anderson was working under ground. He sent up a pan of gravel taken from the end of the drift. This pan contained more than two dollars in gold. A second pan contained eight dollars. Investigation revealed the edge of an old beach deposit in which the sands glistened with gold. In sixty days a dump was taken out which, when cleaned up, yielded $413,000. It was the richest gold placer ever discovered.
NOME AND SEWARD PENINSULA, 1905

MORTON E. ATKINSON

Morton Atkinson is manager of the Nome Trading Company, a mercantile corporation that has been doing business in Nome since 1900. He was born December 27, 1875, at Port Discovery, Washington, and received his education in the public schools of the State of Washington. His father, J.M.E. Atkinson, conducts an extensive insurance business in Seattle, and the con's business training was obtained in his father's office.

M.E. Atkinson first came to Nome in 1901, but did not assume the management of the business until the fall of 1903. In the early spring of 1903, before the snow disappeared, he made a trip with a dog team to the Tanana

Region which is 850 miles from Nome. Returning that summer by steamer he, at the close of navigation, took charge of the company's business in Nome and has been ever since the manager. The Nome Trading Company is one of the leading mercantile institutions of this country.

M.E. Atkinson was married October 21, 1896. His wife was formerly Miss Mary M. Gullison of Portland, Oregon.

NOME AND SEWARD PENINSULA,   1905

FREDERIC NELSON ATWOOD

Fred Atwood was born in Boston, Mass. Early in life Fred studied decorative art, attending several art schools in the East. Later, under the guidance of his father, who had attained national prominence in that line, he specialized in fresco decoration and beautified many of the theatres in the cities of America. A desire to pioneer brought him to the Pacific coast in 1890. His first job on the coast was the decorating of Ezra Meeker's home at Puyallup. In 1892 Fred homesteaded on the Queets river on the western slope of the Olympics, later returning to Seattle, where he acted as a physical instructor in the Y.M.C.A.

Returning to Chicago in 1895, he became associated with his father in the theatre decorating business. While in Chicago he married a Seattle girl, Mary C. Taylor, the daughter of Prof. Joseph Marion Taylor, who for many years was connected with the University of Washington as instructor of mathematics and astronomy. Leaving Chicago in the fall of 1897, Fred headed for the Klondyke, packing his three-year outfit over the Chilkoot Pass. Making thirty-five trips over the pass, packing the whole outfit on his back; piloting boats through the rapids; were all a part of his adventurous life in the Northland.

After three years of fruitless prospecting Fred took up his old profession and managed to accumulate enough money to start a decorating, paper handing and paint business in Dawson. When he came outside to purchase the stock Mrs.

Atwood returned to Dawson with him. Four of their six children were born in that city. Always active in theatricals, athletic and lodge work, Fred became Arctic Chief of the Dawson Camp of the Arctic Brotherhood.

He returned to Seattle in 1912 with his family where he is now living at 1918 North 82nd street. Since 1912 he has been connected with the New York Life Insurance Company.

ALASKA WEEKLY, August 30, 1929

AMOS M. BABER

Amos Baber was born in Kansas, Ill., on November 18, 1864. After leaving college his first business experience was as cashier in the bank of an uncle, Asa Baber, who was president of the First National Bank of Paris, Illinois.

In 1897 at the first news of the gold strike in the Klondike, the young bank teller organized a trading company which late in the fall of '98 established a trading post at Rampart on the Yukon, that being as far as they could get that year after bucking the flow of ice. In 1899 he sold the trading post and went on to Dawson. In 1900 he went down the Yukon in an open boat to St. Michael and on to Nome where in 1901 he together with W.J. Barnes, published the first YUKON TERRITORY AND ALASKA DIRECTORY. In 1902 he sold the directory to F.R. Barnes and A.A. Bass, and the same year became post manager of the Eastern Siberian Trading and Transportation.

In 1906 he bought the sailing ship SOFIA JOHNSON and became a traveling trader for two years, during which time he brought to Seattle fifty-five Eskimos and erected an Eskimo village which merited such wide attraction that people from all over the world came to the Alaska-Yukon Exposition in 1909 to see them.

At the close of the Fair he journeyed to Europe, where he joined Carl Hagenback of Hamburg, Germany, in reproducing the world's famous Tier Garden of that city in Rome, Italy. At the conclusion of this enterprise he went to London, England, and then in 1920 to Paris, France where he entered into a contract with the Park Board to secure for them a colony of the famous Philippine Igorote head-hunters fifty of whom he delivered to them in 1911 at almost the cost of his life. That same year he returned to London and became associated with Frank Bostock, known as "the Animal King." After the death of Mr. Bostock in 1912, Captain Baber returned to New York, bringing with him half of the Bostock animals, and opened a show in New York. The advent of the World War closed the show business for awhile, and in 1914 he organized the Bronx International Exposition Co., which was also forced to close at the time the United States entered the world conflict. At this time he moved to Chicago, then to Portland, Ore., and back to Seattle in 1926.

Captain Baber, during his later years became interested in the lumber and oyster business in the Northwest. He died in Seattle, Wa., September 22, 1933. He is survived by his widow, Mrs. Helen S. Barer.
ALASKA WEEKLY, September 29, 1933

J. E. BAKER

J. E. Baker was born in Wisconsin in 1860. Before going North, he had lived for many years in Eugene and Salem, Oregon.

Mr. Baker soon after his arrival in the Northland, in 1898, worked for the Alaska Commercial Company at Fortymile and at Dawson, from 1898 until 1904. From Dawson, he went to Fairbanks, where he was with the Northern Commercial Company in that camp and in Hot Springs until 1908, when he was transferred to Ophir, in the Innoko district, and later to Tarotna, in the upper Kuskokwim. He remained at these two posts from 1908 to 1912. Later, he went with the Kuskokwim Commercial Company and was with that concern from 1912 to 1914. For the past ten years, Mr. Baker had lived at Ophir and at Tacoma. Two years ago, he was a candidate for the territorial legislature from the Fourth division of Alaska.

Mr. Baker died in Seattle, Washington, February 6, 1925. He is survived by two daughters, Mrs. L. Marsters of Eugene, and Mrs. Maybelle E. Hughes of Salem, Oregon, and by a brother Will V. Baker of Crescent City, California.

ALASKA WEEKLY, February 13, 1925

LEONARD D. BALDWIN

Leonard D. Baldwin was born in Cortland, New York, on May 29, 1867, where he spent his childhood days. He later entered Cornell University, from which institution he graduated in law with the same class as his brother, Arthur J. Baldwin. Both started in the practice of law at North Tonawanda, moving to New York City later. Mr. Baldwin was the senior member of the well known law firm of Griggs, Baldwin & Baldwin.

Active in civic affairs of his community, Leonard Baldwin headed the campaign of the Welfare of the Oranges. He was president of the Y.M.C.A. and speaker of the Men's Bible Class of the Methodist Episcopal Church of East Orange.

Eight years ago he became interested in the reindeer industry of Alaska and was associated with the Lomen Reindeer Corporation as their financial head. He devoted much time money and energy to develop the raising of reindeer, and made an intensive study of conditions in the Northland where he made several trips for that purpose.

Leonard D. Baldwin died in New York City in January, 1932.

ALASKA WEEKLY, January 27, 1932

M. D. BALL

The Honorable M.D. Ball was born on the 23rd day of June, 1835, in Fairfax county, Virginia. He was educated at the Episcopal High School, near Alexandria, and at William and Mary College, receiving the degree of Master of Arts from the latter institution. He then taught school until the war broke out.

He raised a company of cavalry, after the John Brown raid, and was mustered into the Confederate service April 25th, 1861, and ordered to Alexandria. He was captured with part of his company when that town was occupied by the Federal forces in May, 1861, owning to orders given him to stay behind and remove stores under a supposed agreement under flag of truce. Being exchanged at the first regular cartel, September, 1862, he reorganized his company and was assigned to the Eleventh Virginia Cavalry. He saw continued service from that time, was three times wounded, and at the close of the war was Colonel of his regiment.

Retiring to civil life he practiced law in Alexandria from 1865 to 1872, then founded the Virginia Sentinel, and conducted it as an independent political paper, successfully, until 1876. In January, 1878, he was appointed Collector of Customs for Alaska, and held the office until removed by President Garfield, June 2nd, 1881. In 1885 he was appointed to the position of United Stated District Attorney for the District of Alaska.

Colonel Ball died September 13, 1887 aboard the steamer Ancon in the Tongass Narrows, enroute to California. He is survived by his wife and children; a married daughter, Mrs. Gilmore, who lives in Washington, D.C.

ALASKAN, Sept. ?-Oct. 1, 1887

JOHN E. BALLAINE

A large number of men write history, but only a few men make history. John E. Ballaine, of Seattle and Seward, is one of the few men on the Pacific Coast who have made permanent history that will continue to grow larger through the centuries. Without his foresight and planning and work, there would be no Alaska Railroad, no Seward, no Anchorage, no Wassilla, nor any of the other thriving towns up and down the 467 miles of the Alaska Railroad. When he started promoting and building the Alaska Central Railway in 1902, and founded Seward as its terminus in 1903, later to have them incorporated in the Government-owned Alaska Railroad, he foresaw that Alaska's future would be built largely on agriculture, gardening, dairying, coal and copper mining, timber developments, and kindred industries, and not on placer gold mining alone, as then was popularly believed.

When John Ballaine started his numerous Alaska projects, all of which he has put over, he was barely turned thirty years of age, but he had then attained high distinction. Left an orphan at 13 by the death of his father, a Civil War veteran, he helped to support his widowed mother, worked his own way through school, and became one of the best known newspaper men in the state before he was 26 years of age. At 27 he was secretary to Governor John R. Rogers, and at 29 was Adjutant General of the State of Washington with the rank of Brigadier General. He served as an officer in the 1st Washington Infantry regiment in the Philippines through the Spanish American War and the Philippine Insurrection. Back of that, he had a long ancestry of Norman Huguenot parentage from the Isle of Jersey and from Normandy. Both of his parents were natives of the Isle of Jersey, and came to America in their childhood in 1848, locating in Iowa, where John was born in 1868. The families of both of his parents were near-blood relatives for many centuries of other Isle of Jersey families that figure prominently in American affairs--the Carterets, of whom George Carteret was founder of New Jersey; the Cabots and the Thoreaus of New England; the Poindexters and the Le Boutilliers. Former Senator George Turner of Spokane said recently, "John Ballaine has more varied and accurate information on more subjects, such as history, philosophy, law, geography, world conditions, and the sciences, and his mind works with clearer logic and precision, than any other man I have ever known."

ALASKA WEEKLY, May 31, 1929

ESTHER QUINER BARBER

Esther Barber, as a young bride, left her home in Iowa, and in a covered wagon, traveled the Oregon Trail and into Oregon. The trip over the plains was made in the days when the Indians were dangerous.

Her first husband having passed on, Mrs. Barber married Abraham Barber in Portland, Oregon, in March 1895, and as a wedding trip, they elected to go to alaska. Three days later, they took passage on the steamer Alki and landed in Juneau, where they built a 16x30 foot house and started a restaurant. Business was not brisk in those pioneer days and the Barbers decided to take a trip to Kansas to visit Mr. Barber's folks. They were back in Juneau late in the fall, fully determined to go to the Circle City camp on the Yukon. They sold their restaurant, bought an outfit and headed for Dyea.

Their trip over the Chilkoot and down the Yukon to Circle City was a piece of real pioneering. It was made during the winter of 1895-6, during a time when there were no roadhouses along the trail; no stores at which to purchase supplies; no accommodations whatever. They lived in a tent; slept on boughs; endured extreme cold; had several narrow escapes from the elements. Mrs. Barer's three children by her first husband, Rita, aged ten, and Henry and John, made the trip with them.

On arriving at Circle City in the spring of 1896, they opened a restaurant. Mrs. Barber attended to the restaurant, while Mr. Barber worked for the N.C. Company and the N.A.T. Company. They lived in Circle City until George Carmack brought in the Klondike camp. In the spring of 1897, Mrs. Barber went to the new Eldorado, bringing provisions, and opened a restaurant.

In 1900, Mrs. Barber had a restaurant at Nome. In 1901, they went to the Koyukuk, by dog team, traveling by compass. Later, they had a roadhouse at Cleary Creek, at the mouth of Chatham, which they sold to George Addington in 1903. In 1904, they had a store at Grael, near Fairbanks. In 1907, Mrs. Barber had a clothing store in Fairbanks. From there, they went to Cordova and opened an apartment house.

That was in 1910.

Off and on since 1910, the Barbers lived in Oakland, California, where they had a beautiful home. "Ma" Barber was always thrilled when she could give nuggets to friends who appreciated them, while traveling about. She had lived in practically every interior camp in the North; was known to most of the oldtimers, and was loved by them for her pioneering spirit, her generosity, her many charitable deeds.

Esther Quiner Barber died February 23, 1926 in Prince Rupert, B.C., Canada.
ALASKA WEEKLY, March 26, 1926

WILLIAM HARRISON BARD

W. H. Bard is a pioneer lawyer of Nome, a prominent member of the bar of Northwestern Alaska, and has the distinction of having been the fourth mayor, under municipal organization, of the city. He was born February 13, 1860, and is a native of Genesee, Illinois. His parents moved to Iowa during his infancy, and his father enlisted in the Union army and was killed at the battle of Gettysburg. In 1868 the family moved to Nebraska where Mr. Bard resided until he was sixteen years old. He then went to the Black Hills, and served two years as courier of the U. S. scouts under Captain Jack. In '78 he went to Denver and worked at the freighting business, driving one of the first mule teams from Denver to Leadville. Later he mined near Georgetown, and was the discoverer of the Little Florence Silver Mine which he sold for $3,000. Six weeks after the sale, the property was resold for $60,000. With the money from the sale of the mine he went to Europe.

Returning to Chicago he found employment in a music store, and applied himself by attending night school to the acquisition of a better education than the opportunities of a frontier life afforded. He studied law in Danville, Ill., in the office of Judge J. W. Lawrence, subsequently attending Ann Arbor, and was graduated from the law department of that institution. He practiced law in Chicago for a time. Through an operation for tonsillitis he was unable to speak above a whisper for more than a year, and was forced to temporarily abandon his practice. During this affliction he went to Cumberland, Maryland, and founded the Kennedy Manufacturing Co., wholesale grocers, but recovering the use of his voice he went back into the practice of law, opening offices in Pittsburgh, Pa., and devoting his time entirely to the specialty of insurance law.

In 1897 the reports of the new Eldorado in the Yukon Territory revivified the germs of the gold fever. He accordingly started west again and went north over the White Pass, reaching Dawson that year. Being one of the first lawyers in Dawson he was permitted to practice by the Dominion Government, but devoted most of his time to mining. He was the first discoverer of gold in the benches of Lower Bonanza, and owned an interest in eight claims opposite 46 below, left limit of this stream. The property was very valuable, but being undeveloped its value was unknown. The owners of the property got into a wrangle and Mr. Bard sold his interest for $8,000. Half a million dollars was afterward taken out of these claims.

The favorable reports received from the Nome camp induced him to join the stampeders to the new diggings. Arriving in Nome September 30, 1899, he opened a law office in the Muther building, in a room about as big as a dry goods box, furnished with a crude table and stools made out of boxes, and began the practice of law. His library consisted of the Criminal Code and the Code of Oregon. He filled the position of acting U. S. Attorney and discharged the duties of this office until the arrival of District Attorney Joe Wood, July 15, 1900. During his incumbency he prosecuted 110 criminal cases before U. S. Commissioner Rawson, the only court here at that time.

Mr. Bard was elected to the common council

at the municipal election in 1903, and in September of that year was unanimously selected by his associates to preside over the deliberations of that body, and discharge the duties of mayor of Nome. During his incumbency the council took the first steps toward securing a patent for a townsite, constructed a city hall and added to the equipment of the fire department. Mr. Bard, both as a lawyer and as the leading official of the municipality, took an active part in getting the measure before Congress permitting municipalities to handle misdemeanors. As the Alaska Code provided penalties for misdemeanors, it was not unusual in the earlier history of Nome for a person to be arrested and fined under the city ordinance and re-arrested and fined for the same offence by the federal authorities.

W. H. Bard and Miss Gussie Saunders were married in Dawson in 1898. Mrs. Bard is a native of Tampico, Illinois, which is only twenty miles from the town where Mr. Bard was born, but they never knew each other until they met in Dawson. They have one child, Edgar Burton Bard, now in his third year.

In 1888 Mr. Bard joined in Cumberland, Maryland, the following orders: Masons, Knights of Pythias, I. O. O. F., and Chosen Friends. As a Mason he has taken the Knight, Templar and the Mystic Shrine. He is a member of Nome Camp, Arctic Brotherhood, and has served two terms as Worthy President of Nome Aerie, No. 75, F. O. E., being at this writing District Deputy Grand President of the order at Nome.

NOME AND SEWARD PENINSULA, 1905

CALVIN H. BARKDULL

Calvin H. Barkdull first went to Southern Alaska in 1894, and his first mining venture was the location of mining claims on Annette Island. The Rev. Father Duncan, who had established a native colony on the island, aided him in running the lines. Later, he relocated the old Russian copper properties at

Kassan Bay. In June of that year, he joined the gold stampede to the Unuk river country, being one of the twenty who went in there. He went to Juneau in 1895, and was in Sundum Bay when the Bald Eagle mine was discovered. Later, he went to Unga, Southwestern Alaska, where he helped to install the chlorination works and dam and pip line in the Apollo mine, operated by the Alaska Commercial Company. Going outside from Unga, Mr. Barkdull was again attracted to the Northland by the discovery of gold in the Klondike. With a partner, he engaged in freighting over the White Pass and Chilkoot Pass. In July, 1898, he went to the Atlin, B.C. district. He owned and operated the Golden Gate group of claims above Nugget Point, on Pine Creek. In 1900 he located the Columbia Hydraulic Mines claims on upper Spruce Creek. In 1902 located the marble mines at Red Bay, on Prince of Wales Island, and two years later located a garnet mine at the mouth of the Stikine River. He owned and operated a fox farm on Sockeye Island, S.E. Alaska, for several years. In 1907 he was exploring in the Valdez country, was interested in mines at Kuperanoff in S.E. Alaska in 1909-10. At present, Mr. Barkdull is operating mines in California.
ALASKA WEEKLY, May 3, 1929

GEORGE HIRAM BARNES
George Barnes was born in Erie County, Ohio in 1864. At the age of 22 he came to Wrangel, to take charge of the Presbyterian mission farm for boys at Farm Island at the mouth of the Stikine river. Two years later he married Miss Ella Robinson, who had come from Pennsylvania as a worker in the Presbyterian mission school.

After leaving mission work Mr. Barnes entered the logging business and in 1912 with his brother-in-law, the late O.A. Brown, built the Sanitary Packing Company Cannery which they operated until the plant was destroyed by fire in 1923.

During all the years that Mr. Barnes was a

resident of Wrangell he was active in civic and church affairs. He served for several years as United States Commissioner, as mayor of Wrangell and at various times as a member of the town council and school board.

George Barnes died in Modesto, California, May 16, 1932. He is survived by his wife and son, Elton.

WRANGELL SENTINEL, May 20, 1932

GEORGE T. BARRETT, SR.

George Barrett, Sr. was born in New Brunswick, Canada. Mr. Barrett spent his early youth in hazardous occupations in the Minnesota woods. From there he went to Montana where he served as a scout in the Indian wars, first under General Custer and then under General Nelson A. Miles. He bore to his death bullet wounds received when captured by the Indians before the historic Custer's Massacre. In the fall of 1878 he decided to seek adventure further afield and went to San Francisco. The next spring shortly after his 25th birthday he shipped for the Pribilofs under a three-year contract with the old Alaska Commercial Company which had the concession for the seal rookeries, and owned a number of trading posts. Mr. Barrett represented his company for years mainly at ports in westward Alaska. He then bought a trading schooner of his own which he operated for several years and the latter years of his half century of residence in the Territory were spent at Katalla.

George Barrett, Sr. died March 20, 1939 at his son's(George T. Barrett) home in Wrangell, Alaska. Two sons and two daughters survive Mr. Barrett; George T. of Wrangell, Don of Seattle, Mrs. Otto Kulper of Cordova, and Mrs. Paul Succsini, Meriden, Conn. Two sisters live in Minneapolis. There are several grandchildren, nieces and nephews.

ALASKA CATHOLIC, April 8, 1939

J. A. BAUGHMAN

J. A. Baughman, M.D., was born in 1855. He is a native of Michigan (some sources give

Ohio), where he practiced medicine for eighteen years after graduating from Bellevue Hospital Medical College in 1880. He joined the Klondike rush in the spring of 1898 and went to Dawson, returning to Skagway in 1899 where he remained, practicing his profession, for six years. In 1906 he moved to Seward with his wife and daughters, Beatrice and Dorothy.

He was interested in the Oracle mine with bert Higgins, and also ran a small private hospital at the rear of the Van Gildren hotel.

Dr. Baughman also operated several drug stores in Seward, and he was physician for the Alaska railroad with his headquarters at Seward.

A graduate of Bellevue Medical College, New York, Dr. Baughman went to California before the Southern Pacific was connected with San Francisco.

Mrs. Baughman, who was preceded in death by Beatrice, passed away seven years ago. Dorothy is married and living in Juneau.

John Albert Baughman died in Juneau, Alaska, November 1937.

ALASKA-YUKON MAGAZINE, July 1911
VALDEZ MINER, Dec. 10, 1937

MICHAEL JOHN BAVARD

Michael Bavard was born in Greece, March 3, 1891. When he was sixteen years old he came to the United States and spent the years between 1907 and 1917 in Portland, Oregon, and Vancouver, B.C. In April, 1917, he came to Alaska and established the California Fruit Company, which later became the California Grocery. His younger brother, Nick Bavard, who had followed him to this country in 1910, joined him in Alaska a few months after his arrival here and has been associated in business with him since that time.

Mike Bavard entered the army during the World War in May 1918,, and spent the duration of his service at Fort Seward.

He was married to a Juneau girl, Edith Messerschmidt, daughter of Gus Messerschmidt.

In 1927 Mike Bavard decided to leave the

business here and seek other field. Mr. and Mrs. Bavard made a six months tour of Europe and after visiting the Bavard's former home in Greece, returned to the united States and lived for some time in Los Angeles. They returned to Juneau in August, 1929, and have since made their home here.

Mike Bavard died April 20, 1933. The only surviving relatives of Mr. Bavard are his widow and his brother, Nick.
Relatives-in-law in Juneau are Gus Messerschmidt, father of Mrs. Bavard, Henry and George Messerschmidt, her brothers, and Mrs. George Shaw and Mrs. Jack Schmitz, sisters of Mrs. Bavard. Mrs. L.C. Nelderhelman of Chicago is a sister of Mrs. Bavard and William Biggs, of Hirst-Chichagof, is a brother. Mrs. Nick Bavard, formerly Mary Conner, is also a member of a pioneer Juneau family.

Mike Bavard was prominent in the local Elks lodge and in the American Legion.
ALASKA WEEKLY, April 28, 1933

JOSEPH A. BAXTER
Mr. Baxter was born in Boston in 1852 and removed to San Francisco in his early youth. He lived in that city until he went to Nome in the early days . He was engaged there in mining for several years when he went to Valdez. About ten years ago he came to Juneau.

He was always interested in political matters, and for many years was an important member of the Democratic organization in San Francisco, during the days that Chris Buckley was the Democratic leader there. After coming to Alaska he continued his interest in politics, and was a delegate to several Democratic Territorial conventions. He was elected Chairman of the Democratic Territorial Committee in 1914 and served in that capacity until succeeded by the late William T. Burns in 1916. He was an assistant in the Publicity Bureau, under E.J. White. He served as Sergeant-at-Arms in the Senate during the session of 1923.

Joseph Baxter died on June 8, 1927. He is

survived by his widow and a son, residents of San Francisco.
    ALASKA WEEKLY, June 17, 1927

ISADORE BAYLES

Was born in Libau, Courland in the year 1876. He came to America over thirty years ago, and for awhile worked in Victoria, G.C. In 1898 he started for Alaska, reaching Dawson in the spring of '99. Here he remained in business for six years, later going to Fairbanks. After six years in business here he took in the Iditarod, arriving there in 1915. From Iditarod Mr. Bayles came directly to Anchorage, where he is engaged in the clothing business, under the firm name of Jaffe & Bayles. He is president of the Anchorage school board.

Mr. Bayles was married in 1909, in New York city, to Miss Beatrice Schwartz. They have two girls, Edith and Dorothy.
    PATHFINDER, November 1919

B.M. BEHRENDS

B.M. Behrends was born in Hanover, Germany, in 1862, and came to the United States with his parents, locating in Nebraska City, Neb. where several relatives still reside.

In 1884 he went to California and in 1887 he landed in Alaska, at the age of 25 years. He first went to Sitka but after a few months, was appointed manager of the Sitka Trading Company, doing business in Juneau. For four years he held this position and then went into the mercantile business in Douglas in 1901. In 1904 he incorporated the mercantile business, and in 1904 incorporated the banking business which bears his name.

He was appointed Director of Savings for alaska during the World War, and served in that capacity with great credit. In politics he leaned toward the Democratic side. He was a member of the Presbyterian church but his gifts to other denominations ran up into the thousands.

Mr. Behrends was married in 1889 at Sitka

to Miss Virginia Pakke, a government school teacher. She was a native of West Virginia and came to Alaska in 1886. One child, Beatrice Margaret, now the wife of J. F. Mullen, was born to them. Three grandchildren also survive.

Mr. Behrends was instrumental in having the capital removed from Sitka to Juneau, its present site.

B.M. Behrends died in Cordova, Alaska, in August of 1936.

VALDEZ MINER, August 21, 1936

JAMES W. BELL

J. W. Bell is one of the bright young lawyers of Nome. He is a native of Newburn, Tenn., and was born August 2, 1870. When he was thirteen years old he moved to California. He attended Stanford University, and was graduated in 1897. He resided, while in California, in Fresno and Visalia. During Cleveland's administration his father was receiver in the land office at Visalia.

After his graduation he took an elementary course in law, and subsequently read law in Visalia. He was admitted to the bar March 13, 1900, and on April 21 succeeding, left California for Nome. When he arrived in the new mining camp he took a flyer at mining, but did not strike anything rich. October 2, 1900, he entered the District Clerk's office as assistant, and was appointed deputy district clerk February 19, 1901, to succeed John T. Reed, who went outside that winter. He resigned in July of that year and went to San Francisco with Judge Noyes, attending the famous trial in the contempt cases in the United States Circuit Court at San Francisco. He returned to Nome on one of the last steamers of the season, and has since engaged in the practice of his profession. He was city attorney in 1903.

NOME AND SEWARD PENINSULA, 1905

BURTON ELLSWORTH BENNETT

Burton Ellsworth Bennett was born April

17, 1863, at North Brookfield, Madison County, New York. After passing through the common schools of his native village he entered the Brookfield Academy at Brookfield New York, and graduated therefrom in his seventeenth year. He successfully passed all the examinations required by the Regents of the university of the State of New York and received its diploma. In the fall of 1881 he matriculated at the Cornell University at Ithaca, New York, and graduated therefrom in 1885 with Honors for General Excellence, being one of three in his course to obtain so high a standing. He was elected orator of his class and delivered the class day oration at commencement. In 1884-5 he was one of the senior editors of the Cornell Daily Sun, then, as now, the leading paper of the university. During his senior year he was also president of the Irving Literary Society. Always having the profession of the law in mind, Mr. Bennett, during the latter part of his course, turned his attention especially to international and constitutional law, American law and jurisprudence, modern history and political science.

After leaving the university he entered the law offices of E.H. Lamb of Waterville, New York, and after about a year went to Utica, New York and continued his reading with S. M. Lindsley one of the leading lawyers in central New York. Mr. Bennett was admitted to practice in all the courts of the state of New York in the fall of 1887. The same fall he came to Seattle, Washington and, except for a short time spent in California with an invalid brother, practiced his profession there until appointed United States District Attorney for Alaska by Ex-President Cleveland in 1895 to fill out the term of Lytton Taylor who had resigned.

The politics Mr. Bennett has always been a Democrat and his services have always been at the disposal of the Democratic party. In Seattle he established his home in Latona in the Ninth ward of that city and assisted in organizing the first Democratic club there. As long as he lived there he represented his ward in every city and county convention held. Mainly through his efforts the Ninth ward, which is normally Republican, went Democratic in 1892. The incoming administration made him a member of the Board of Park Commissioners of the city of Seattle which position he filled creditably during the years 1892-3-4. In 1892 he was one of the delegates from King county to the Democratic state convention at Olympia and in 1894 he was a member of the Yakima convention. From 1892 to 1894 he was a member of the Democratic executive committee of King county and also of the county central committee. In 1894 he was unanimously nominated by his party for representative from the Forty-third representative district of the state of Washington.

In 1895 he was appointed United States District Attorney for Alaska and shortly thereafter came to Sitka and has made his official residence here ever since. At his first term of court Judge Warren Truitt was on the bench.

Although Mr. Bennett was a new man in the country, and to our people, he was most successful. The Alaska Searchlight, then the leading paper of the territory, on December 7, 1895, had this to say about the term of court just ended: "United States Attorney Bennett has won the complete confidence of our people as none of his predecessors have ever been able to do. His success marks a distinctive era in the administration of civil law in Alaska...."

In 1896 he was appointed by Ex-Governor Sheakley one of the delegates from Alaska to the Mexican International Exposition to be held in the City of Mexico and this year he was appointed by Acting Governor Elliott one of the delegates from the territory to the International Mining Congress held in Salt Lake City. Mr. Bennett is a member of the Episcopal church and is the lay Delegate from the Diocese of Alaska to the General Convention of the American Church which meets in Washington city in October of this year. In masonry he stands high have had conferred upon him the 32nd degree.

ALASKAN, August 6, 1898

GEORGE L. BENNING

George L. Benning, former Alaskan, now engaged in the automobile business in Seattle, was born in Boone, Iowa, April 25, 1895. In 1900 the family moved to Colorado. After going through school, young Benning entered the employ as an accountant, of the Santa Fe Railroad, at Pueblo, Colorado, where he remained until the United States entered the World War. He enlisted in the U.S. navy and was assigned to the U.S.S.SATURN. The SATURN was sent to Alaska to visit all the radio stations, carrying supplied and making repairs. This was George Benning's first trip to the Northland. The SATURN, upon completing the Alaska trip, went to the Orient and to Vladivostok, Siberia, where a radio station was built, establishing the first direct radio communication between Siberia and the United States. While on the SATURN, Benning made five trips to Alaska.

Returning to private life after the signing of the armistice, Benning, in 1919, went to Alaska to work in the stores department of the Alaska Railroad, at Seward. Later he became auditor of the supply division, with headquarters in Anchorage. In 1922 Benning returned to the States and entered the automobile field at Portland, Oregon, selling Chevrolets. Since then he has been successively used car manager and sales manager with the Chevrolet organization in Portland, Spokane, and Seattle, and is now general manager for the Seattle Chevrolet.

ALASKA WEEKLY, November 22, 1929

EDWARD BENSON

Edward Benson has been a pioneer all his life, beginning on the prairies of Minnesota in 1873. When Minnesota became too thickly populated young Benson left his home state and moved to Washington state, then a territory.

There was plenty of pioneering to be done in the coast regions, but the mountains held a fascination. Consequently, in the spring of 1892, he traveled from Ellensburg to Lake Chelan and there received his initiation as a prospector, which occupation he has followed for thirty years. Benson heard of the Klondike strike while prospecting on Graham Island, northernmost island of the Queen Charlotte group. He was the first in the Northland during the great rush. He counts as an outstanding achievement the discovery and exploration of the Upper Donjek river region in 1905. This region is probably one of the best stocked big game regions on the North American continent. He has guided many expeditions of big game hunters, reconnaissance surveys, and Mounted Police patrols. He was married in 1919 and is now a resident of Seattle. Is associated with the United Groceries, a chain store organization, and is a pioneer in the upbuilding of that chain.

ALASKA WEEKLY, July 19, 1929

IDA MONTAGUE REESE BENTON

Mrs. Benton, whose maiden name was Ida Montague Reese, was born in Quincy, Ill., the daughter of Mr. and Mrs. William Armstrong Reese, pioneers of that state who trekked westward from Pennsylvania. mrs. Benton was educated in Wichita, Kan. and afterward came to Seattle and for years was a teacher here in the old Pacific school.

In June of 1914, she married Marvin Benton of Dawson City, Yukon Territory. They remained in Dawson and vicinity where Mr. Benton was one of the best known of gold dredging experts until 1922 when they came to the coast and after a time went to California. Later they went to Malay where they both spent some three years.

Ida M. Benton died in Seattle, January 15, 1932. She is survived by her husband, Marvin W. Benton, for many years dredgemaster on the Klondike Creeks for the Yukon Gold Co., and now serving in the same capacity for that company

in its extensive tin dredging operations in Malay. Mrs. Benton is also survived by two sisters, Mrs. James Stuart Ball, of Portland, Ore., and Miss Nell Reese of the same city.
ALASKA WEEKLY, January 22, 1932

JACOB BERGER
   Mr. Berger is a native of Germany and thirty-four years of age. He left the old country when he was a small boy. When twelve years old he sold newspapers in St. Paul and Philadelphia. Since the age of eighteen he has been engaged in mining, his first mining venture being in British Columbia. He went to Dawson via Juneau in 1897, and came down the Yukon of Nome in 1899. He began mining in the Nome country on the beach. During this summer he and J. T. Sullivan located property on Daniel's Creek in the Topkuk country.
NOME AND SEWARD PENINSULA, 1905

BRAXTON BIGELOW
   Braxton Bigelow was graduated from Harvard in 1905 and from Massachusetts Institute of Technology in 1910, and was employed in Peru as a mining engineer at the outbreak of war. He returned to New York and sailed to England on December 26, 1914. He first served with the American Ambulance Field Service and later in Siberia with a hospital unit. For bravery and unselfish work he received a medal. Returning to England in April 1916, he obtained a commission in the British army as lieutenant in the Royal Artillery and was sent to the front. Later he was transferred to the Royal Engineers, 170th Field Co., and early in the summer he was promoted to be captain. In August Captain Bigelow was slightly wounded and received six weeks leave. After his return to France he was near Lens when there was a suspicion that the Germans were engaged in mine work at a particular point in his sector. On the night of July 12, Captain Bigelow volunteered to head a small party of sappers to investigate, and was killed in action. He was mentioned in dispatches for bravery and

distinguished service. Captain Bigelow was the son of Major John Bigelow, U.S.A., retired and grandson of the late John Bigelow, author and minister in France under President Grant. He was a member of the American Institute of Mining Engineers.

Captain Braxton Bigelow was formerly a Douglas Island man who worked in the Mexican mine from December 1910 to May, 1912 and in the cyanide plant and 300 mill before leaving the Island in 1912.

ENGINEERING & MINING JOURNAL, May 4, 1918
DAILY ALASKAN, May 17, 1918

WILLIAM A. BISHOP

Born in Bishopville, Maryland, 1842. As a member of the Sixty-third First Maryland Infantry, he entered the Civil War when 21 years of age. In 1866 he entered the Quartermasters service in the regular army and for forty eight years served his country. He helped build Fort Phil Kearney Dakota, in 1866 and served at Ft. Smith on the Big Horn. From there to Ft. Lyons and from there to Texas, serving at Ft. Concho, thence to Ft. Davis, then back to Texas. Next he was with Roosevelt as a Rough Rider, later in the Third Cavalry. He next shows up at Manila and was at Leaty among the Moors. From there he was stationed at Panama, where he fell sick with a fever after nine years service. He then tried several climes endeavoring to regain his health. He wears a half dozen medals of honor, for heroic service. This war veteran of half a century's service came to Alaska directly from Texas, arriving here 1915 with the first settlers.

PATHFINDER, November 1919

WILLIAM J. BLACK

W. J. Black is one of the successful miners of this country. He is a native of Massachusetts, and went to Alaska from San Francisco in 1895. He has been in the Forty-Mile country and in Circle, and has mined in both of these regions. He came to Nome over

the ice in the winter of 1899-1900, and since his arrival has been actively engaged in mining, most of his work having been done on Dexter Creek and Arctic Creek.
NOME AND SEWARD PENINSULA, 1905

RINGWALD BLIX
Ringwald Blix was merchandising in Minneapolis, Minn. when gold was discovered in the Klondike. He went to St. Paul where he joined the Scandinavian Alaska Colonial Association, as its secretary-treasurer. The association numbered forty-nine members, nearly all of them being Scandinavians from the middle western states. The party took passage on the steamer PROTECTION from Seattle, March 1, 1898, en route to the Copper River country. The party landed at Valdez, then a tent town, and made their way over the Valdez glacier as far as the Klutina river. On a site selected for the purpose the town of Copper Center was founded. Mr. Blix built and opened up the first roadhouse and general merchandise store at that point, and filed on and secured a U.S. patent to the first homestead in Alaska. In 1904 he was appointed U.S. commissioner at Copper Center, and also had the post office. During the boom days of Fairbanks the Richardson Highway, then running between Valdez, on the coast, to Fairbanks, was the winter means of transportation which made of Copper Center an important point on the highway. In addition to his other activities Mr. Blix raised the first vegetables ever grown in the Copper River valley. Mr. Blix remained in Copper Center for twenty years; then came south to Seattle, where he now makes his home.
ALASKA WEEKLY, September 27, 1929

MEYER BLUM
Meyer Blum was 55 years of age and was born in Alsace, France, coming to this country 35 years ago. Since 1898, Mr. Blum was concerned in industrial and financial interests in Alaska, being associated with a cousin, Samuel blum, a widely known Alaskan figure, who

died some years ago.

Meyer Blum went to Valdez many years ago, to join the firm of S. Blum & company, in which he was financially concerned. Soon after his arrival there, Samuel Blum, the senior partner, started a mercantile establishment in Cordova with branches at Chitina and McCarthy, in the Copper river valley, and thereafter made his headquarters in Cordova, Meyer Blum taking charge of the business in Valdez. When Samuel Blum moved to Seattle to reside, Meyer Blum assumed charge of both the Valdez and Cordova interests, which included mercantile and baking businesses.

Mr. Blum moved to Seattle some two years ago and opened offices in the Lowman building. He died in August 1926.

ALASKA WEEKLY, August 13, 1926

S. BLUM

S. Blum is a native of California. He was born in San Francisco in 1868 and was educated in the public schools there and in Germany. He engaged in business in San Francisco when he was twenty-one years old.

In 1898 he located in Juneau, Alaska, having purchased the business of the firm of Kohler & James, one of the oldest concerns in Alaska and in 1900 he started a branch store in Valdez. In 1901 he closed out his business in Juneau and spent a couple of years in Seattle.

In 1903 he moved to Valdez where he took an active part in the management of this store and bank which were established the same year and he has lived there and in Cordova continuously since that time. In April, 1909, he started a store and bank in Cordova.

Mr. Blum is married and has two sons who were born in Valdez. He has a residence in Valdez and one in Cordova and divides his time between these two places which are only 75 miles apart.

Mr. Blum is one of the largest individual property owners on the west coast and is one of the original townsite owners of Cordova.

ALASKA-YUKON MAGAZINE, December 1910

GEORGE V. BORCHSENIUS

George V. Borchsenius was born in Madison, Wis., July 15, 1865. When he was twelve years old he moved with his parents to Baldwin. He attended the public schools of Wisconsin and subsequently was graduated from the law department of the State University. While a resident of Baldwin he learned the printers trade. At a later period he engaged in the hardware and general mercantile business, and subsequently, with his father and brother, conducted a real estate and loan agency under the firm name of H. Borchsenius & Sons. In 1885 he returned to Madison and assisted in the compilation of the state census. Following the completion of this work he was employed in the executive office by Governor Rusk, and at a later date was connected with the land office.

In 1891 he returned to Baldwin, and for a period of four years was in the real estate and loan business. In 1895 he went back to the capital as assistant to the state treasurer. He was here in 1899 when the reports of the wonderful Eldorado at Nome reached the states, and he determined to try his fortune in the newly discovered gold fields. In the spring of 1900 he received the appointment of Clerk of the U. S. District Court, and arrived in Nome and entered upon the discharge of his duties July 19. July 15, 1901 he was retired by Judge Noyes, but one year later he was reappointed to the office by Judge Moore.

Mr. Borchsenius has acquired by purchase considerable mining property in the vicinity of Nome, and has expended near $25,000 in its development. He is the owner of No. 12 Anvil Creek and three benches adjoining and near the famous and very rich Mattie claim. He has a controlling interest in Specimen Gulch property from Anvil Creek to Summit Bench. Besides these properties Mr. Borchsenius owns some quartz claims between Rock and Lindblom Creeks.

September 14, 1887, Mr. Borchsenius and Miss Lula M. Bockus were married in Baldwin, Wis. Harold, their only child, was born December 4, 1891. The father, mother and sister of Mr. Borchsenius reside at Madison, Wis. His father has retired from active business. His brother resides in Baldwin and is engaged in the real estate and loan business.

NOME AND SEWARD PENINSULA, 1905

R. J. BORYER

R.J. Boryer, the head of the legal department of the Copper River * Northwestern Railway in Cordova, is a Virginian, having been born in the northern part of the state.

Mr. Boryer was educated at Roanoke College and is also a law graduate of the Dickinson College of Carlisle, Penn. Previous to coming north he practiced in Pennsylvania and Seattle. He accepted a position with the present road in 1906 and was first stationed at Katalla, then the headquarters for the railway company.

When the base of operation was changed to Cordova, he removed to that city.

ALASKA-YUKON MAGAZINE, December 1910

ALBERT E. BOYD

Mr. Boyd is a native of County Grey, Province of Ontario, Canada, and was born in 1862 within a mile and a quarter of Georgian Bay. His father was born in Manchester, England, and his mother was Scotch, a sister of the Rev. Geo. McDougall, the pioneer missionary of the Northwest Territory who founded missions from Lake Superior to the Rocky Mountains. Albert was the youngest in a family of six boys and two girls. His early education was acquired in a log school house, but he never attended school after he was fourteen years old. When he was sixteen years old he determined to go to the Northwest Territory. One of his sisters had married the Rev. John McDougall and then was located at Morley Mission. His parents decided to go with him. It was a long journey, by boat to Duluth, by train to Bismarck, Dakota, by boat to Fort Benton, and thence 600 miles across country and into Canadian territory - into a new, wild country where white men's habitations were hundreds of miles apart.

The story of one incident is told here because it illustrates the character of the man. When twenty-one years old he made a trip of 262 miles in two days and thirteen hours and a half, and during this trip he drove three teams that had never been in harness before. He made this ride to get a doctor for a women who was ill. The nearest doctor was the Army surgeon at McCloud, 131 miles away.

He left Canada and went to the United States, arriving in Seattle in 1888. Here he bought and sold stock, broke many wild horses; also conducted several other kinds of business. In May of 1900, he sailed for Nome on the eighty-ton schooner Laurel. The vessel carried a cargo of lumber and other supplies. He was the managing agent of the schooner. It was in the latter part of the season of 1901 that he began the work of constructing a long-distance telephone line. With more than 250 miles of wire connecting the principal camps of the peninsula and with the system in the city of Nome, he organized a company in New York in 1905, the Alaska Telephone and Telegraph Company, and is prepared to extend the line to any part of the country.

A. E. Boyd and Miss Avaloo M. Steel were married in Victoria, B. C., August 31, 1899.
NOME AND SEWARD PENINSULA, 1905

RALPH BOYKER

Ralph boyker, pioneer of the Northland, was born in Maine in 1874. He reached the gold diggings in the Circle City district, Alaska, in 1896, where he mined on Deadwood Creek. In 1897 he went into the newly discovered Klondike diggings and opened the first restaurant in Dawson. This business, operated under the name of the Northern Cafe, flourished under the competent management of Boyker and his partner, the late Lon Griffin, and was noted as being the best eating place north of 53. Boyker imported the first eggs into the Klondike camp, landing with the precious cargo on the 17th of May, 1897.

Coming to Seattle from Dawson in 1902, he leased the Northern Hotel which he has conducted continuously up to the present time. Last year, he purchased the Stevens Hotel property, at First and Marion, and at this time he is operating both hotels. He enjoys the longest hotel operating record in the city of Seattle.

ALASKA WEEKLY, June 8, 1928

EDWARD V. BOYLE

Edward V. Boyle was born in Dover, in the state of Delaware. He migrated to Valdez, Alaska in January, 1904, where he was employed by his brother, Dr. F.M. Boyle who owned the Owl Drug store in that town. After the Fairbanks rush, Ed went to Seward and opened the Seward Drug company store; from thence he went to Katalla, where he opened the Katalla Drug company store. In 1908 he opened the Cordova Drug Company store at the old town of Eyak; later in the same year, he moved the store to the present town of Cordova. Ed started in by being a small stockholder in his first venture, and slowly, but surely, he grew until finally he became the controlling owner Cordova store. This he operated successfully until 1926, when he sold out and moved to Seattle. During his stay of twenty-two years in Alaska, Mr. Boyle took a prominent part in the moulding of affairs in the territory. He was a member of the first territorial board of pharmacy; was mayor of Cordova five successive terms; was chief of the Cordova branch of the Alaska Pioneers.

ALASKA WEEKLY, March 22, 1929

JOHN G. BRADY

John Green Brady arrived in Sitka in March of 1878 and immediately called the natives together in the old Baranoff Castle building, announcing his mission to educate them.

On April 17, 1878, Mr. Brady and Miss Fannie Kellogg opened the first Protestant native school in Sitka, in an upstairs room of the soldier's barracks. The present Sheldon

Jackson School is the lineal descendant.

Governor Brady was a firm believer in industrial education. So strongly was he of the opinion that this type of work was of first importance, that he withdrew from the mission, and devoted himself to industrial training. He started a sawmill, took a homestead, and in many other ways stimulated the movement toward individual homes and self support.

In 1897 he was appointed Governor of Alaska by President McKinley, and held this office for nine years. The remainder of his life was spent in active efforts to build the civil and commercial interests of the Territory.

His death occurred on the evening of December 17, 1918 at his homestead in Sitka.

ALASKA WEEKLY, June 11, 1926

ROBERT S. BRAGAW

Robert Bragaw was a direct descendent of the family of Bourgon Brouchard and his wife, Catherine Le Febre, French Huguenots from Manheim on the Rhine, who landed on Manhattan Island in 1675. They bought an estate in old Nassau and there established the family whose members are now variously known as Bragau, Bragaw and Brokaw. During the revolutionary war the old home, then owned by Richard Bragaw, was a rendezvous for patriots and all the members of the family bore arms in the struggle for independence.

Robert Bragaw was born at New London, Conn., October 1, 1851. He was educated in the public school of his native state and his first occupation was in a wholesale grocery house in New York City. At the age of 23 he moved west to Denver and engaged in the mining and real estate business. In 1883 he cast his destiny with the Couer d'Alenes and two years later married.

The official career of Mr. Bragaw began when he was appointed recorder of Kootenai county and he served in that capacity until 1890 when he was elected clerk of the district court and ex-officio county auditor and clerk of the county commissioners. He held that office until 1899. In that year he was appointed forest supervisor of the Priest River forest reserve and resigned that office in 1904 to become state auditor, in which office he was elected by a majority of 20,000 votes.

In 1906 Mr. Bragaw moved to Spokane, and engaged in the real estate business with his son. He moved to Los Angeles later and went to Anchorage in 1917, Having resided there since that time.

Robert Bragaw died in Anchorage, Alaska in March 1928.

ALASKA WEEKLY, March 9, 1928

JOHN BRANNEN

John Brannen was elected to the common council at the municipal election in 1903. In 1902 he filled a short term as chief of police for the city, and subsequently, as councilman, was appointed chairman of the police committee.

John Brannen was born in Pennsylvania in 1852. He is of Celtic ancestry and the son of a farmer. His education was obtained in the public schools and in a business college. Fourteen years of his life he spent in British Columbia as a coal miner. He went west with his mother when he was six years old, and followed the business of farming and mining until 1889, when he was appointed to a position on the police force of Seattle. He was subsequently promoted to lieutenant and finally to captain of police.

He came to Nome in 1900, and is in the liquor business. He is largely interested in mining in the Nome country. Mr. Brannen was married thirty years ago to Sarah McCool, of British Columbia. They have a family of seven children.

NOME AND SEWARD PENINSULA, 1905

HENRY BRATNOBER

Mr. Bratnober was born in Castrine, Prussia, in 1849, and immigrated with his parents to America in 1854. The family located in Galena, Illinois, and a year later moved to

Wisconsin. In 1864 Mr. Bratnober joined the army. He was a private in the Thirty-sixth Wisconsin, Second Corps of the Army of the Potomac. In 1866 he journeyed across the plains to Montana, and began his career as a miner.

In 1894 he visited Australia, where he remained a year and a half engaged in quartz mining. He began his life work as a miner in the placer camps of Montana, but has had a varied experience, which includes every kind of mining. In 1897 he went to the Klondike country, and has been identified with the northern gold fields ever since. The trip in '97 was an historic journey as he accompanied Jack Dalton, the man who blazed the trail from Haines Mission to Dawson. The following year Mr. Bratnober took another journey across country through an untraveled and unknown region in Alaska. This trip was from Haines Mission to the head-waters of White River. In 1903 he made a journey from Valdez to Eagle City, on the Yukon. In 1904 he went from Skagway to Tanana, and thence to St. Michael. A part of his travels in Alaska this year will consist of short journey's from the main trail to regions in Central Alaska, where prospecting parties sent out by Mr. Bratnober are exploring the country and hunting for the yellow metal.

Mr. Bratnober was married in Greenville, Illinois, in early life, and with his wife resides in Piedmont, California, where they have one of the most beautiful homes in that part of the country.
NOME AND SEWARD PENINSULA, 1905

LEO W. BREUER
Leo W. Breuer, the new commissioner of education of Alaska, was appointed to that position by the Territorial Board of Education.

Mr. Breuer, who is 32 years old and married, received an elementary and high school education in the schools of Whatcom County, state of Washington. In 1919 he graduated from the Washington State Normal School at Bellingham, Wash., and holds a life diploma from that institution. In 1926 he graduated from the Washington State University, receiving an A.B. degree in education. His educational work at the university was largely with the administrative phase of education.

His experience covers ten years in the schools of Washington and Alaska. He held positions as an elementary school teacher, beginning in a one-room school of eight grades; has taught in high school and has held positions as principal and superintendent.

His last position in the state of Washington was superintendent of a consolidated district. His experience in Alaska covers three years, Mr. Breuer having gone to Nome in 1926 as superintendent and remaining there for two years. Then he accepted a like position at Cordova for the year 1928-1929.

ALASKA WEEKLY, October 18, 1929

JOESPH H. BROOKS

Joseph Brooks was born in Manitoba, Canada, in 1860. He early became a butcher in his home town, and some time later he was married.

Later he and his wife traveled to San Francisco, where he worked as a butcher for the Bay City Meat Market until news came of the great strike in Alaska.

Lured by tales of great discoveries here, he left San Francisco and landed in Skagway July 12, 1897 with the seventeen mules which later became the cornerstone of his fortune.

When he landed here there was but one small cabin in Skagway, owned by Capt. Moore. Brooks and a man named Turner blazed and cleared the trail of '98. This route was so successful that the gold seekers diverted from Dyea and the Chilkoot Trail. Joseph Brooks was largely responsible for the founding of Skagway.

He increased his 17 mules to 335 animals and began packing over the pass. He recalls those early days:

"I carried over the goods of the Northwest Mounted Police at a fabulous price, often making as much as $5000 in a day."

After the White Pass and Yukon Route Railroad came to Skagway, he moved to Atlin with his mules, leaving there in 1905 for Vancouver.

In that city, besides engaging in the freighting business, he also built the Vancouver Post Office. In 1934 Joseph Books returned to Skagway to hike over a portion of the Trail. His party made camp at White Pass City, one of the stops on the Trail of '98. He commented to his companion: "If I had my wish and my selection of the manner of my passing, my greatest desire would be to pass away on the old trail."

Then he said "Good night" and went to sleep, to fulfill his last desire. Joseph H. Brooks died July 13, 1934 at White Pass City on the Trail he pioneered in 1897.

MIDNIGHT SUN, July 4, 18, 1934

CHARLES E. BROWN

Charles E. Brown was born in New York state, August 17, 1873. His parents, pioneer residents of Quebec, Canada, were visiting the Empire State when the son was born. It was in Quebec where his father was a wealthy and prominent citizen that Charles Edward Brown grew to manhood. When the Klondike was discovered, young Brown joined a large party of gold hunters from Quebec, going into the goldfields via the Edmonton route, reaching Dawson in 1898.

Brown, after passing nearly two years in Dawson, went down the Yukon River and up to Nome, reaching that point early in 1900. Here he went into the mercantile business, with a store on the shore of Snake River.

In 1903 Valdez was attracting attention as the gateway to the newly discovered Fairbanks goldfields, and Mr. Brown and Thomas W. Hawkins, whom he had met in Nome, went there and established a store under the name of Brown & Hawkins. That same year Mr. Hawkins went to Seward and installed a branch store there. Work on the old Alaska Central Railway was the reason. Things began to boom in Seward, while Valdez already had too many mercantile houses, and Mr. Brown closed the Valdez house and joined his partner in Seward. That was late in 1903. Here the firm has remained in business.

Brown was also the president of the Bank of Seward.

Charles E. Brown died September 21, 1920 in New York city. He is survived by his wife, Athel Van Devere Brown, and by his father.
ALASKA WEEKLY, September 27, 1929

FRANCES KNEELAND BROWN

Frances Brown was born in Iowa Hill, Placer country, California. She can trace her ancestors back to John Kneeland who landed in Boston Harbor in 1630. Her father John Kneeland came from the Sate of Maine to San Francisco in '49, making the trip in a sailing vessel around Cape Horn. Her mother, Anne Kinney, came across the Isthmus of Panama to 'Frisco in the same year when a mere child and upon reaching womanhood, married John Kneeland. Here the family home was built in the mining camp and the daughter, Frances, was born and reared. On June 14, 1900, she landed in Nome, thus making her not only a Pioneer of California, but a Pioneer of Alaska as well It was in Nome that she met and wedded Felix Brown, clothing merchant. They have no children.

Frances Brown was with her husband in his famous sea voyage in 1903, when they were adrift in mid-ocean for ninety days, and she stood by the pumps as bravely as any sailor aboard until their arrival in Seattle.
PATHFINDER, November 1919

J. C. BROWN

Mr. Brown was born at Fort Worth, Texas, in 1860, but his youth was spent on a farm near Argentine, Kansas. In early manhood he removed to the city and conducted a feed, fuel and builders' supply business and was associated with the city bank. His townsmen elected him a member of the city council, of which body he was president until he left the city. In 1898 Mr. Brown decided to go to Dawson. He arrived at Chilkoot Pass on the momentous day of the snow-slide which caused such loss of life at Sheep Camp. After this catastrophe he was one of the first to cross the pass. He underwent the awful hardship incident to overland travel to Dawson at that time, but not finding the place to his liking traveled farther down the Yukon. During the summer he prospected in the vicinity of Eagle City, and in 1899 was chosen mayor of the town he had helped lay out and plat. Here he met his first mining difficulties.

    He had located some property when a party of English capitalists came down the river and in utter disregard of the rights of the resident miners and United States law, began to locate tracts of land hundreds of square miles in area. Mr. Brown called a miners meeting, one of the first and largest ever held in Alaska, and demanded justice and protection against the intruders. The result of the meeting was an order issued to the men to vacate the country on three days' notice. In the fall of 1899 Mr. Brown returned to the states, but the rush of 1900 carried him to Nome, where he has since been a permanent resident. His first operations were unfortunate. He bought a lay of property on Mikkilai Gulch, and afterwards found that he had paid the wrong man, but was unable to regain the money. He spent the remainder of the season prospecting, and went as far north as the Good Hope District.

    The summer of 1902 found him working on Dorothy Creek, and the following season he was associated with a company that put in a ditch on Cripple River. In 1904 Mr. Brown mined Claim No. 1, sometimes known as Railroad Claim, on Little Creek. Commencing at one end of the claim, he put down a series of six holes through solid frost. In all fair prospects were found, but not until the last was the rich gravel found. In this main shaft, pans of pay gravel chosen at random yielded from $150 to $180. Both fine and coarse gold was found, the largest nugget being worth fifty dollars. Five different lays were worked during the winter of 1904-'05. The cluster of camps with those of men who worked adjoining property was called Brownville.

Mr. Brown's efforts to secure law and order in a mining camp are well illustrated by the following incident. In the winter of 1900 he was robbed of nearly all he owned. Believing the thief would return, he lay in wait and caught the man and forced him to divulge the names of the persons aiding in the robbery. Through his determined prosecution a gang of robbers was broken up and six men were went to McNeil's Island.

NOME AND SEWARD PENINSULA, 1905

JAMES BROWN

Mr. Brown was born in Galena, Ill. July 17, 1845. He worked with Hugh Kirkendall, a contractor engaged in hauling supplies to the soldiers of the Union throughout the Civil War. At the close of the war he emigrated westward with Kirkendall. they operated freighting outfits from Corinne, Utah, the end of the Union Pacific railroad, into Montana. Kirkendall established headquarters at Helena, and freighted from Fort Benton, the head of navigation on the Missouri, as well as from Corinne.

In the 80s Kirkendall withdrew from he business and Mr. Brown carried on the freighting concentrating the business in Butte where he hauled supplies to the mines, and ore from the mines to the smelters.

In 1900 Mr. Brown joined the Alaska gold rush. In Alaska he made his headquarters at Bluff City, 52 miles east of Nome, where he operated placer properties. In 1924 he started fox farming. His illness began last winter at Bluff City and he was removed to a hospital in Nome.

Last summer his son, James H. Brown of the Mountaineer Welding company here, went to Alaska and brought his father to Seattle, where he remained with his daughter, Mrs. Albert Payne, until a month ago when he was brought to Butte.

James Brown, 83, pioneer Butte Teaming contractor, who joined the Alaska gold rush in 1900, died Saturday morning at the family home at 1011 South Wyoming Street, Butte, Montana, December 1928(?). Mr. Brown is survived by his widow, Mrs. Ida Brown and his son and daughter.

ALASKA WEEKLY, December 21, 1928

ALBERT G. BROWNE

A. G. Browne is a prominent young business man of Nome. He is a native of Canada and was born in Serbrook, October 1, 1876. His parents went to the United States in 1877 and resided on Staten Island, New York, until 1889. In 18889 the family moved to Tacoma, Washington. In 1892 the young man obtained a position with the Northern Pacific Steamship Company, and for five years was the steerage passenger agent of this company in Tacoma. Subsequent to this he was aboard the City of Seattle as freight clerk. He contracted the Alaska fever in 1897 and started for Skagway. From Skagway he went over the trail to White Horse, and became interested in the White Horse Tram-road. He followed the business of a pilot for near two years, making 108 trips of 180 miles each trip. August 1, 1889, he left Bennett as pilot of Ore & Turkey's outfit which consisted of nine scows and three steamers. He had previously made three trips to Dawson.

Hearing of the Nome strike he concluded to go to the new camp. He arrived in Nome September 17, 1899. He immediately went to work on the beach, and with two partners cleaned up $5,400 in two weeks. He subsequently mined on the creeks. In the summer of 1903 he fitted up a shop for the manufacture of hydraulic pipe and fittings, and is now the owner of the biggest establishment

of this kind in Alaska.
NOME AND SEWARD PENINSULA, 1905

FREDERICK D. BROWNE
Frederick D. Browne, formerly District engineer for the Alaskan Engineering Commission, in charge of the construction of the Alaska Railroad, with headquarters at Nenana, interior Alaska, died at Merced, California, January 19, 1926. San Raphael, California has been his home most of the time since he severed his connection with the Alaska Railroad project. Up to the time of his death, he had been connected with the Southern Pacific railroad.

Mr. Browne went to Alaska to take charge of the construction work in the interior when former Governor Thomas Riggs resigned from the Alaskan Engineering Commission to assume the governorship.

Mr. Browne was born September 24, 1865, in Montreal, Canada. He was a member of the Alaska Scottish Rite Bodies of Juneau and Lompoc Lodge No. 262, F. and A.M., of Lompoc, California.
ALASKA WEEKLY, February 12, 1926

ALVIN J. BRUNER
A. J. Bruner is a son of Joseph A. Bruner, a Methodist minister who for thirty years followed his ministerial calling in the state of California. His mother was Margaret Morris, who was a member of the McArthur family of Ohio.

The subject of this sketch was born in Circlesville, Ohio, August 7, 1852. He is one of a family of seven children, five boys and two girls. When he was four years old his father moved to California, locating first in Marysville. After obtaining a grammar school education, Alvin J. Bruner attended the preparatory department of the University of the Pacific at Santa Clara, California. He was graduated from this University in the class of 1872 with the degree of B. A., and received the honor of valedictorian of his class. He was the youngest member of the class. He studied law with a firm in San Jose, California. Mr. Bruner was admitted to the bar April 11, 1877. In 1876 he and Miss Martha H. Hayden, of Gilroy, California, were married and after his admission to the bar he moved to Arizona on account of his wife's bad health. He resided in Arizona three years and while there organized the Oro Bonita Mining Company to operate mines in the Bradshaw Mountains near Prescott. Returning to California in 1879 he located in Sacramento. The death of his wife in 1880 caused him to go to Idaho where he established an office in Hailey.

While a resident of Idaho he opened the Big Copper group of mines on Lost River and erected a smelter, but lost his investment in the fall in the price of copper. In 1889 he returned to Sacramento and resumed the practice of law in that city, being associated with his brother, Elwood Bruner. This association was terminated in 1900 when Mr. Bruner came to Nome.

During his last residence in Sacramento he promoted and organized the Dutch Flat Blue Lead Mining Company to mine Blue Lead of Tuolumne County, California. Mr. Bruner has a reputation as a miner and mining expert as well as a lawyer. He is the owner of some promising property in the Nome country.

Mr. Bruner was married a second time in Sacramento in 1900. Mrs. Bruner was formerly Miss Mary Putnam, a lineal descendant if Israel Putnam.

NOME AND SEWARD PENINSULA, 1905

JOHN BRYNTESON

John Brynteson came to Alaska in the spring of 1898. He had been a worker in the iron mines in the northern part of the United States. His first prospecting in Alaska was in the Fish River country.

He then joined a party that started from Golovin Bay to investigate a report brought by natives of gold on the beach at Sinuk. This party, on account of rough weather, was forced to make a landing at the mouth of Snake River, and during their detention at this place they prospected some of the adjacent country. Mr. Brynteson found encouraging prospects on Anvil Creek August 1, and it was these prospects that induced him to return to this place accompanied by Lindeberg and Lindblom in September following when the great discovery was made by which the Nome country became known, and developed into one of the notable gold producing regions of the world.

Mr. Brynteson is a native of Dalsland, Sweden, and was born August 13, 1871. His father was a farmer and the subject of this sketch received his education in the public schools of his native land. He came to America in 1887. He was one of the original members, and one of the organizers, of the Pioneer Mining Company, and he is now a director in that corporation.

Mr. Brynteson was married May 2, 1900. Mrs. Brynteson was formerly Emma Forsborg. Three children, one son and two daughters, have been born to them.

NOME AND SEWARD PENINSULA, 1905

JOHN S. BUGBEE

John Bugbee was born in Boston, Massachusetts(the ALASKA MINING RECORD lists Nova Scotia as his birthplace) in 1842. He has lived in San Francisco from his boyhood. His father, Sumner C. Bugbee was a well-known architect of that city, who died there on September 1, 1877. He had studied architecture and become proficient as a draughtsman in his father's office, but changed his purpose to the legal profession.

John Bugbee graduated from the Harvard Law School and returned to San Francisco to practice. Very soon after entering on the practice he was employed by the law firm of Doyle & Barber and remained with them about five years. He then formed a law copartnership with Henry D. Scripture, which lasted until 1875. Mr. Bugbee then tiring of law practice went into the brewing business. This firm owned and operated the Swan Brewery, located at Fifteenth and Dolores Streets, for two years, when Mr. Bugbee withdrew and went back to the law. He and Clark Churchill(since Attorney-General of Arizona) practiced together a year, when Mr. Churchill left the State. Mr. Bugbee continued practice alone until 1885, when he became Assistant City and County Attorney. He served as such for two years and since has been associated with Mr. Love.

John Bugbee married Anna Maxwell, a native of Rhode Island. This union produced Bessie and Arthur Bugbee. Ann Maxwell was related to Julia Ward Howe. She was also a niece to the wife of William W. Story, author and sculptor. Anna Maxwell Bugbee died in San Francisco on March 18, 1895. The funeral was held at the home of her sister, Mrs. Sidney M. Smith.

In 1889, John Bugbee was appointed District Judge for the District of Alaska by President Harrison. Judge Bugbee held this position until 1892. Since his retirement from the bench, he has practiced law in Juneau.

John Bugbee died in Juneau in May 1896.
ALASKAN, Nov. 16, 1889; May 24, 1890;
     May 23, 1896
ALASKA MINING RECORD, May 20, 1896

GEORGE DOW BUNKER

George D. Bunker is associated with the early history of Northwestern Alaska, and has been identified with mining interests of the Council District since 1897. He is the son of a pioneer businessman of San Francisco, and was born in that city June 6, 1870. He attended the San Francisco public schools and subsequently Brewer's Academy, San Mateo. Mr. Bunker's grandfather was Cromwell Bunker, one of the first whalers to sail in Alaskan waters. The date of his whaling cruises was near seventy years ago. The family at that time resided in Nantucket. R. F. Bunker, father of the subject of this sketch, came to San Francisco in the early days of the Western metropolis, and engaged in the butcher business. In 1897 when Captain Libby was outfitting to go to Alaska George D. Bunker grub-staked Louis F. Melsing to accompany him. Captain Libby and Louis Melsing are both brothers-in-law of Mr. Bunker. Their group was the original discoverers of gold in the Fish River country, and were prospecting in this region at the time the strike was made on Anvil Creek.

Mr. Bunker has been interested in mining in the Council District ever since the historical trip of his brothers-in-law. At one time he owned 106 mining claims in Seward Peninsula, but now he concentrates on Ophir Creek.

He was one of the first arrivals in the Nome country in the spring of 1899, being a passenger on the steamship Garonne. Mrs. Bunker accompanied him on this trip, and she was one of the first white women in Council City. Mr. Bunker has had a varied and interesting experience in the Northland. He has been with the country since the earliest days. In 1899 he set up and operated the first gasoline engine on Ophir Creek, which was probably the first engine of this character brought into the country.

Mr. Bunker was married December 18, 1890, to Miss Dora Melsing. The issue of this union is one girl, Alfarretta, twelve years old.
NOME AND SEWARD PENINSULA, 1905

CHARLES E. BUNNELL

Doctor Bunnell was born January 12, 1878 on a farm near Dimmock, Pa. His parents were Lyman Walton Bunnell and Ruth Tingley Bunnell.

He entered Montrose high school in Susquehanna county when he was 13 and worked on the farm during his spare hours. In 1894 he entered Keystone Academy at Factoryville, Pa. in preparation for his study of Greek and Latin at Bucknell university, which he entered in 1896. He was active in Bucknell student activities and played on the football team. He supplemented his income for four years by waiting upon table in a private boarding house.

He graduated summa cum laude on June 20, 1900. Shortly after his graduation he received an appointment to the U.S. government school on Wood Island across the strait from Kodiak, Alaska.

The young teacher devoted his time toward working on a masters degree which he received in 1902. A year earlier he traveled to Pennsylvania where he married on July 24, Miss Mary Ann Kline, a classmate who had also graduated from Bucknell with honors. Both Mr. and Mrs. Bunnell taught at Kodiak until 1903 when they transferred to Valdez. They taught there another two years. When Mrs. Bunnell resigned, he became principal of the Valdez public schools for two years.

Bunnell resigned his position in 1907 and took charge of the Reynolds Alaska Development Co. Bank.

He managed the Phoenix Hotel until April 1908. The following spring their only child, Jean was born.

Bunnell studied law and was admitted to the Alaska Bar Nov. 21, 1908, while working with a Valdez attorney, Edmund Smith. The two men practiced law together until May, 1912, when Bunnell purchased his partner's interest in the firm. During this time Bunnell also owned half-interest in both the Copper river Lumber Co. and the Valdez Sheet Metal Works.

In 1914 Bunnell was nominated on the Democratic ticket to run against the late James Wickersham, Republican, for Delegate to Congress. He lost the election, but in 1914 President Woodrow Wilson appointed him District Judge for the Fourth Division. He took the oath of office on his 37th birthday, Jan. 12, 1915. Judge Bunnell completed one four-year term at Fairbanks and three years of a reappointment until he was seceded by a Republican selected by the Harding administration.

On Dec. 7, 1921 the board of trustees of

the then Alaska Agricultural College and School of Mines appointed him president. Bucknell University awarded him an honorary doctor of law degree in 1925.

Dr. Bunnell died in Burlingame, California, November 1, 1956. He is survived by his daughter, Jean.

FAIRBANKS NEWS-MINER, November 1, 1956

THOMAS H. BURMAN

Thomas Burman, born in England in 1879, came to this country at the age of seventeen, where he spent two years on a farm, after which he joined the Canadian Northwest Mounted Police and was in the service for five years, being three years in the Northwest Territory and two years in Dawson, Y.T. After taking his discharge from the police force, Mr. Burman decided to try mining in the Koyukuk in 1903, where he spent two years; from there he went to Fairbanks and engaged in mining in that camp and the Beaver district until 1914. In that year, Mr. Burman bought out the business of W.E. Phillips of Fort Yukon, Alaska. In 1923, Mr. Burman sold his business in Fort Yukon to the Northern Commercial Company and moved outside to Seattle, where he is now in the wholesale business. Mr. Burman makes his annual trip to Alaska buying furs, leaving Seattle about may and returning in August. He covers the Yukon in his own gas boat from Dawson to St. Michael.

ALASKA WEEKLY, February 8, 1929

JOHN EDGAR BURTON

He is one of the strong men who is assisting in the development of the resources of Seward Peninsula, Alaska.

John Edgar Burton, miner, was born October 19, 1847, in New Hartford, Oneida County, N. Y. He organized the American Fiber Company, which aims to produce merchantable fiber from any form of vegetation which contains fiber, and became the chief promoter of the Aguan Navigation and Improvement Company, whose object is to connect the Aguan River of

Honduras with the Caribbean Sea.

Mr. Burton was educated at the Cazenovia Seminary and at Whitestown, N. Y. He won first prize for oratory in the Cazenovia Seminary, and was graduated from the Whitestown school with high honors in June, 1868. He began life as a school teacher in Cazenovia and during two years following was principal of the public schools in Richmond, Ill. In 1870 he became principal of the public schools in Lake Geneva, Wis. In 1872 he established the Geneva Herald and a year later resigned from his school work to fill the position of editor of this paper. He followed journalism for three years when he sold his paper and devoted his time to the promotion of the manufacturing interests of Geneva.

Mr. Burton's next important work was a general agent and manager of the Equitable Life Assurance Society of New York for the state of Wisconsin. He was very successful in this field of endeavor. He was then promoted by the company to general manager for Wisconsin, Minnesota and Northern Michigan and increased the business to $3,000,000 in one year. In four years his total business exceeded $6,500,000.

In 1885 Mr. Burton resigned this position and undertook the work of promoting the iron mining interests of the Gogebic and Penokee Range. He made an exploration of this country in February of that year, traveling by rail to the end of the railroad line and the balance of the journey on foot and snow-shoes. His investigation satisfied him of the great value of some of the properties, which he secured, and their development within three years made him a millionaire and the acknowledged chief promoter of the Gogebic Range. He gave Hurley, Wis., its place on the map, being its pioneer promoter, and erected the Iron Bank Building, thirteen stores, thirty-five dwellings, the big foundry and the Burton Hotel. Since this period he has followed the business of mining with the exception of the effort directed to the construction of the Aguan Canal. He devoted five years to mining in Calaveras County, California, developing and operating a crystal mine, taking out the largest rock crystals recorded in geology, the product of twelve tons being sold to Tiffany & Co., New York. He also opened the Green Mountain Hydraulic Mine and extracted from this property gold to the value of over $40,000.

His attention having been directed to the Northern Alaskan gold fields, he accordingly acquired extensive interests of both gold placer and tin properties in this region. The gold mines are situated near Nome in the most promising part of the Nome District, and the tin properties are near Cape Prince of Wales on Cape Mountain.

Mr. Burton is a thoughtful man and a student. He owns a private library of 11,500 volumes, which is said to be the finest in the state of Wisconsin. This library represents the careful and constant accumulation of more than thirty years. It contains 2,160 volumes of Abraham Lincoln and Lincolniana. Everything that has ever been published about the president may be found in this collection.

Mr. Burton's ancestors were natives of Conningsby, Lincolnshire, England. His father and grandfather immigrated to the United States in 1829. His father married Ruth Jeannette Allen, the daughter of a soldier in the war of 1812. She was a devout woman. Her son's religious training was in accordance with the Methodist Episcopal Church. For sixteen years he was a member of this church, but drifted into agnosticism. Mr. Burton is a Royal Arch Mason, and also a life member and vice-president of the State Historical Society of Wisconsin.

December 7, 1869, John E. Burton married Lucretia Delphine Johnson, of Killawag, Broome County, N. Y., his schoolmate at Cazenovia. The issue of this marriage is four children - Howard E. and Warren E., both graduates of the University of Wisconsin, and now in business, and Kenneth E. and Bonnie E., Kenneth being superintendent of the Madonna Mine, Monarch,

Col., and the daughter is the wife of Prof. Edmund D. Denison.
NOME AND SEWARD PENINSULA, 1905

RICHARD C. BUTTON

R.C. Button was born in Hamlin, Mo., in 1887; he was working in the mint in Denver at the age of 17 years, and before his eighteenth birthday went to Alaska. He was at Nome from 1904 until 1911 as bookkeeper in the Miners' and Merchants' Bank, whence he was called to Iditarod by Charles Ross, a banker, on the colonization of that mining town. Starting as bookkeeper, he eventually attained a partnership in the enterprise, with Mr. Ross and Claude Bacon.

In 1920 he married Mrs. E.L. Byers who came in over the trail on a dog team to meet him. they left Alaska for the "outside" in 1923, coming to Seattle where they have resided since. Mr. Button went into the insurance business.

Mr. button died at his home in Seattle in November of 1926. He is survived by his widow in Seattle, and by a sister, Mrs. Burt Ritter; a brother, William, and parents, Mr. and Mrs. J.C. Button, all of Denver, Co.
ALASKA WEEKLY, November 19, 1926

HARRY BUZBY

Harry Buzby was born in Burlington, New Jersey, on October 12, 1863. Mr. Buzby removed to Illinois with his parents, when a lad of nine years of age and later the family went to Nebraska. There Mr. Buzby grew to manhood.

When he started live on his own he traveled west to Montana and for several years followed surveying and was in the cattle ranching business there.

Soon after the Dawson stampede he moved his family to Willamette, Oregon, and when Nome was struck he went there in 1901. In 1901 he moved his family to Skagway, where he was interested in a molybdenum mine.

Not long after the Fairbanks stampede Mr. Buzby came here and moved his family here in

1904. He was one of the very earliest ranchers in the interior.

Mr. Buzby took up a homestead soon after coming to Fairbanks on the banks of the Chena, one and a quarter miles above the wireless station. He cleared land and started a market garden, growing many vegetables which at that time it was thought impossible to grow in the Interior. He has contributed much to the knowledge of farming and stock raising in Alaska.

In 1920 he was forced to move to California on account of Mrs. Buzby's health. They lived near Sacramento until 1923 and then moved to Tillamook, Oregon, where he engaged in the dairy business. In 1925 the family came back to Fairbanks and Mr. Buzby ran the Buzby dairy until his health failed a year ago.

Harry Buzby died in Fairbanks, February 4, 1931. He leaves five children, Mrs. C. T. Spencer of Fairbanks, Jason, manager of the Northern Commercial Company store at Hot Springs, Mrs. James Ewart Crowell of Los Angeles, Elton of Fairbanks, Theodore of Tillamook, Oregon, and Robert of Fairbanks.

ALASKA WEEKLY, Feb. 27, 1931

J. K. CALLBREATH

J.K.Callbreath, commonly known as "Cassiar Jim," was born in LaGrange, California on April 7, 1857, and was taken into Caribou, B.C. by his father, being the first white boy in Caribou. He left B.C. in 1871, going east to attend a commercial college. He came to Fort Wrangell in Alaska on board the G.W. ELDER, May 20, 1876, going immediately into the Cassiar mining district to take a position of receiving and forwarding agent for the Diamond C firm owned by Callbreath, Bacon & Cook. In 1881 he made a trip overland to Frazer river and return--a distance of 1,000 miles.

In the spring of 1897 he started for Dawson with four tons of ham and bacon. He remained at Dawson until 1899, when he left for Rampart, where he mined until 1900, when he left for the upper Koyukuk country where he

prospected and mined with varying success until 1920, when he left the Koyukuk for Nenana, where he resides at this time.
PATHFINDER, December 1922

ADOLPHUS CALVERT

Adolphus Calvert, a full-blood Tsimpsian Indian was born at Ft. Simpson, British Columbia, at the time of the full moon of March, 1847, and his long life has been bound up with the missionary work of William Duncan, the "apostle" to the Tsimpsian Nation

Ft. Simpson had been established by the Hudson Bay Company but a few years previous to Mr. Calvert's birth and the village of his ancestors had moved from Old Metlakatla to Ft. Simpson. In 1857, when Mr. Calvert was ten years of age, came the young man, Mr. Duncan, sent by the Church of England to work with the Indians.

When 18 years of age, Mr. Calvert left Ft. Simpson for Old Metlakatla and attended Mr. Duncan's school.

After attending school one year Mr. Calvert was baptized and given the name of "Adolphus Calvert." At the same time that he was baptised, a young Indian girl of the same age was also baptized and given the name of "Matilda." These two young people were married.

To this marriage four children were born: Mary Ann, the wife of Robert Ridley and a communicant of St. John's; Walter, a member of the Salvation Army; Matilda, the wife of Silas Booth and a communicant of St. John's; and Florence, who died.

Mr. Calvert served as constable in Old Metlakatla for ten years. In 1885 when Mr. Duncan moved over to New Metlakatlas on Annette Island belonging to the United States, Mr. Calvert with his family moved to the new village.

In New Metlakatla Mr. Calvert continued to serve the church and the village, being Elder in the church for seven years, member of the village council six years and mayor of the

village for four years.
ALASKA-YUKON MAGAZINE, Oct. 1907

SARANTIS CARLLIS

Sarantis Carllis was born at Tripoli, Greece, in 1860. His father was a farmer, who owned a small place in the outskirts of the city. Mr. Carllis' early schooling was acquired at Tripoli and Athens. Circumstances compelled him to give up school and begin work. He clerked in a dry goods store in Athens for a short time, and at the time of the British-Egyptian difficulty he left Athens for Egypt, where he stayed for two years, leaving there in 1885 for San Francisco by way of Liverpool and New York. Soon after arriving in San Francisco he secured work in a commission house, and later went to Los Angeles, where he opened a commission store of his own.

During the Dawson excitement Mr. Carllis outfitted his brother with merchandise and sent him to the gold fields, but the adventure was a failure. In 1900, when the Nome excitement swept over the country Mr. Carllis brought a big stock of merchandise to Nome. The first summer he conducted his business in a building that had rough boards for a floor and a tent roofing. The same fall he erected a substantial building that he has added to yearly ever since. His profits the first year were very satisfactory, and the business was rapidly expanded until he had three stores in Nome and one in Solomon.

Mrs. Carllis outfitted prospectors for interests in claims acquired by them until he has many valuable properties. He has property on Seattle, Willow, Flambeau and other creeks, which are producing considerable gold.
NOME AND SEWARD PENINSULA, 1905

GEORGE CARMACK

Born in Contra Costa county, California, September 24, 1860, Carmack spent his early years prospecting in that state. He went North in 1885 and hunted, fished, trapped and traded with natives for several years.

In 1896, in company with an Indian, "Skookum Jim," he went up the Klondike River and found gold on Bonanza Creek. When word reached civilization of the discovery the great Klondike gold rush started, and $200,000,000 in yellow metal was added to the world's wealth.

Carmack came out of the North in 1900 and made his home in Seattle. He sold his northern holdings to Howard Hamilton Hart, who, in turn, relinquished to the Guggenheim interests.

For the past three years he has been engaged in mining operations on claims at Forest Hill, near Placerville, California.

For many years, until 1909, Carmack saved his first 22 nuggets. In that year he gave them to President Taft on a nugget-studded telegram key, with which the President opened the Alaska-Yukon-Pacific Exposition here.

George Carmack died in Vancouver, B.C. in June 1922.

Carmack had thousands of friends on the Pacific Coast and in the North. He was a member of the Yukon Pioneers, and one of the charter members of the first lodge organized in Dawson in 1897.

ALASKA DISPATCH, June 9, 1922

JULES BERTRAM CARO

Mr. Caro was born in 1871 in San Francisco. He went to Alaska early in 1898, first to Juneau and then into Dawson, as representative of the Joseph Myers Tobacco Co. and Kreilsheimer Bros.

About 1900 he associated himself with Charles E. Hooker, formerly of Kelly, Clark & Co. and since then Mr. Caro had been head of the wholesale brokerage business of the company which he developed into one of the largest establishments in the Territory.

Mr. Caro was also interested in the cannery business, having purchased the Auk Bay Cannery from the John Carlson Co. six years ago.

Jules B. Caro died in Seattle, April 24, 1933. He is survived by his widow, Mrs. Laura

R. Caro of Juneau; a son Bertram of Juneau; a daughter, Mrs. Georgia Kraft of San Francisco; and a sister, Miss Tillie Caro of San Francisco.

ALASKA WEEKLY, March 3, 1933

HERBERT CHAPMAN CAROTHERS

Dr. Carothers was born in Chicago in 1888. After an eight-year course in medicine he graduated from the State University Medical School of Chicago. He also took special courses in Rush Medical School.

He went to Alaska in 1919, locating at Petersburg where he spent a year-and-a-half. He then returned to Seattle and associated with Dr. William C. Heussy. Dr. Carothers specialized in diabetic cases. He married Rena West at Brookville, Indiana in 1919.

Dr. Carothers returned to Alaska in 1924 and established his practice in Ketchikan. He became physician for the Fraternal Order of Eagles, and this duty took up a large part of his time.

Dr. Carothers died on December 15, 1926 in California. Besides Mrs. Carothers and their six-year old daughter, Mary, Dr. Carothers is survived by his father, Frank Carothers, and by his grandmother, Mrs. Minnie Dolliver. Mrs. Dolliver raised the doctor from his boyhood, and assisted him in his medical and musical education.

Dr. Carothers possessed a rich, deep baritone voice, and had received training as a singer, and on the piano. He was much in demand to entertain local audiences.

ALASKA WEEKLY, December 24, 1926

MILLY D. CARR

Milly Carr was born in 1883 at Smith's Ferry, near Elkton, Oregon, of pioneer stock, her people having crossed the plains in 1847 from Virginia. Her mother was the first white child born at Umpqua, Oregon. Her girlhood days were spent on the family homestead at Smith's Ferry, and upon her marriage to Ralph

Carr, she moved with her husband to San Francisco, where in 1906 the great fire and earthquake left them penniless. Again she struggled with her husband and built a home and ranch near Red Bluff, California. And again they lost everything to fire.

Mrs. Carr came to Alaska to teach in the Territory's public schools, her wages going to help pay for another farm at Yoncalla, Oregon.

Mrs. Carr had taught at Kasaan for the last two years. Before then she had been a teacher at Girdwood, Fairbanks Creek, Tenakee and Sanak.

Mrs. Carr died January 12, 1929 in Ketchikan.

ALASKA WEEKLY, January 25, 1929

JULIUS C. CARSTENS

Julius C. Carstens is one of Nome's business men who has been here since 1900. He is a member of the firm of Carstens Brothers & Dashley, wholesale and retail butchers. Mr. Carstens was born in Germany, July 2, 1872, and went to America when he was fifteen years old, locating first in Wisconsin. He arrived in Seattle in 1890 and for a period subsequent to 1903 conducted a butcher shop in that city.

In 1899 he took forty head of cattle to Dawson. In the spring of 1900 he and his associates established a business in Nome. During the seasons prior to 1902 live stock was shipped to this firm at Nome and killed in the fall of the year for the winter's meat supply. In 1902 the firm installed a cold storage plant of 200 tons capacity, and now deals in both fresh and cold storage meats.

Mr. Carstens was married November 4, 1896, in Fon du Lac, Wisconsin. His family, consisting of his wife and two sons, Clarence T. and Ernest J., aged six and two years respectively, are in Nome with him.

NOME AND SEWARD PENINSULA, 1905

NEVILLE H. CASTLE

N. H. Castle was born in San Francisco, February 15, 1863, and was graduated from Yale

College with the degree of B. A. in the class of '84. He read law in the office of Doyle, Galpin & Scripture, of San Francisco, and was admitted to the bar in 1886. He practiced law in San Francisco and San Jose, Cal., and came to Alaska in the spring of 1900. He became associated with Laurier McKee, another Yale man and established an office, and Mr. Castle has remained faithfully at this post of duty ever since. In addition to building a lucrative practice he has acquired interests in valuable mining property. Mr. Castle's father is a prominent merchant of San Francisco, a member of the firms of Castle Brothers and Macondray & Co.

NOME AND SEWARD PENINSULA, 1905

ENDRE MARTIN CEDERBERGH

Captain E. M. Cederbergh has been identified with Northwestern Alaska ever since the great rush in the spring of 1900. The favorable reports that reached the states from this region in the fall of 1899 caused Captain Cederbergh to go to Alaska. In addition to these encouraging reports, he was induced by Eastern capitalists to take charge and manage some investments in this part of the country, of which they thought favorably. He acquired the property of the Arctic Trading & Mining Co. for the people he represented, and subsequently reorganized this company, naming it the New York Metal and Reduction Co. The capital stock was subscribed by citizens of New York. In 1902 Captain Cederbergh was solicited by friends in Chicago to obtain some property in the Nome country.

He bought mining claims for them on Dick and Reindeer Creeks, in what was then known as the Good Hope Mining District. In January, 1904, he was asked to go to Chicago and assist in the organization of the Good Hope Bay Mining Co., and was elected president of this corporation.

During the winter of 1904 and 1905 Captain Cederbergh was appointed to the position of

Vice-Consul of Sweden and Norway for the State of Oregon. His office is in Portland.

E. M. Cederbergh was born in Stavengar, Norway, November 11, 1853. His early education was received in the schools of his native land. When twelve years old he was sent to Germany and received three years' schooling in that country. In 1870 he went to sea, shipping as a sailor before the mast. He followed the sea for a period of twelve years. In seven years he had attained to the position of captain, and during the last five years of his life on the sea he was master of the vessels in which he sailed.

The history of his family is a part of the annals of Norway. His grandfather was a member of the Norwegian Parliament. His father was a manufacturer, and the subject of this sketch received his early business training in a mercantile house and was associated with the mercantile business at the time of the death of his father, just prior to the time when he became a sailor. He immigrated to America in 1883, and after a brief stay in Chicago went to Portland, where he has resided ever since. During his residence in Portland he has engaged in the mercantile and real estate business, and at one time was employed in the tax department of the sheriff's office.

April 25, 1880, Captain Cederbergh and Miss Marie Nyman were married in Stavangar, Norway. Mrs. Cederbergh has accompanied her husband on all of his ocean voyages.

NOME AND SEWARD PENINSULA, 1905

DR. W. d'ARCY CHACE

Dr. W. D'Arcy Chace was born in San Francisco, Cal., on Halloween, 1873. He attended the public schools of San Francisco, and was graduated by the Medical Department of the University of California in the class of '96. In the month of June of the year of his graduation he accepted the position of company surgeon of the A. C. Co., and immediately sailed for the company's post at St. Michael.

In 1897, when his contract expired, he

quit the employ of the company and prepared to return to San Francisco, but while waiting for a steamer, news of the Klondike strike reached him. He changed his plans and went to Dawson, arriving in July of '97. After a summer's work, the robbery of his cache and a threatened shortage of provisions caused him to go to Circle. He practiced medicine in Circle during the winter of '97-'98, and in the early spring returned to Dawson over the ice with a dog team. During the summer of '99 news of the strike at Nome was confirmed in Dawson, and Dr. Chace and his party started for Nome in a small boat. Twenty miles below the mouth of the Tanana the Yukon froze.

They went into camp, and remained here until the middle of January, when they made another start for Nome with two sleds loaded with their supplies.

Dr. Chace went to the Kougarok country soon after his arrival in Nome, and helped to organize that district. He returned from the Kougarok the middle of April, and during the summer of 1900 practiced his profession in Nome, and subsequently conducted Cribb's drug store. He was acting city physician and health officer in 1901-'02 during the smallpox scare, and was assistant city physician in 1903-'04, and the city council elected in April, 1904, appointed him city physician.

December 3, 1903, Dr. Chace was married to Debra Body, of Seattle.

NOME AND SEWARD PENINSULA, 1905

JOHN WIGHT CHAPMAN
   By the Rev. Henry H. Chapman, son of John
   Wight Chapman

John Wight Chapman was born in Pikesville, Maryland, June 2, 1858; the third son of Albert Chapman and Matilda Grace (Mulchahey). On the outbreak of the Civil Way Albert volunteered for service in the Union army, but was rejected as physically unfit for the rigorous life of a soldier. Soon afterward, the family returned to Vermont, Albert Chapman's native State, and

made their home in Middlebury. Albert Chapman
was a devout churchman and served for many
years as a vestryman and warden of At.
Stephen's Church, Middlebury. It was his habit
to read a portion of the Bible daily, following
the table of Lessons appointed in the Prayer
Book.

Albert and his father, Wightman Chapman,
were farmers and sheep breeders. Albert
Chapman was the founder and, until his death,
the secretary of the Vermont Merino Sheep
Breeders' Association. As boys John and his
brothers, Charles and William, helped to take
care of their father's flock of Merino sheep.

John attended school and college in
Middlebury, and received his A.B. from
Middlebury College in 1879. During the next
two or three years he taught school. He became
a candidate for Holy Orders from St. Peter's
Parish, Westchester, New York. He graduated
from the General Theological Seminary in 1886,
was ordained Deacon by Bishop Potter of New
York, and served for a year as an associate of
the New York City Mission.

In 1887, John Wight Chapman was advanced
to the Priesthood by Bishop Bissell of Vermont.
The ceremony took place in St. Stephen's
Church, Middlebury. The day after his
ordination to the Priesthood he started for his
chosen field.

Before leaving for Alaska, John had become
engaged to Adelaide May Seely, daughter of
Henry Martyn Seely, at that time head of the
Department of Natural Science in Middlebury
College. For six years, from 1887 to 1893 John
was separated from his betrothed, at a time
when communication with Alaska was so difficult
and so infrequent that he received mail but
once or twice a year. In the summer of 1893 he
went back to Vermont on his first furlough, and
was married in October of that year. The
following summer he took his bride to Alaska
with him, and she has shared his life in the
wilderness ever since.

In 1915, John W. Chapman received the
honorary degree of Doctor of Divinity from

Middlebury College.
ALASKAN CHURCHMAN, July 1930

Z.R.CHENEY

Z.R. Cheney was born about forty-two years ago[1877] in Medelia, Minnesota, and was raised there. He served in the army during the Spanish-American war. About sixteen years ago he came to Alaska and opened a law office in Douglas, later moving his office to Juneau. He has been a prominent member of the Alaska bar since he became a resident of the Territory.

Mr. Cheney married Miss Pearl Ziegler in Juneau in 1909.

Z.R. Cheney died in Seattle, Washington July 12, 1919.
He is survived by Mrs. Cheney, their son John, two sisters, Mrs. Bradford of Grants Pass, Oregon, mother of Z.M. Bradford, Postmaster in Juneau; Mrs. Lincoln of Sioux Falls, South Dakota, and a brother A.W. Cheney of Vader, Washington.

ALASKA DAILY EMPIRE, July 12, 1919

BENJAMIN A. CHILBERG

In 1898 B. A. Chilberg went to Dawson. He came down the Yukon the following year on his way to the states. He paused in his journey when he reached St. Michael, and made a brief trip to Nome. He returned to this camp in 1900 and has been identified with the country ever since. Mr. Chilberg is a native of Ottumwa, Iowa, and was born February 22, 1848.

He is a brother of the Seattle banker, and two of his nephews are connected with the Pioneer Mining Company. He is of Scandinavian ancestry, his father being a pioneer of Iowa.

When twenty-one years old B. A. Chilberg came to the State of Washington and engaged in farming. In 1876 he started the first grocery store in New Tacoma. Three years later he moved to Walla Walla and pursued the same line of business, subsequently returning to La Conner, where he first settled, and going back to the farm. In 1889 he engaged in the real estate business in Tacoma. Two years later he

moved to Seattle, and was in the grocery
business until 1897. During this year he went
to Skagway, and from this place to Fort
Wrangell, where he conducted a grocery
business. In '98 he sold out and went to
Dawson with a stock of window glass, which sold
for two dollars and three dollars a pane. He
made some money out of the venture and lost it
mining with a steam thawer on Cheduko Hill.

In the spring of 1900 he returned to Nome,
and he and his brother, N. Chilberg, mined with
a rocker on Cooper Gulch. At the close of the
season N. Chilberg returned to Seattle, but Ben
Chilberg remained on Cooper Gulch for the
purpose of taking out a winter dump. January
19 of this winter is the date of the severest
blizzard in the history of Nome. Mr. Chilberg
was working alone in a drift of his mine, 600
feet from his cabin. When he came to the
surface at 5 o'clock to go to his cabin, the
night was dark and the wind was blowing with
such force that he found it difficult to stand.
The air was filled with flying snow, and he
debated whether he should go back into the mine
or try to go to the cabin. In the mine he knew
there was safety, although the cabin was only a
short distance away and he might miss it and
perish in the furious storm. The thought that
his cabin mates might attempt to hunt for him
and lose their lives, impelled him to go
forward. When he had covered half the distance
he observed a corner stake which he passed
daily, and saw he was off his course. Taking
his bearings again, he went on and reached the
spot where the cabin ought to be, but found no
cabin. He called at the top of his voice, but
there was too much noise made by the elements
for his companions to hear him. Bewildered, he
stood still for a few minutes, but the
penetrating cold warned him that he could not
stand still and expect to be alive when
daylight returned. He went on, and a short
distance ahead found another landmark that
enabled him to retrace his steps and find the
cabin door. Next day when the storm had abated
he found the spot where he had stopped and

stood and called for help, and it was on top of the cabin. This cabin was a sort of a dug-out in the hill-side, only the face of it being visible in the winter time.

This experience caused him to make provision for another such contingency. He constructed a windmill with a tick-tack, and when the wind blew hard it made a noise that could be heard a couple of miles away. One bad night during this winter, when the wind was howling there was a knock at the door of the cabin. Hastily getting out of his bunk and opening the door, a man, nearly exhausted and half frozen, stumbled inside. He had been lost, and was about to give up in despair when he heard the noise of the windmill. The windmill saved his life.

In 1901 Mr. Chilberg was foreman for the Pioneer Mining Company on Mountain Creek. In 1902-'03 he was connected with the Nome Exploration Company. In 1879 he married Miss Lina Woodward. They have two daughters, one of whom is the wife of Frank Victor, manager of the Moore Jewelry Company of Seattle.

NOME AND SEWARD PENINSULA, 1905

EUGENE CHILBERG

Eugene Chilberg's first identification with Northwestern Alaska was as the treasurer of the Pioneer Mining Company, a position he still holds. He was an operator of the Hot Air Mining Company on Glacier Creek, and was one of the operators of the Bella Kirk bench claim on Dry Creek. In the fall of 1904, and upon the organization of the Miners and Merchants Bank of Nome, he was selected as the president of this institution.

Mr. Chilberg was born in Seattle, Washington, October 29, 1875. He is the son of A. Chilberg, president of the Scandinavian-American Bank of Seattle. Eugene was educated in the common schools and in the high school of Seattle. He also attended the State Agricultural College, and the School of Science at Pullman, Washington. In 1893-'94 he was a student in the State University of Seattle, and left the university to accept a position in the Scandinavian-American Bank, which position he held until he became treasurer of the Pioneer Mining Company at Nome, Alaska.

NOME AND SEWARD PENINSULA, 1905

WILLIAM A. CLARK

W. A. Clark is a member of the firm of Tanner & Clark, owning and conducting the largest lumber business in Northwestern Alaska. The foundation of this large concern, owning its sawmill plant and timber lands in Washington, and lumber yards in Nome, Alaska, where from five million feet to six million feet of lumber is kept in stock, was laid by L. B. Tanner, the senior member of the firm, in 1900.

Mr. Clark is a native of Youngstown, Ohio. He was born October 10, 1870. When six years old he moved with his parents to Portland, Oregon, where he attended public school. When eighteen he began an apprenticeship to learn the iron molder's trade. After serving his time he took a course in a business college at Seattle, and then worked for about six years at his trade. In 1897 he caught the Klondike fever, and started for Dawson over the White Pass route. He and a companion packed 1,200 pounds over the pass on their backs the greater part of the distance to Bennett, thirty-seven miles. Then made eleven round-trips for every relay, and were from the middle of July until October accomplishing this task. After reaching Bennett a boat was purchased.

That winter Mr. Clark mined on Bonanza. The following spring he went out and bought a stock of merchandise, which he took into Dawson. He made three round-trips that season, taking each time a stock of goods to Dawson. During the last trip he and Miss Laura Johnson were married in Seattle. Mrs. Clark did not accompany her husband to Dawson but he came out after he in the spring of 1899. Returning to Dawson, he found the Nome excitement at its height, and determined to go to the new camp. He arrived in Nome September of 1899, and

earned his first money in this town ferrying people across Snake River. The receipts from his ferry in seven days were $190. In the spring of 1900 he opened a road-house on Anvil Creek, and later in the season built a home in Nome. During the winter he also mined on the beach. He followed mining and conducted the road-house until the fall of 1901, when he went to Nome and went into partnership with L. B. Tanner. One member of the firm lives in Seattle and attends to the manufacturing and forwarding of the lumber; the other in Nome attends to the sales and distribution.
NOME AND SEWARD PENINSULA, 1905

C. R. CLARKE

Mr. Clarke was born in Kingston, Ontario.

In 1896 when Mr. Clarke reached the place where the town of Skagway is now located, there were only two buildings there, one of which was the cabin lived in by Capt. Wm. Moore the original owner of the Skagway townsite and family, and a small saw mill, also the property of Capt. Moore. The valley where it was not traversed by primitive logging roads was covered with a heavy growth of timber and dense underbush.

Mr. Clarke was put in the whole of that time in the roadhouse business between Whitehorse and Dawson, but has been at his present location only about five years. Prior to coming to the Yukon the ran a roadhouse on the Valdez trail to the interior.

At Yukon Crossing, Mr. Clarke has several acres of ground under cultivation, raises all his own vegetables and last year sold a quantity of potatoes of excellent quality and size at a good price in the Whitehorse market.
WEEKLY STAR, December 22, 1916

M. J. COCHRAN

M. J. Cochran, lawyer and journalist, is a member of the Nome bar and has filled the office of United States Commissioner for the Kougarok District. He was born April 1, 1854, at Evansville, Indiana. His grandfather was a pioneer who came from East Tennessee to this region before Indiana was a state. Mr. Cochran belongs to an old Scotch family that was forced to leave the old country on account of the persecution of the Covenanters in the days of King Charles. He was educated in the public schools. He studied law at Rockville, Indiana, under David H. Maxwell, late Chief Justice of the Supreme Court in Indiana, and was admitted to the bar in May, 1875. He went to Kansas in 1877, locating in Woodson County; thence he went to Medicine Lodge, Kansas, where he edited a newspaper for the period of a year, and was assistant prosecuting attorney. In 1879 he was in New Mexico, and subsequently was deputy clerk of the District Court of the Fifth Judicial Division at Buena Vista, Colorado. After the election of 1882, he practiced law in Buena Vista for six years, and was also associated with A. R. Kennedy in the publication of the Buena Vista Herald.

In 1880 he went to Washington Territory, and was nominated as one of the candidates for the first legislature, but was defeated. In the spring of 1890 he located in Aberdeen, and practiced law there for six years. In 1896, when the Populists elected a superior judge, he moved to Spokane, preferring to seek new fields rather than practice in a court presided over by a Populist. He was subsequently associated with C. S. Warren of Butte, in mining. He cam to Alaska in January, 1898, locating first at Fort Wrangell, where he practiced law. In 1899 he went over the trail to Atlin, and the following season he came to Nome. He was appointed United States Commissioner for the Kougarok District in the spring of 1901, and held the office one season. The balance of his time in Nome has been devoted to the practice of law.

During the first legislative session of the State of Washington, Mr. Cochran was clerk of the Senate Committee on Education and the Joint Committee on Tide Lands. He reported this session of the legislature for the Tacoma Globe. Mr. Cochran has been a very successful lawyer, and has made an exceptional record in criminal practice. In eighteen murder cases which he defended, there was only one conviction, but there were three reversals by the Supreme Court.

NOME AND SEWARD PENINSULA, 1905

ORVILLE D. COCHRAN

His is a native of Virgil City, Southeastern Missouri, and was born in 1871. His education was obtained in the public schools of his native state and in the high school of Parsons, Kansas, his parents have removed to the latter state when he was sixteen. At the age of nineteen he began work for the Missouri Pacific Railroad. In the spring of 1890, having been continuously in the service of the company until this date, he started west, and settled in Huntington, Oregon, where he obtained a position as car inspector of the Union Pacific. At a later date he was transferred to the O. R. & N. Railway Company at Portland, where he followed the same line of work. In 1895 he began to take a course in the law department of the University of Oregon. His work for the railway company was a night shift of thirteen hours. He attended the lectures at the college in the afternoon. At half-past 6 o'clock he would take his lunch pail and law books and go to his work, reading during the night whenever leisure afforded an opportunity. For his services the railroad company paid him a salary of $2.10 a day. At the end of two years he graduated and passed the supreme court examination.

In 1898 he opened a law office in Portland, and found a good clientage among railroad men. In 1900 he came to Nome.

NOME AND SEWARD PENINSULA, 1905

ALBERT J. CODY

Mr. Cody is a native of Auburn, Oregon, and was forty-two years old November 10, 1904. He is a member of an old English family that came to America about 200 years ago. His father was a pioneer of California who emigrated from Indiana in 1849. A. J. Cody was educated in the public schools of Oregon, and began the serious work of life riding the range on a cattle ranch in Big Lake County, Oregon. At a later period he was engaged in the fish cannery business on Columbia River. From 1883 to 1889 he was in the hotel business in Portland. He then became an officer of Multnomah County, by appointment as deputy sheriff. Subsequently he was appointed to a position on the police and detective force of Portland, Oregon.

In 1898 Mr. Cody was appointed deputy collector of customs for Alaska. He came to St. Michael and ascended the Yukon to the boundary line, establishing customs houses at Rampart, Fort Yukon and Eagle. He resigned this position the following year and came to Nome, engaging in mining. In the fall of 1900 he was appointed to the position of deputy marshal by U. S. Marshal Vawter.

Being a field deputy in the office of the U. S. Marshal Mr. Cody had the privilege of conducting a detective agency, and was employed by all the big companies to protect their interests. He resigned as field deputy and devoted his time to the work of his detective bureau and to his mining interests. In 1903 Marshal Richards tendered him the position of office deputy, which he accepted, and filled until the close of navigation, 1904, when he resigned to return to the states, the main object of his going being to give his son a collegiate education.

Mr. Cody owns extensive and valuable mining interests in the Nome District. He owns all of Extra Dry Creek, comprising fourteen claims, and owns property on Anvil Creek. He and Miss Alice V. Campbell were married in Portland, Oregon, in June 1884. They have one son, Albert R., a man twenty years old.

BARNEY COGGINS
Barney Coggins was born in Ireland on June 25, 1871, and came to the United States at a

very early age, settling in Butte, Montana, where he became a hard rock miner, and worked for a number of years for Marcus Daly. He left Butte in 1896 for Juneau, Alaska, and worked in the Comet mine at Berners Bay, until the spring of 1897 when he left for Dawson, remaining in that camp until the spring of 1900.

After arriving in Nome he became actively identified with the mining activities of the new camp. He was one of the first discoverers of the second beach line and during the winter of 1904 and '05, he mined successfully on the second beach line below Ft. Davis. He was frequently in charge of mining operations for Jas. O'Sullivan on Dexter Creek, and during the third beach line excitement was foreman for P.D. Winters and Sons, on ground adjoining the Portland bench; he was also identified with Joe Crabtree in the Summit beach. In the winter of 1915 and '16 he was one of the lucky laymen on the rich Dexter Creek strike.

ALASKA WEEKLY, September 17, 1926

JAMES H. CONDIT

In 1887, James H. Condit was graduated from Parsons College, then attended McCormick Theological Seminary where Presbyterian ministers are trained, and in 1891 he was graduated from that school.

After a pastorate in an Iowa town, Dr. Condit went to Alaska arriving in Juneau in 1896 to take over the pastorate of the once famous Log Cabin Church were he remained until 1899. He then returned to Iowa on account of the ill health of his wife, who passed away shortly after his arrival in Iowa. Dr. Condit remarried and the year 1901 found him back in Juneau as pastor of the Northern Light Church, which had replaced the old Log Cabin Church during his absence. He remained in Juneau until 1908, when he was called to Fairbanks where he stayed for the next five years, returning to Juneau in 1913 as the General Missionary in Alaska for the Presbyterian Church, traveling throughtout Alaska.

In 1921 he became Superintendent of the

Sheldon Jackson School at Sitka, a Presbyterian institution for the training of native youth. When he left Sitka there were no pupils below the fifth grade level and a complete high school course had been established with fifty pupils enrolled. Under his superintendency the Russel Sage Memorial Building was completed and equipped with modern machinery for the establishment of an industrial school.

Dr. Condit's remarriage produced three children; Faith (Mrs. Nicholson), Ruth (Mrs. Gare), and Craig C. Condit. Mrs. Nellie Condit died in August 1950 in Pasadena, California at 82 years. She was born August 20, 1868.

ALASKA WEEKLY, December 5, 1930
(Newspaper?) August 19, 1950

CHARLES EDWARD CONE

Charles Edward Cone was born in Union town, Bourbon Co., Kansas, on the 9th day of August, 1862. In 1865 his parents moved over the line to Jasper County, Missouri. As a young man he moved west to California in 1882.

There he soon drifted to the mining district of Dogtown, Butte County. He then prospected for a year, and ended up in Virginia City, Nevada.

From there he headed north into Idaho, thence over the Cascade Range by way of Natchez Pass and down the old "Military trail" to Tacoma, Washington, landing there in October, 1885.

The following March he headed for Alaska, and in company with three other adventurers, went up the Stikeen River took the old "Telegraph trail" to the Cassiar, thence to Hootalinqua lake and down the Hootalinqua river to the Yukon, arriving on the Yukon the 10th day of August, 1886. After two years prospecting in the Interior he headed back to the coast and for several years fished and prospected all along the coast of B.C. In the spring of 1896 he went to the Arctic on a fishing trip and knew nothing about the great Klondike strike until he came down in the fall of 1898. After a short stay in San Francisco he started for Dawson, but switched off and went into Atlin where he located several claims. Selling his holding in Atlin he headed for the Interior again going to the Koyukuk. From the Koyukuk he crossed over into the Arctic again, prospecting to Noatak and Kobuk Rivers, thence to the Bucklin and down the Bucklin to the Kotzebue and into Nome. Nome did not know him long, but broken in health, and badly crippled financially, he came south, stopping at Ketchikan, where he engaged in quartz prospecting. In 1903 he received an injury which necessitated his going outside for a surgical operation.

In May 1905 Mr. Cone returned to Alaska and was one of the early men in the Cache Creek district, where he made the discovery of Poor Man creek. During the summer of 1907 he and his partners took out $20,000 in 41 days. He sold his interests in the Cache creek district to his partners and went over the Alaska Range into the then little known Kuskokwim Country. Discovering some gold on the Hartman river, he came back to Susitna river.

In February, 1910 he went back to the Hartman river again and stayed in the Kuskokwim country until 1916 when he came out to Anchorage.

While in the Kuskokwim country Mr. Cone gained the title of "the Bard of the Kuskokwim" on account of his propensities for writing verse.

PATHFINDER, Jan. 1920

J. H. CONRAD

Col. J. H. Conrad was born in Virginia about 1855. When fifteen years of age he went to Fort Benton, Montana. Young Conrad, big and strong for his years, cast his lot with that thriving settlement. Here the Hudson's Bay Company had a large trading post and the young Virginian took a job with that fur house. He stayed on this job until he was made manager of this post. Later, he organized the Conrad Trading Company and established trading posts at intervals from Fort Benton to where the city of Calgary, Canada now stands.

Col. Conrad began to venture in mining enterprises. He owned and operated several coal mines in the west. He operated stores at Virginia City and Alder Gulch when that great placer camp was in the flower of its production. He was a member of the vigilance committee that preserved order in those hectic days. In company with Phil Armour, he bought twenty thousand head of cattle in Texas and drove them into Montana for beef purposes.

During his pioneering days in Montana he won the friendship of General Sherman, General Custer and the great Indian chief, Sitting Bull; in Canada he was the friend of Lord Strathcona, head of the Hudson's Bay Company, and Sir Donald Mann and Sir Alex Mackenzie, the Canadian railway builders.

In 1898, Col. Conrad went into Alaska. For two years he did some exploration work around Ketchikan, when he was called further North by the big stampede to Nome. He remained there only a year and then went to the Yukon territory and into the Porcupine country back of Haines, Alaska. Here col. Conrad was concerned in the Porcupine Gold Mining Company.

He then got interested in lode properties in the Windy Arm section of the Yukon territory in what is now called the Conrad district. He started development work on a big scale on two lode properties, the Venus and the Big Thing, and shipped about 500,000 tons of ore to the smelters from them. A town, called Conrad City, was started as a result of the mining activities there.

Col. Conrad was a member of Arctic Brotherhood, Camp No. 1 at Skagway.

During his long busy and adventurous career, Col. Conrad had won and lost fortunes. At one time he was a member of the New York Stock Exchange, and the Chicago Stock Exchange.

Col. J. H. Conrad died in Seattle(?) November 27, 1928. He was 73 years old at the time of his death. He is survived by a daughter and a son, who live in San Francisco, California.   ALASKA WEEKLY, Nov. 30, 1928

JOHN S. COPLY

J. S. Coply is prominently identified with the mercantile interests of Nome. At the municipal election in April, 1904, he was selected by the people to fill a position in the Nome Council, and was elected mayor of Nome in 1905. Mr. Coply was born May 3, 1863, in West Salem , Ohio. He is of English ancestry, and a descendant of John Singleton Coply, at one time Chief Baron of the Exchequer and Lord Chancellor of Great Britain. Mr. Coply's father was a merchant who went to Southern Michigan during the boyhood days of the subject of this sketch. In 1877 he removed to Eastern Washington.

John S. Coply was educated in the public schools of Washington, and the Portland Business College, and was graduated from the latter institution. His work has been in the mercantile and shipping lines. In 1892 he went to San Francisco where he engaged in the shipping business. He came to Alaska in September, 1899, and has made Nome his headquarters ever since. He has seen Nome in nearly all of its phases of growth and development.

April 8, 1900, he and Miss Minnie H. Harrington of Oregon City, were married. They have one child a daughter, Lois H., four years of age.

NOME AND SEWARD PENINSULA, 1905

CALEB CORSER

Caleb Corser was born in Minneapolis, Minn., and has been interested in railways from the time he received his first toy train many years ago. His first work was that of an axeman in a railway engineering party, and he later followed railway maintenance and construction work on the Northwestern lines for several years in the capacity of rodman, instrumentman, draftsman, resident engineer and chief draftsman.

Mr. Corser first came to Alaska in 1907, as resident engineer for the Copper River & Northwestern Railway, landing at Katalla, where he was assigned to work in the Abercrombie canyon. The following year he was transferred to work out of Cordova, and from that time until the completion of the road was in the employ of the railway company as resident engineer and chief draftsman. Recognizing his energy and resourcefulness, at the close of construction, Mr. Corser was made engineer of maintenance of way, and steadily worked up to the top of the ladder until 1913, when he was made superintendent of the road, a position which he has since occupied in a manner acceptable to the general public and the railway management.

In 1909 Mr. Corser was united in marriage to Beatrice M. Potter, of Seattle. Two children have arrived to bless the union, both daughters, and thorough Alaskans, being born in Cordova.   PATHFINDER, July 1920

JOHN W. CORSON

John W. Corson has been identified with mining in the Nome country ever since 1900. He is associated with Capt. E.W. Johnston in the Cooper Gulch properties. These properties contributed more than half a million dollars to the gold product of the Nome country last year. He is a native of Maine and forty-seven years old.

By his own industry and thrift he obtained enough money to acquire an education. He was graduated from Kent's Hill Academy in 1881, and afterward entered the Wesleyan University and subsequently read law with Baker, Baker & Cornish, at the time the leading law firm of the State of Maine. Mr. Cornish is now Chief Justice of the Supreme Court.

Mr. Corson and Jane Perley were married in 1893. Mrs. Corson is the daughter of Asbury Perley, a prominent citizen of New Hampshire and a member of one of the oldest families in the East.

ALASKA-YUKON MAGAZINE, Feb. 1908

PORTER J. COSTON

Porter J. Coston, born in Ashtabula

County, Ohio, August 29, 1849; when three years of age his parents moved to McDonough County, Illinois. In the fall of 1859 his father moved, overland, to Kansas, settling first in Linn County, but the following year the great drouth that prevailed in that state, drove him to Fort Scott, which has been the residence of the family ever since. In those days there were no schools in Kansas, and the father of young Coston put him in a printing office to learn the trade, thinking that the best substitute for a school. He served his apprenticeship of four years, and subsequently became identified with newspapers in Southeastern Kansas and Western Missouri as printer, publisher and editor. At the time of the Gunn City massacre, in Cass County, Missouri in 1872, he was publishing the Harrisonville Democrat, a Republican paper in that town, and had many thrilling experiences during the excitement connected with and following the murder of the County Court by a mob. His newspaper plant was burned by the same mob in the fall of 1872. He then went to Colorado, where he remained a couple of years, when the "law fever" developed in him, and he returned to Fort Scott, where he read law in the office of W. J. Bawden, and was admitted to the bar. He has been actively engaged in the practice ever since in the State of Kansas, Colorado and Missouri, except seven years, during which time he held the office of assistant attorney in the Interior Department in Washington City. He cam to Nome in July, 1900, and immediately started in the practice.

In 1903 the City of Nome concluded to make an effort to get a patent for the townsite, the titles of lots at that time being held only under the settlement laws of the United States, and Mr. Coston was employed by the city for that purpose. To do this involved a visit to Washington, where he spent four months in perfecting the details. He was appointed trustee by the Secretary of the Interior for the purpose of making this entry for the benefit of the occupants.

Mr. Coston married Miss Kittie E. Gibson in Buena Vista, Colorado, in 1882. Their oldest son is now in the sophomore year in the Kansas University, and Mrs. Coston and two younger children are residing in Nome.
NOME AND SEWARD PENINSULA, 1905

CHAUNCEY G. COWDEN

C. G. Cowden is the cashier of the Miners and Merchants Bank of Nome. He as served three years as city treasurer of Nome and is treasurer of the Northwestern Ditch Company; and is also interested in a number of mining properties. He comes from the Jersey shore, where he was born February 22, 1865. His boyhood days were spent in Pennsylvania, and his education was obtained in a Kentucky university. He is the son of a Christian minister.

His first business venture was in the real estate line in Pittsburgh, Pennsylvania. In 1888 he went to Tacoma, and was employed in the land department of the Northern Pacific Railway Company, mapping and appraising the value of lands. After two years of this work he was employed by the National Bank of Commerce of Tacoma, working for this institution in various capacities for ten years. Just prior to his going to Alaska, he was chief deputy county treasurer of Pierce County, Washington. He resigned this position to accept the position of cashier of the Alaska Banking and Safe Deposit Company of Nome corporation in June, 1901. He resigned September 1, 1904, and helped to organize the Miners and Merchants Bank of Nome.

Mr. Cowden has been twice married. His first wife, whom he married in Tacoma in 1891, was Miss Florence Lithgow. A son, Parker, who is now a boy of thirteen years, is the only issue of this marriage. In 1902 Mrs. Cowden died suddenly while visiting friends in the states. During the winter of 1904-'05 Mr. Cowden and Miss Hattie V. Thompson were married in Nome.
NOME AND SEWARD PENINSULA, 1905

CHARLES CRAWFORD

Charles Crawford was born in Quincy, Illinois, on June 23, 1856. He went to Colorado in 1870 and to Arizona and Mexico in 1879. He built the first iron-clad coaches that run from Cheyenne to Deadwood. He came to Fort Benton, Montana, in 1883, and was one of the early locators in Neihart, Montana, one of the richest silver camps in the west. Mr. Crawford came to Alaska in 1900 and for some time was in Dawson, later in Valdez, finally settling in Seward. He is a blacksmith by trade. For six years he served on the City Council and during the year 1913 was mayor of Seward.

PATHFINDER, May 1920

PETER M. CREPEAU

Mr. Crepeau was born in Minneapolis, and moved to Montana when the first railroad was built across the Treasure State. In Montana he met and married Miss Abbie McCarthy in 1888. Three children, Charles Edward, Louis Arthur, and Abbie Agnes (now Mrs. Victor L. Sparks of Skagway) were born to them.

In 1897 a year of great significance to the North country, Mr. Crepeau joined the gold rush to Dawson, building a boat at Lake Bennett, and with his pack followed the lake and Yukon River, shooting the dangerous rapids, not knowing what lay ahead. He spent a year in Dawson and in the Fall of 1898 returned to his home in Seattle. In the winter of 1899 he made the long and cold trip to Dawson by dog team over the ice, spending another season in the Klondike Camp.

When gold was discovered in Nome he joined the big stampede, yielding to the irresistible urge that lures a miner on. Mr. Crepeau again returned to his home in Seattle without a fortune, but carrying with him an intense love for the Great Northland. Another rumor of a strike brought him North in 1913, and in 1914 his wife and family joined him in Skagway, where they lived four years. Two of the children, Louis and Abbie, were married in

Skagway.

In 1918 the Crepeau family moved to Bainbridge Island where Peter Crepeau died on March 22, 1939. He is survived by his wife, children, and grandchildren--Charlotte and Peter Sparks.

ALASKA CATHOLIC, April 8, 1939

ULYSSIS GRANT CROCKER

Ulyssis Grant Crocker was born in Placer county, California, September 14, 1864. At eleven years of age he went to Colorado, and later followed placer mining. When 18 years of age he came to Seattle, and was on he Pacific coast until 1898 when he came to Alaska with the "Big Crowd." Went into Dawson and same year went back to Seattle after a stock of goods. Sold out stock and went to Nome running a bakery on a scow as it floated down to the new gold camp. Started the first bakery in Nome. Spent two winters in the Koyukuk, did well and had to go back to Seattle again. Was in Valdez a year, then went to Cordova to help Heney build the railroad. Was in the furniture business. He then went to Idaho and farmed for two years. From there he went to Chicago in hope that Mrs. Crocker's health might be recovered but she died there. Crocker then came back to Seattle and on up to Seward Alaska. In 1915 he came to Anchorage and opened up a furniture store, which business he still follows. He has married again and has a son.

PATHFINDER, December 1919

FRED E. DAGGETT

F. E. Daggett is a pioneer hotel man of Nome, and although his Golden Gate Hotel has been twice destroyed by fire he has rebuilt it and is still engaged in the business. He conducts the leading hotel of Nome, which in furnishing and equipment is equal to many first class hotels in far more pretentious cities.

He was born in Hammond, Wisconsin, August 23, 1864. He left home when he was fourteen years old and worked his way west. At Spokane,

Washington, he was employed for two years at the Windsor Hotel. He was subsequently connected with hotels in Portland, San Francisco and Northern California. He was employed in the Southern Pacific Commissary Department for four years, and was also connected with the commissary department of the California Navigation and Improvement Company. In 1898 he went to St. Michael, Alaska, with the Alaska Exploration Company, Captain Hibbard, manager. He resided in St. Michael until the spring of 1900, filling the position of post steward besides having charge of the commissary department for the company. Going to Nome in 1899, he saw an opening for a hotel. He purchased a lot and went "outside" to obtain the necessary money for the construction of the building. He and A. J. Johnson built the first hotel in Nome. They charted a vessel to take to Nome the material and equipment for the hotel, the cost of which was $35,000. Arriving in Nome they discovered that the lot upon which the building was to be erected had been jumped and sold many times. Rather than seek to recover it by litigation another lot was purchased, which is the site where the hotel now stands.

The Golden Gate Hotel was completed on May 25, and at 1:30 p.m., after the last carpet was laid, a fire broke out by 3 o'clock the hotel property was entirely destroyed, entailing a loss of $40,000. They started to rebuild, and two weeks later the new building was open for the reception of guests.

July 5, 1904, at 5 o'clock in the morning, another fire destroyed the Golden Gate Hotel, and what was worse than the destruction of the property, destroyed three lives. This fire left Mr. Daggett with but $70 in cash and without a change of clothing. By the assistance of the public-spirited citizens of Nome he has erected a third building which with its furnishings has cost $43,000.

NOME AND SEWARD PENINSULA, 1905

REGNAR DAHL

Regnar Dahl was born in Norway in 1849 and came to Seattle just before the great fire of 1889. He remained here until 1898, when he was employed by United States Government under the supervision of Dr. Sheldon Jackson, at that time general agent of education in Alaska, to assist in an attempt by the War Department to furnish relief to miners in the Yukon Valley by bringing in a herd of reindeer.

Dr. Jackson and 20 young men, including Mr. Dahl, left Seattle on March 19, 1898, for Haines Mission with the deer. Eventually the party reached St. Michael, and en route down the Yukon River, prospected many of the rivers and creeks they encountered.

Mr. Dahl spent several years around St. Michael and in the Seward Peninsula country before and after the discovery of gold at Nome, before returning to Seattle to make his home in this city. He conducted a store in West Seattle for some time and later for several years was employed in the city light department in Seattle.

In 1910 he went to Petersburg and engaged in the mild curing of salmon for eight years, returning to Seattle in 1918 to become associated with the Skandia-American Bank, and remaining with the bank until it wound up its business four years later, since which time he had lived in retirement in his Seattle home.

Regnar Dahl died in December 24, 1932. He is survived by his wife, Martha Dahl; and son, Regnar Dahl; a daughter, Mrs. Sigrid Larson of Seattle; and a son, Sheldon Dahl of Los Angeles.

ALASKA WEEKLY, December 30, 1932

FRED W. DASHLEY

Fred W. Dashley is a member of the firm of Carstens Bros. & Dashley, wholesale and retail butchers, and is one of the successful business men of Nome. He was born in Oswego, New York, August 4, 1859, and educated in the public schools of his native city. He has been identified with the butcher business ever since early boyhood. This business was the one in which his father was engaged. In 1877 he started west, and stopped first in Chicago where he was employed by Libby, McNeil & Co. He subsequently lived in Colorado and in Nebraska, and at a later date went to Montana, where the alluring prospect of mining caused him to invest the little capital he had accumulated and in the language of the West "go broke."

He arrived in Seattle in 1891 and started a butcher and grocery business in South Seattle on a capital of $4. With the exception of another unfortunate mining venture in the Atlin District of Alaska in 1899, when he lost $1,000, he has shown commendable thrift. He came to Nome in the spring of 1900 and has been identified with the Nome country ever since. Besides being one of the substantial business men of Nome, he is the owner of valuable mining property on Seward Peninsula, notably in the Inmachuk region.

Mr. Dashley and Miss Christina Schlax were married in Seattle, November 24, 1891. The issue of this union is two children, Leo, age thirteen, and Hazel, age ten.

NOME AND SEWARD PENINSULA, 1905

JAMES M. DAVIDSON

Mr. Davidson was born in 1853 at For Jones, Siskiyou County, California, where he grew to manhood, studied civil engineering in the University of California, held political office for several years in his home county, and later engaged in mining and civil engineering.

When the news of the Klondike gold strike reached the outside, Mr. Davidson's interest was enlisted, and in the spring of 1898 he made his way over famed Chilkoot Pass and thence down the lakes and the great Yukon River to Dawson. He stayed there but a short time. He went to Circle City where he mined on Mastodon Creek. Upon the opening of navigation in the spring of 1899 news of the Nome strike reached him and he went to the then practically unknown

Seward Peninsula, landing at Nome July 4th.

His first work was that of a civil engineer surveying lots in the Nome townsite and mining claims on the contiguous creeks.

With two partners, W.H.Illiss(?) and W.I. Leland, also Californians, the mining firm of Davidson, Leland, and Illiss was formed and out of this partnership the Miocene Ditch Company was organized. Water from the Miocene Ditch made possible the development of Nome's famous "beach lines" and added many millions to the wealth of the nation. Mr. Davidson's work and investments in the Seward Peninsula netted him a substantial fortune and after leaving Nome, he went to Alberta, Canada and engaged in ranching on a large scale. His venture in farming--largely wheat raising--was not successful, due to frost and lack of rain, and he returned to California, with his family, and located in Oakland and San Francisco, where he made his headquarters until he gain returned to mining, principally to British Columbia, with more or less success.

From British Columbia, he returned to Alaska, going into the Fairbanks country, where he achieved notable results. The Fairbanks Exploration Company which through Mr. Davidson's efforts has acquired large placer holding, water rights and ditch rights of way is now developing on an extensive scale by installing dredges at an expense of some $15,000,000.

Mr. Davidson came of a family of pioneers. His father, William Davidson, a native of Virginia, crossed the plains from Indiana in 1850, arriving at Hangtown in the fall of that year. He died in 1915 at 88 years at Mr. Davidson's San Francisco home.

Mr. Davidson, while active in mining developments, never lost his interest in the soil, having been born on a farm, and among his holdings at the time of his death was a ranch in Montana. He was twice married and leaves two children, Helen Irene and Philip, who live in Oakland.

Mr. Davidson a few years ago married Mrs.

Sophia J. Rice of Yreka, Calif, who survives him, the Seattle home being on South street.
ALASKA WEEKLY, May 4, 1928

HERMAN CARLISLE DAVIS

Herman C. Davis was born on Lopez Island, Washington in 1890. He was a pioneer in the salmon canning business on Puget Sound. His sons, James V. Davis and Lisle Davis joined him in that business and came to Alaska with their father twenty-five years ago. Lisle resided in Alaska, at Juneau and vicinity since that time, and has always been engaged in the salmon fisheries. He was a Superintendent for the Pacific Alaska Fisheries and went from that company to join the Burkhardt's in the Alaska Consolidated.

A few years ago, in connection with his brother, James V. Davis, and George Franklin, Herman acquired fish trap locations, and he had been an independent trap operator since that time. He made the business a success. He was regarded as one of the best cannerymen and trap operators in the North.

Herman C. Davis died in Juneau, December 24, 1932. He is survived by his widow, Mrs. Winnie Davis of Juneau, his father and mother, Mr. and Mrs. Raleigh E. Davis of Cordova, two sisters and four brothers. The brothers and sisters are Capt. James V. Davis of Juneau; R.I. Davis of Anacortes, Washington; P.H. Davis of Security Bay; Don S. Davis with P.E. Harris, Alaska canneryman of Seattle; Mrs. Louis Lemieux of Petersburg; and Ruth Davis, who married some years ago and lives in the states.
ALASKA WEEKLY, January 8, 1932

JEFFERSON C. DAVIS

Although still in the prime of life, for he had not completed his fifty-second year, General Davis was a veteran of the Mexican and civil wars. Born in Indiana, March 2, 1828, he, at the beginning of the war with Mexico, enlisted in Colonel Lane's Indiana regiment. For conspicuous gallantry at the battle of Buena Vista he was, in 1848, given a second lieutenant's commission in the 1st regiment, U.S. artillery. In 1852 he became 1st lieutenant, and in April, 1861, was one of the garrison of Fort Sumter. In the following month he was made a captain, and given leave to raise a regiment of volunteers, the 22nd Indiana infantry, of which he became colonel. For the capture of a superior force of the enemy at Milford, Missouri, Colonel Davis was made a brigadier general of volunteers, December 18th, 1861. In March, 1862, General Davis commanded a division at the battle of Pea Ridge; in April he took part in the battle of Corinth. Shortly afterward General Davis was assigned to duty in the army of the Tennessee. In September of the same year he shot his commanding officer, General Nelson at the Galt House in Louisville, after an altercation in the course of which he had been grossly insulted and finally struck by Nelson. For this he was arrested, but was never tried, and soon returned to duty.

In 1862-3 General Davis commanded a division in the battles about Murfreesborough and at Chickamauga; in 1864 he was commander of the 14th corps in Sherman's army, taking part in the Atlanta campaign, and in the subsequent march to the sea. He became major general by brevet in 1865, and colonel of the 23rd U.S. infantry July 28, 1866. From 1867 to 1870 he commanded the forces in Alaska. During this time he made an expedition against some rebellious Indians on the main land, and quelled some disturbances at Sitka. After the murder of General Canby, in 1873, General Davis took command of the forces operating against the Modoc Indians, and compelled their surrender.

General Davis died in Chicago, Illinois, November 30, 1879.

ALASKA APPEAL, December 15, 1879

LISLE DAVIS

Lisle Davis was a native of Lopez Island, Washington, where he was born 42 years ago.

Lisle's father was a pioneer in the salmon

canning business on Puget Sound. His sons,
James V. Davis and Lisle joined him in that
business and came to Alaska with their father
twenty-five years ago. Lisle resided in
Alaska, at Juneau and vicinity since that time,
and has always been engaged in the salmon
fisheries. He was a Superintendent for the
Pacific Alaska Fisheries and went from that
company to join the Burkhardt's in the Alaska
Consolidated.

A few years ago, in connection with his
brother, James V. Davis and George Franklin he
acquired some excellent trap locations and he
had been an independent trap operator since
that time. He made the business a success. He
was regarded as one of the best cannerymen and
trap operators in the North.

Lisle Davis died December 24, 1931 in
Juneau, Alaska. He is survived by his widow,
Mrs. Winnie Davis, of Juneau, his father and
mother, Mr. and Mrs. Raleigh E. Davis of
Cordova, two sisters and four brothers. The
brothers and sisters are Capt. James V. Davis
of Juneau; R.L. Davis of Anacortes, Washington;
P.H. Davis of Security bay; Don S. Davis with
P.E. Harris, Alaska canneryman of Seattle; Mrs.
Louis Lemieux of Petersburg; and Ruth Davis,
who married some years ago and lives in the
states.

ALASKA WEEKLY, January 8, 1932

CLARA S. DEDMAN

Mrs. Clara S. Dedman, one of Skagway's
most prominent business women, as well as one
of the earliest settlers of the community,
arrived in Skagway on July 5, 1898. Her first
home--one of the best in Skagway at that time--
was a rough board structure of two small rooms,
the sole furnishings consisting of three built-
in bunks, a table, and three apple boxes which
served as chairs.

Mrs. Dedman's first work in Skagway was as
housekeeper at the old Pacific Hotel. this was
the city's finest hotel., at that time,
providing seven or eight rooms, each 8X10, with
built-in bunks, washstand, and coal oil lamps--

and nothing more.

the following winter brought hordes of people on their way in to the gold fields and Mrs. Dedman soon found her housekeeping duties extended to helping outfit those travelers. She estimates that she lined about 500 parkas with fur that winter. the hardships of the trail were followed by an epidemic of spinal meningitis and erysipelas. The hospitals were full, and the hotel became an informal emergency hospital, with Mrs. Dedman attending to broken bones, frozen feet, and victims of snow blindness as well as caring for the sick.

Mrs. Dedman claims the distinction of importing the first bathtub in Skagway, and the Pacific was the first "hotel with bath"--an innovation that immediately met with enthusiasm and popularity, trail-weary travelers gladly availing themselves of this none too exclusive luxury.

Through all her busy days, Mrs. Dedman has taken a very active part in all public enterprises. She was a member and for several years Commander of the Lady Maccabees, prominent in the Idle Hour Club of early days and, following a return from South Pasadena, organized the Woman's Improvement Club, whose object was the beautifying of the city. They planted many trees to replace in part the beautiful growth that had been ruthlessly sacrificed in the first mad settlement days.

Mrs. Dedman has always been prominent in the activities of the Alpine Club, and was largely instrumental in securing the Government grant to the tract generally known as the Alpine Park, and the bridge over the Skagway River, leading to the park, call the Alpine Bridge.

The Skagway Women's Club counts Mrs. Dedman one of it earliest members. Her greatest interest in the club work has been perhaps in the Annual Harvest Fair, a feature of Club activities which she has enthusiastically advocated and assisted with for a number of years.

In 1910 Mrs. Dedman's husband, Mr. George

R. Dedman, and Mr. Ed Foreman purchased the Golden North Hotel, which has from that time on been the scene of Mrs. Dedman's activities. Following the death of Mr. Dedman in 1925, Mrs. Dedman has been proprietor of the hotel.

For nearly 34 years Mrs. Dedman has been a real Alaskan.

STROLLER'S WEEKLY, April 1932

EDWARD deGROFF

One of the oldest and most prominent citizens of Alaska is Edward deGroff, the leading merchant of the capital city. Mr. de Groff came to Alaska in 1880 and to Juneau in March, 1881. He was the first postmaster at this place, which was then known as Harrisburg, the name being changed to Juneau in December of that year, and fulfilled the functions of the office in addition to his duties as resident agent in charge of the extensive business of the Northwest Trading company. In 1882 he was transferred to Killisnoo by his company, superintending their operations there until 1886, when he removed to Sitka and established the business which he still owns and conducts. Mr. deGroff was one of the commissioners appointed to represent Alaska at the late World's Fair. He holds the agency at Sitka for the Pacific Coast Steamship company and for the Alaska Commercial company, the latter operating a line of steamers to the westward and north to the mouth of the Yukon River. In 1900 Edward deGroff received a commission as United States Commissioner at Sitka.

He married Mrs. Lena Vanderbilt, the widow of his partner, in 1894. She died in Los Angeles, California in February 1928. Mrs. deGroff is survived by a son, John Vanderbilt and a daughter, Mrs. Nance Macado.

Mr. deGroff is a native of New York, born at Snug Harbor, Staten Island in that state, October 25, 1860. He died in Sitka, Alaska, April 7, 1910.

    ALASKA MINING RECORD, January 1896
    VERSTOVIAN, April 1910
    ALASKA WEEKLY, February 8, 1928

ARTHUR K. DELANEY

Arthur K. Delaney was born at Fort Ticonderoga, on Lake Champlain, January 10th, 1841. In 1845 he removed with his father's family to Wisconsin, then one of the new and coming territories of the United States. He resided in Wisconsin continually until april 1887, when he came to the coast. He received a common school educations, working his way through one of the high school of Wisconsin by teaching school at odd times and devoting his energies to any work which might give him funds to complete his academic course. He also read law from time to time in the office of Amos J. Rising, later one of the judges of the supreme court of the state of Colorado. In 1865 he was admitted to the bar, and the same year married Anna J. Wallwork. After his admission, the judge became quite active in the practice of law as well as in public matters. In 1869 he served as a member of the Wisconsin assembly, and at the expiration of his assembly term was three times consecutively elected county superintendent of school for his old county of Dodge. In 1881 and 1882 he served the state senate of Wisconsin and on the election of Mr. Cleveland to the presidency, was appointed in 1885 District Attorney at Milwaukee, Wisconsin, which position he resigned in 1887 to accept the office of collector of the Port of Sitka, Alaska, where he arrived in April of that year.

He started for the North, reaching Sitka on the 16th day of April, 1887, since which time he has been a resident of Alaska. In 1889 the administration having changed, the judge removed to Juneau and opened a law office, readily obtaining a very active practice. Mr. Cleveland again exhibited his confidence in the judge by appointing him December 1895, U.S. Judge for the District of Alaska which position he held until after the inauguration of President McKinley.

Judge Delaney died in Pasco Robles, California, January 21, 1905.

KETCHIKAN MINING JOURNAL, Jan. 20, 1905
ALASKA MONTHLY, May 1906

DR. ALBERT L. DERBYSHIRE

During the past three years Dr. A. L. Derbyshire has filled the position of Assistant Surgeon of the U. S. Marine Hospital Service in Nome. This position places him in charge of the hospital and quarantine work, and requires him to inspect all vessels arriving at Nome.

Dr. Derbyshire is a native of Franklin County, Indiana. He was born May 23, 1851. When a young man he learned telegraphy, and was employed as a telegraph operator on the Wabash Railroad for a period of six years. It was during this time he began the study of medicine. He afterward completed his medical education in the Ohio Medical College at Cincinnati and Indiana Medical College at Indianapolis, and was graduated from the latter institution Feb. 18, 1886. He began the practice of medicine in Connersville, Ind. In 1887 he moved to San Diego, Cal., and practiced in San Diego and El Cajon Valley. He spent a year at Cedrous Island, Mexico, as physician for a mining company, and moved to Oregon in 1893, locating at Stayton, seventeen miles from Salem. Five years later he moved to Portland where he resided until the spring of 1900, when he came to Nome. He tried his hand at mining for a couple of years, but resumed the practice of his profession in 1902, subsequently receiving the Government appointment heretofore noted.

Dr. Derbyshire was married in 1879. The issue of this marriage is a daughter, Laura, now twenty-three years old. Mrs. Derbyshire died in 1882. Thirteen years later he contract a second marriage with Miss Francis A. Briggs, of Stayton, Oregon.

JOHN A. DEXTER

John A. Dexter is one of the earliest pioneers of Seward Peninsula. He first came to this country in the steam whaler Grampus in 1883. In 1890 he came to Alaska to work in the Oomalik silver mines, and has been a resident of Seward Peninsula ever since. He conducted a trading station on Golovin Bay at the place now known as Cheenik. For many years this station was known as Dexter's. As early as 1895 he prospected on Ophir Creek.

Mr. Dexter was born on Barton Heights, Virginia, December 9, 1852. He went to Boston after the surrender of Richmond, and in 1870 went to sea. For a period of twenty-one years he sailed the seas. During an interval he was engaged in putting down torpedoes for Chili and Peru. He served as paymaster clerk in the Shenandoah.

Mr. Dexter has had some thrilling experiences in the Northland, one of which came near costing him his life. In 1894, while traveling from St. Michael to his home on Golovin Bay, he got caught in a blizzard while on the ice. This was the worst blizzard he ever saw in the country. It lasted near three weeks. The ice broke and he and four natives were afloat for nine days. They dug a hole in the snow and put a cover over it. This dug-out was their only protection from the furious storm. When the ice finally drifted back there was a chasm of sever feet of water between it and the anchored ice. He attempted to jump the chasm, but miscalculating the distance, fell in the water. He was able to grasp the anchored ice and pull himself out. He was wet to the waist, and with the thermometer at forty degrees below zero was instantly covered with a solid sheet of ice. His legs were blistered by the intense cold and he was saved from freezing only by a change of clothing. Before he arrived at home he got in an overflow and had another narrow escape from freezing. Mr. Dexter still suffers from his misfortune, but is able to travel and attend to his business affairs.

No man in the North country is better acquainted with the Eskimo, no man knows more of the true life of the native of this country than Mr. Dexter. His wife is an Eskimo woman.
NOME AND SEWARD PENINSULA, 1905

WILLIAM DON DICKINSON

William Don Dickinson of Ketchikan has been endorsed by the union local at Petersburg and by the republican club of that place as a candidate for representative. The announcement of Mr. Dickinson came too late to get his name on the official primary ballot, but will make a bid for votes.

Mr. Dickinson is well known, having been a resident of Alaska for the past 44 years. He helped explore the Yukon country with Lieut. Swatke in 1881. Two years previous to that he was with Prof. Muir in his second explorations of the glaciers of Alaska. He also worked for the government a number of years, under the republican administration, and was court interpreter in Alaska for treasury officials before any courts were established by enactments.

Mr. Dickinson was an officer in the marshal's office of the first division, was chief of police under former Governor John Brady, for the part of Alaska now the Ketchkian district, and has been always active for public improvements and institutions.

Mr. Dickinson is now engaged in the fishing trade.

DAILY ALASKA EMPIRE, March 30, 1920

JOSEPH C. DIERINGER

Joseph Dieringer was born at Morchois, Columbia County, Ohio, March 12, 1851. In 1864 he removed to Wisconsin with his parent. Mr. Dieringer left home when he was but 11 years of age and worked in a store at Schleisingerville, Wisconsin. In 1864 he went to Milwaukee, where he attended school evenings, and was later appointed messenger in the House of Representatives at Madison. He was here employed by the State Auditor, for whom he worked six years. He attended the University of Wisconsin, taking up civil engineering; graduated in 1876.

In 1882 Mr. Dieringer landed on the Pacific Coast. He worked for the Northern Pacific for a time running a line from Meeker

Junction to Seattle. In 1883 he followed the restaurant business in which he was highly successful. In 1886 he engaged in farming in the Stuck Valley, clearing and draining 180 acres.

Leaving his farm Mr. Dieringer trekked to the Caribou mining district on Williams Creek. In 1900 Mr. Dieringer and a Mr. W.R. Henning, a partner, arrived at Nome with a team of horses, a wagon, and a complete outfit for sluicing. A storm destroyed their equipment and Mr. dieringer returned to the States.

In April, 1901 he went to Dawson, Yukon Territory, taking in some milch cows and beef cattle, together with other perishables. Here Mr. Dieringer opened up a restaurant on Craig street, selling out August 1, 1902; left Dawson on the steamer CASCA, and arrived in Valdez September 23, 1902. He makes his home in Valdez.

PATHFINDER, March 1920

HENRY J. DIETER

Henry J. Dieter is a well-known mine owner and operator of Seward Peninsula whose connection with this industry in this part of Alaska dates from the fall of 1900. He went to Dawson in 1898, where he was engaged in mining for two years. He came down the Yukon to Nome in 1900.

Mr. Dieter was born in St. Paul, Minnesota, October 15, 1862. His father was the proprietor of the oldest shoe establishment in Minnesota, and the son acquired a thorough knowledge of this branch of the mercantile business, with which he was associated until he was twenty-three years old. At the age of twenty-three he went west and engaged in quartz mining in Lower California and Arizona. He resided five years at Mercur, Utah, where he learned the cyanide process, the method for treating low-grade gold ores. Subsequently he went to the Northwest and prospected in Rossland, British Columbia. He was in this region during a period of two years, and sold two good prospects. At a later date he was connected with the construction of the Great Northern Railroad. In the early nineties he returned to Utah, and at this early date became interested in Alaska. When he heard the news of the Klondike strike in 1897, he started immediately for the northern gold field. He got over the pass that season, but was compelled to make a winter camp on Lake Bennett. He returned to St. Paul that winter and again started for Dawson in February, arriving at his destination June 11. To borrow his own language, he "never made a big thing in Dawson, but met with fair success." He came near striking it rich in a fraction off 28 above Bonanza, but failed to find pay in any of the many holes that he sunk. After he sold the property a "lucky Swede" located the pay-streak and extracted gold dust to the value of $380,000.

He had sent a man to Nome in 1899, to prospect. He arrived in Nome late in the season of 1900, and learned that property had been staked for him on the Bluestone in the Port Clarence country. Prospecting this property, he obtained pans of gravel that yielded as much as $313 the pan. But the pay was in pockets, and the result of operation was not commensurate with the alluring prospects. He mined successfully two seasons on a claim at the mouth of Alder Creek. He is the discoverer of a big ledge in this vicinity which appeared to possess the possibility of a great mine.

Before leaving Dawson he was shown stream tin from the York region, and after arriving in the Nome country he kept men in this part of the peninsula prospecting for tin ledges. The result of this prospecting has been the location of a large number of tin claims on Cape Mountain.

In the fall of 1903 he went to Milwaukee and obtained financing. He was also involved in the organization of the United States-Alaska Tin Mining Company. Arrangements have been completed for the erection of a smelter at Seattle, Washington, for the smelting of all the ore from this mine.

He became a benedict last spring. Mrs. Dieter was formerly Miss Blanche Seepluch, of Milwaukee, Wisconsin.
NOME AND SEWARD PENINSULA, 1905

JOSEPH F. DIGGS

Jos. F. Diggs, the postmaster and pioneer merchant of Cordova was born in Leadville, Col.

He was educated in the public schools in Seattle and moved with his parents to Juneau in 1895 where he also attended school.

Mr. Diggs first worked for B.M.Behrends whose firm has the oldest bank in Alaska. Mr. Diggs later worked in Juneau for S. Blum and in 1899 went to Dawson. He returned to Juneau in 1901 and accepted a position with the Ross Higgins Company, the successors to Decker Bros. Thereafter he had charge of the grocery department for c. Gold stein and he and Mr. Goldstein incorporated the Western Trading Company. Mr. Diggs came to Eyak, or old Cordova, in 1906 in the interests of the firm, and the following April purchased the interests of his partner.

Mr. Diggs was elected to the first council after Cordova was incorporated, but resigned as councilman in order to serve as postmaster. He was married to Rose Schweitzer in 1907 and his two daughters were born in Cordova.
ALASKA-YUKON MAGAZINE, December 1910

EDWARD A. DIXON

Edward A. Dixon is a native of the province of New Brunswick where he grew to young manhood, coming to what is now the province of Alberta in 1892 as a member of the then Northwest Mounted Police. He was stationed at Fort McLeod until 1897 when he came with a detachment of police to Yukon.

In 1897 Mr. Dixon opened the first police post at Canyon City at the head of Miles Canyon. Remaining with the police until the following year, he was honorably discharged when he engaged in the perilous calling of piloting scows and barges through the renowned Miles Canyon and Whitehorse Rapids which he followed all during the period of the Klondike rush in '98, '99 and during 1900 until the railroad was completed from Bennett.

In 1900 Mr. Dixon erected and operated the Pioneer hotel, the first building in Whitehorse. The same year and in partnership with Cariste Racine he started the Whitehorse Steam Laundry with which he was associated until 1903 when with his present partner, Chas. H. Johnston, he erected and opened the Regina hotel.

WEEKLY STAR, March 12, 1915

BEVERLY B. DOBBS

Beverly B. Dobbs is a photographer who has been identified with Nome since the beginning of 1900.

He was born near Marshall, Missouri, in 1868. He is a farmer's son. He moved with his parents to Nebraska in 1876, and learned photography in Lincoln. He went to Washington in 1888, and located in Bellingham, where he conducted a gallery for twelve years.

Attracted by the Nome gold fields, he went north in the great stampede of 1900, and has been every summer since then in Nome. He probably has the largest collection of Seward Peninsula views that ever have been made. His studies of the Eskimo show careful and painstaking work. The best evidence of the character of his work is the fact that he received one of the six gold medals awarded at the St. Louis Fair. Dobbs began experimenting with the newly invented motion picture camera. in 1910 he showed the first motion pictures of Alaska in Seattle, at the old Grand Theatre.

In 1911, he sold his business at Nome to the Lomen Bros. and devoted two years in exhibiting his work in the largest American cities. In 1913, returning to Seattle, he established a motion picture laboratory which has since occupied his time.

May 20, 1896, Mr. Dobbs and Miss Dorothy Sturgeon, of Bellingham, were married.

NOME AND SEWARD PENINSULA, 1905
ALASKA WEEKLY, Aug. 23, 1929

DOLLY SMITH DONALDSON

Dolly Smith Donaldson was born at what is known as Smith's Ferry near Elkton, Oregon, December 9, 1885. She was the eighth and youngest child of a pioneer family in early Oregon history. Her grandfather, I. Wells, was one of the early pioneers crossing with ox team and covered wagon the Oregon Trail in 1847. The father, J.L. Smith a Virginian, immigrated to Oregon with his parents in 1852. He proceeded this daughter in death when she was but three years old. The home of J.L. Smith and his wife, Esther Wells Smith, was situated on the banks of the Umpqua, near Elkton. The mother was the first white child born in this region of western Oregon. They moved to Roseburg in 1897, where the mother established and still maintains a home. There she entered her children in the Roseburg schools. From these school and Monmouth Normal, Mrs. Donaldson graduated and took up the work of teaching. She taught at Roseburg Salem High, Douglas and La Touche. Going to Alaska in 1920 she met and married William Donaldson, an engineer in the Government employ.

Dolly Smith Donaldson died in Roseburg, Oregon on March 11, 1928. She is survived by her husband, William Donaldson of Juneau, Alaska; two brothers, Lewis and J.P. Smith of Roseburg and Oakland; and three sisters, Mrs. Carr of Sanak, Alaska, Mrs. Toner of Yoncallar, Oregon, and Mrs. Goodman of Roseburg. Ex-Governor Stephen F. Chadwick, deceased, was her uncle, and Stephen Chadwick of Seattle, now a candidate for governor, was a cousin.

ALASKA WEEKLY, March 30, 1928

ROBERT S. DONALDSON

Robert S. Donaldson was born in Ontario, Canada. As a young man he went to Dawson, Yukon territory, in the spring of 1905, worked at mining. In the spring of 1916, Mr. Donaldson was appointed district storekeeper of the Alaskan Engineering Commission, with headquarters at Talkeetna. When the U.S. entered the World War, he resigned, enlisted in the 31st Engineers and was regimental supply sergeant of this organization until after the signing of the armistice, after which he joined the North Russian Expedition and was in complete charge of the base supply warehouse of the expedition at Murmansk, North Russia, for which service he received a commission and citation for efficiency. Returning from Russia, he was appointed general storekeeper of the Alaskan Engineering commission on the northern division, with headquarters at Nenana, Alaska. In the spring of 1921, Donaldson resigned his position with the Alaska Railroad to devote his time to the promotion of the Healy river Coal Corporation, of which he was the vice-president. Mr. Donaldson is now engaged in the development of the talc deposits of Skagit and Whatcom Counties, in the state of Washington.

ALASKA WEEKLY, October 4, 1929

ROBERT L. DOUGLASS

Robert C. Douglass was born in Nova Scotia, Canada, 1871.

Mr. Douglass had a remarkable career, being a veteran of four wars, according to E. Valentine, a friend. As a boy of 15, Mr. Valentine said Douglass joined the Canadian forces as a soldier bugler and served through what is known as the "Red Rebellion." He received a silver medal for these services.

Shortly after this campaign he is said to have attended the famous English military school at Aldershot, England, from which he graduated. Following this he joined British forces and served with them through the "Punjab War" in India. While in England later, the Boer War broke out and he was again found in the British forces in South Africa, servicing through the period of hostilities.

After this he returned to Canada, studied optometry and established himself in business at Nelson, B.C.

He was married and had two children at the outbreak of the World War. Commissioned a captain in the British army, he left Canada with the first contingent and was a member of the Eighteenth Battalion in France. He took part in battles on the Somme, and around Ypres until badly wounded by shrapnel. He lay on the field for 24 hours until the Canadians drove back the Germans and rescued him and others. After 10 months in a hospital, he recovered and returned to the front where he remained to the end of the war. He was decorated for gallantry in action. While Mr. Douglass was in France, his wife and children died. He came back to Canada and later came to this country.

Mr. Douglass has been a resident of Juneau for the past five years. He was an optometrist by profession and after working for various local firms, followed that trade in offices in the Valentine building during the last three years. He died in Juneau, Alaska, November 1, 1928.

ALASKA WEEKLY, December 7, 1928

BEN F. DOWNING

Ben Downing was born in 1862(?) in New Hampshire. Early in life he lost both parents, and was adopted by a farmer in Maine.

At the age of 12, he ran away and shipped as cabin boy on a Yankee trader. Young Downing followed the sea until he grew to manhood.

Tiring of the life of a sailor, he went to Montana. Here he became a cowboy, and later went into ranching for himself. He then drifted to Mexico, where he engaged in prospecting and mining. Returning to Montana, he was appointed United States deputy marshal. While engaged in this peaceful pursuit he had several engagements with cattle "rustlers," and, as a consequence, carried three bullets in his body until the day of his death. In 1896 Downing went to Circle City, which was then the principal mining camp in Alaska. After mining, in '98 he secured a contract with the United States postal service to carry the mail from Dawson, Y.T., to Fort Gibbon, a distance of 800 miles.

In the summer months the mail was carried on the Yukon steamers, which were very irregular at that time. This made it necessary to often carry the mail the entire 800 miles by "poling" up the Yukon. Downing established a system of relay stations along the Yukon, and had over forty men constantly in his employ.

During the winter the mail was carried by a relay system of dog teams, the entire distance in less than two weeks. Downing, with his picked dog team, was constantly traveling the Yukon in all kinds of weather and over trails that others declared impassable. In fact, it was Downing and his men who made the trails on the Yukon.

In the fall of 1903 Mr. Downing was at Fort Gibbon, the lower end of the mail route, when the river closed. As usual, Ben was the first "musher" to start over the ice for Dawson. On this trip, Ben fell through the ice. It was forty below zero but with the aid of his dogs, he was able to pull himself out of the river. He managed to make his way to a trapper's cabin. On the following morning Ben Downing with his feet and legs swollen, "broke trail" to Dawson, a distance of 288 miles. Upon his arrival at Dawson, Downing refused to go to the hospital and undergo the partial amputation of four toes.

Later, however, he underwent the operation, and nearly died of blood poisoning as a result of his delay. It was due to his procrastination in the matter that eventually caused his death. After leaving the hospital, Downing was able to resume his travels on the Yukon until the close of his contract in 1904. He then went to the Tanana country where he engaged in a general merchandise and transportation business, very much to his profit. In the fall of 1905, Downing sold out all of his interests in Alaska.

Ben F. Downing died in San Francisco, January 11, 1906.

ALASKA MAGAZINE, April 1906

FERRIS "FRED" S. DUNHAM

Mr. Dunham was born in the state of New York in 1847,

and was at the time of his death 79 years old.
He removed to Michigan with his parents when
but a small child, taking up residence on a
farm.
    Mr. Dunham always resided on the frontier.
As a young man he engaged in the cattle
business on the plains, where he hunted
buffalos. At the time of the Custer massacre
he was at an army post nearby. Following the
settlement of the Indian troubles he located in
the Black Hills in North Dakota. While there
he was united to Miss Kate O'Reilly.
    In 1898, Mr. Dunham joined the stampede to
the Klondike, and in 1899 established a grocery
store on Second Avenue, in the rear of Hobb's
sawmill, in Dawson. He went to Auburn in 1911
and ran a grocery store there for many years.
    Ferris "Fred" S. Dunham died on February
17, 1926 in Auburn, Washington. He is survived
by his widow, Mrs. Kate Dunham, two sons,
Sidney Dunham of Yakima, and Michael Dunham,
and two daughters, Misses Rachel and Frances
Dunham of Auburn.
    ALASKA WEEKLY, February 26, 1926

EDWARD R. DUNN

    Mr. Dunn was born in the city of New York,
October 3, 1858. His parents emigrated from
Ireland to this country. Mr. Dunn's boyhood
days were spent in New York, but at the age of
sixteen he left home and went to Texas, where
he rode the range as a cowboy. He mined in
Colorado and New Mexico, and when twenty-one
was a subcontractor on the Atlantic & Pacific
Railroad in New Mexico and Arizona. But with
the exception of a short period of his life
spent in the construction work of railroads, he
has been a prospector and miner for a quarter
of a century. Mexico, Arizona, New Mexico,
Colorado, California, Montana, Idaho and Alaska
are countries in which he has prospected and
mined. In 1879-'80 he operated extensively in
Leadville, and made a big poke, but there have
been lots of times, to use his own expressive
words, when he "had no more money than a
jackrabbit." He and his brother rode across

the desert from Bradshaw Mountains to San Diego, Cal., a distance of about 800 miles. The greatest distance between watering places on this trip was seventy miles. In '83 Mr. Dunn made another long horseback trip, riding from Prescott, Arizona, to Portland, Oregon. He has had three narrow escapes from death on the desert, and on one occasion when thirst had driven him and his companion almost crazy, they found water by following coyote tracks into a little hollow in the scorching hills.

In the spring of 1898 Mr. Dunn went to Dawson over the Chilkoot Pass, and mined on Gold Hill. The following year he came down the river to Nome, arriving June 28, 1899. The next day after his arrival he leased No. 5 Anvil Creek, and on June 30 started the first pack train across the tundra with supplies and sluice-boxes to begin work on the Anvil property. He operated on Anvil Creek during the season of '99. In August of this year he left the work in charge of a foreman and went to Seattle, where he purchased thirty-five head of cattle, 108 sheep, a span of horses, lumber for a house and a quantity of general supplies. This cargo was shipped on the Lauranda, and the vessel was wrecked on St. George Island Sept. 20, while enroute to Nome, and while some of the cargo was removed to the island, shippers sustained nearly a total loss.

He did not complete the journey to Nome, but returned to Seattle on the Townsend. The following season, 1900, he came to Nome, bringing ten head of horses, four wagons and a complete equipment for mining. In 1899 and 1900 he acquired considerable property in the Council and Nome Mining Districts, and since then he devoted most of his time to operations on Ophir Creek. His son, Ed. R. Dunn, Jr., owns a quarter interest in the famous Snowflake Mine on the hill between Dexter and Anvil Creeks.

In the winter of 1903-'04 Mr. Dunn came to Nome from Seattle via Dawson over the ice. He accomplished the trip in fifty-eight days. In the latter part of 1903 he and others bought a quartz mine in Chihuahua, Mexico.

September 23, 1885, Ed. R. Dunn and Miss Abbie Sullivan were married in Butte, Montana. The issue of this marriage has been three children, only one of whom, the eldest son, born in April, 1887, survives.

NOME AND SEWARD PENINSULA, 1905

JOHN H. DUNN

A farmer's son, a school teacher at the age of sixteen, and by teaching acquiring money to obtain a collegiate education, a law student, a lawyer, and finally a federal official in Alaska - this is an epitome of the life of the subject of this sketch. John H. Dunn was born in Mercer County, Pennsylvania, June 18, 1866. His father was a member of an old English family that came to America in the early part of the last century, and his mother was of German lineage.

John H. Dunn was the eldest of the children, and the death of his father, when he was only eight years old, invested him at an early age with the cares and responsibilities of the head of the family. When sixteen years old he taught school, and the following year was a student in the Pine Grove Academy, now known as the Grove City College. After teaching school for another period, he attended the Edinboro State Normal School and was graduated from this institution in 1888. In 1892 he was graduated from the Alleghany College at Meadsvill, with the degree of A. B., having received the classical course. Three years later the degree of A. M. was conferred upon him.

From 1893 to 1895 he was principal of the schools at Monaco, and from 1896 to 1898 he was principal of the schools in Beaver, Penn. In 1894 he began the study of law in the office of John A. Buchanan, in Beaver, and in 1897, while teaching school, was admitted to the bar. The following year he opened a law office in Beaver, and practiced law until 1902, when Judge Moore, who had been appointed from Beaver, Penn., to succeed Arthur H. Noyes as

Judge of the Second Judicial Division of Alaska, requested him to accept a deputyship in the office of the district clerk. He closed his office in Beaver and cam to Nome, and has since filled the position of deputy clerk in the court room.

In the fall of 1904 Mr. Dunn was appointed Acting U. S. Marshal. In the summer of 1905 he was selected as District Clerk.

He is a member of the Knights of Pythias and Woodmen of the World. He was president of the K. of P. club in Nome during the winter of 1903-'04. During the same period he was president of the Nome Literary Society.

NOME AND SEWARD PENINSULA, 1905

THOMAS DWYER

Thomas Dwyer is a well-known miner and merchant of Council City. He came to the Nome region from Circle, on the Yukon, in the early part of the season of 1900. He located in Council City, where he conducted a mercantile business. Realizing that the money to be made must come from the mines, he has acquired extensive holdings on Ophir Creek and Neukluk and Casadepago Rivers. Last fall he closed out his mercantile business and has devoted his time to mining.

Mr. Dwyer is one of the pioneers of Alaska. He went to this country first in 1896, locating in Circle. This trip was made over the Dyea Pass. In 1896 he mined on Haughum or Deadwood Creek, and one of the first men to shoot the White Horse Rapids. He returned to the states via St. Michael, and went back to Dawson in the spring of 1898. He came to Nome from Dawson, over the ice, in 1900.

Thomas Dwyer was born in New York June 30, 1849. He was educated in the Normal State School. For twenty-five years he followed the business of a railroad contractor, and has assisted in the construction of a number of trunk lines in the United States and Canada. In 1889 he located in Superior, Wisconsin, and conducted a real estate business. He went to Everett, Washington, in 1891, and was elected as the first mayor of Everett.

Mr. Dwyer was married in 1880. Mrs. Dwyer was formerly Miss Julia Matte, of Three Rivers, Canada. At the time of his marriage Mr. Dwyer was constructing the North Shore Line, which is now a part of the Canadian Pacific Railway. He has valuable holdings of mining property in Seward Peninsula.

NOME AND SEWARD PENINSULA, 1905

ARTHUR EIDE

Arthur Eide, author, lecturer and educator, who has spent many years in Alaska, studying the strange customs and traditions of the Eskimos is now in Berkeley, California arranging for the publication of his latest book on Arctic Lore. He also gives an occasional illustrated lecture for educational and church organizations.

Eide was in charge of a government school on Diomede Island, 180 miles north of Nome in the Bering Straits. This school was erected by the United States in 1907 but because of the antagonism of the natives toward the white men, it was abandoned a few years later.

Eide is a graduate of the Berkeley Seminary, and was married in San Francisco to Coodlalooq, an Eskimo who was adopted when a small child and brought to the United States by Dr. Sheldon Jackson. Jackson was the man who introduced the reindeer industry in Alaska. Coodlalooq was educated in the United States and after their marriage, Mr. and Mrs. Eide went to Diomede Island, where they reopened the government school and carried it on successfully. During the time he was there Eide made an intensive study of the strange traditions and customs of the people and secured one of the finest and most valuable collections of Eskimo curios, including exquisitely carved pieces of walrus ivory several thousand years old, which he excavated on the island.

Through his wife, Eide was able to secure information and material in his research work which no other white man had been able to obtain.

After leaving the island, Eide was for seven years in charge of the medical and missionary work of the Presbyterian Church at Point Barrows. He has returned to Berkeley recently and resides at 1838 Carlton Street, where he is devoting his time to writing.

The oldest daughter of Mr. and Mrs. Eide died in Nome during the diphtheria epidemic a few years ago, another of his children died there and a third was killed.

ALASKA WEEKLY, March 23, 1928

WILLIAM J. ELMENDORF

William Elmendorf was born in Brooklyn, and completed his training in the Brooklyn Polytechnic. Shortly thereafter he went to Colorado where he engaged in various mining enterprises. He came to the Northwest in 1902 to take charge of the famous Sullivan group of mines in the Coeur d'Alenes. During the years 1904-6 he operated the Arctic Chief Mines in Whitehorse, in the Yukon Territory. Returning to Spokane, he went to the Bunker Hill and Sullivan where he remained until 1910, resigning to go North, as manager of the Portland Canal Mining Co. in whose service he remained the subsequent four years. He then took up his residence in Seattle where he went into private practice. His profession carried him into the mining camps throughout the West and from the Far North to the Mother Lode of California. The last two years he has been associated with L.A. Levensaler, under the firm name of Mining Service Inc.

William Elmendorf died in Seattle, June 26, 1933. He is survived by his wife, Mary J. Elmendorf, and by three children, Julia, Hartwell, and William Elmendorf, all residing in Seattle. He is also survived by one brother, James R. Elmendorf of Nashville, Tenn. and by one sister, Mrs. Margaret O'Brien of Paris, France.

Mr. Elmendorf was a member of the Seattle mining Club, the American Institute of Mining Engineers, and the executive Board of the

Chamber of Mines of Seattle.
ALASKA WEEKLY, June 30, 1933

GUY B. ERWIN
Guy B. Erwin was born in Mount Pleasant, Minnesota, June 20, 1872, and as a young man took up the study of law, and was later admitted to the practice of that profession, which he has ever since followed.

Mr. Erwin first came North in 1898, landing at Dyea on February first of that year. From there he, with the thousands of others who made up the great stampede of that year to the North, mushed over the Pass and boated down the Yukon to Dawson.

He remained in Dawson from 1898 to 1905, when he came to Fairbanks, where he has since made his home, and to the growth and development of which he has given much of his time and endeavor. As Secretary of the Fairbanks Commercial Club, he has taken an active part in those measures initiated for the development of Alaska.

He is also Secretary of the Tanana Rifle Club, an organization affiliated with the National Rifle Association of America.

Mr. Erwin was married at Minneapolis, Minnesota, on October 15, 1905 to Miss Lillian M. Coyle of that city, and 1st October celebrated at Fairbanks the twenty-fifth anniversary of their wedding. In politics Mr. Erwin is a Republican, and has been unanimously endorses by the member of the Republican organization of the Fourth Division of Alaska for the position of United States Attorney for that Division.
PATHFINDER, May 1921

JAMES EDWARD FENTON
James Edward Fenton was born in Clark County, Missouri, April 6, 1857, and crossed the plains in a prairie schooner with his parents in 1865. The family settled in Yamhill County, Oregon, where his father farmed. The subject of this sketch received a public school education and took a classical course in

Christian College, Monmouth, Oregon. He began his career in educational work, and taught in an academy for two years. He subsequently studied law under Judge William Ramsay, of Salem, Ore., and was admitted to the bar in 1882. He practiced law at Eugene, Ore., until 1900, when he moved to Spokane, Washington, and engaged in practice with his brother under the name of Fenton & Fenton. In 1892 he was elected prosecuting attorney for the county.

In 1896 he was elected as a delegate from Washington to the Democratic National Convention at Chicago. He practiced law in Spokane until September, 1899, when he went to Nome. He returned to Washington that winter and went back to Nome the following spring, residing there continuously until the fall of 1902. Since then he has spent his winters in the states returning to Nome each spring where he has a large clientage and a lucrative law practice.

NOME AND SEWARD PENINSULA, 1905

CAPTAIN WALTER H. FERGUSON

Captain W. H. Ferguson was born in Philadelphia in 1860. He was educated in the schools of Philadelphia and vicinity, and in his early manhood adopted a sea-faring life as a profession, rising rapidly to a command. After serving for twenty-two years, he left the sea and joined the rush to Alaska.

In 1897 he was employed by the North American Transportation and Trading Company as superintendent of construction at Dutch Harbor, and supervised the building of the company's river fleet at that place. After completing his work he went to St. Michael in September, 1898. While there he heard of the strike on Ophir Creek in the Council District and he at once proceeded to the diggings.

Arriving at Council City the party found even at that early date that the creeks in the vicinity of Council had been staked and on account of the lateness of the season, the party returned to Golovin Bay. While waiting at the Bay for transportation to St. Michael the Captain heard good reports of this Seward Peninsula and he determined to return to the peninsula in the early spring of 1899.

During the summer of 1899 he prospected and staked claims in nearly every section of the Nome peninsula. In the fall of 1899 he engaged in business in Nome, and took a prominent part in the affairs of that community. He was an active member of the Citizens Committee that deported a number of bad characters that infested the camp, and later, in the spring of 1900, when it became necessary for the citizens to again organize and assist in the government of the place, the Nome Chamber of Commerce was formed and Captain Ferguson was unanimously elected the first president of this organization.

In January 1900, Captain Ferguson was elected the first Arctic Chief of the Nome Camp of the Arctic Brotherhood. In July, 1900, Captain Ferguson was appointed United States Commissioner at Council City. During that entire period he was feared by evil-doers and claim-jumpers. He would not permit any man to go on a claim and endeavor to hold it against the original locator.

Since 1902 the Captain has been engaged in transportation and mining. He is also an attorney-at-law, having been admitted to practice before the courts of Alaska previous to his appointment as United States Commissioner.

NOME AND SEWARD PENINSULA, 1905

GEORGE FITZGERALD

George Fitzgerald is a native of Swansea, South Wales, G. B., and was born November 17, 1873. He learned the grocery and baking business in his native town. Immigrating to the United States when he was twenty years old, he located in San Francisco and found employment in the grocery business in that city, being employed by one firm during the entire time that he was in San Francisco. In 1898 he went to the Klondike. He was in Dawson a year, and came down the Yukon in the summer of 1899, arriving in Nome July 19. He mined on the beach that season and worked on Snow Gulch during the winter. The year following he established the Anvil Bakery in None which is now the oldest and the leading bakery in the town.

Mr. Fitzgerald was married in Nome, November 27, 1902, to Miss Freda Polsky. A son, George Gerald, was born to them in 1904.
NOME AND SEWARD PENINSULA, 1905

EDWIN HENRY FLYNN

Edwin Flynn was born in Ireland in 1835. He migrated to the United States just before the outbreak of the Civil War; enlisted in one of the New York regiments, and went through the war as color sergeant of his company. After the close of the Civil War, Mr. Flynn served as secretary to General George B. McClellan, while that eminent engineer was in charge of the great harbor improvements in New York City.

At the discovery of gold in the Black Hills, South Dakota, in 1876, and before the Indian title to that country was adjusted, Flynn was sent by the war department to take charge of the military telegraph line at Custer, S.D. He was chief operator and lineman and performed every duty pertaining to the operation and maintenance of that line. He was often required to go out and repair the line destroyed by roving bands of hostile Indians. Later, he held several political offices in South Dakota.

Hearing of the gold discovery at Nome, he joined the stampede to that camp in 1900. He engaged in mining on the Seward peninsula for a time. He was then appointed U.S. commissioner for the St. Michael recording precinct. He also established a general merchandise business there, which he successfully operated until 1914, when he sold out to the Northern Commercial company. He then came south to Seattle.

Edward Flynn died in Seattle, Wa. in May 1927. He is survived by his wife, Mrs. Augusta Flynn(whom he married in 1881); two sons,

Robert and Walter Flynn, each in business in Seattle; three daughters, Mrs. Emma Vrooman of Bremerton, Wash., Mrs. Edna Sturdy of Portland, Ore., and Mrs. Clara Hempson of this city, and one grandson, Joseph, son of a deceased daughter of Mr. and Mrs. Flynn, who was adopted by the grandparents following the death of the mother.

ALASKA WEEKLY, May 20, 1927

J. M. "Ted" FORTIER

Mr. Fortier was born in the Province of Quebec in 1850. At an early age he moved to Old Town, Maine, where members of the family still live.

In 1900 he was appointed Deputy U. S. marshal and for the next two years was stationed at St. Michaels, coming to the State of Washington at the expiration of his appointment.

In 1912 he was appointed to the State Fisheries Department, with headquarters at Bellingham, Washington. In 1929 he went to Walla Walla where he had charge of the State Fish Hatchery in the City Park of that city. He died in Walla Walla, Washington, in 1931.

Mr. Fortier is survived by his stepson, Mr. James G. Stephens, of Seattle, Washington, a son, H.H. Fortier of Spokane, Washington, where he has held a position on the staff of the Spokesman-Review for the past fifteen years; a sister, Mrs. Lille La Valle, and two brothers, Michael and L. A. Fortier, of Old Town, Maine.

ALASKA WEEKLY, February 6, 1931

JAMES FRAWLY

James Frawly is a Nome lawyer, but has a business instinct, and is engaged in mercantile lines and mining enterprises as well as in the practice of law. He is a native of Madison, Wisconsin, born January 26, 1860. He was graduated from the University of Wisconsin in 1884. Mr. Frawly took both a collegiate and law course in this institution.

In 1877, and before he attended the

University, he was in the Black Hills. After graduating, he returned to Deadwood. He was in the Cripple Creek country in 1896 where he practiced his profession and engaged in mining. He came to Nome in 1900, and has since been interested in law and mining.
NOME AND SEWARD PENINSULA, 1905

FREDERIC E. FULLER

F. E. Fuller, whose first residence in Alaska was at Juneau in 1897, is a member of the Nome bar. He spent a year at Juneau, Dyea and Skagway, and a couple of months in the Atlin Mining District. He returned to the states from Alaska, practiced law a year in New York, and came to Nome in 1900.

Mr. Fuller was born in West Auburn, Pennsylvania, March 27, 1868. He was graduated from the Wesleyan University of Middletown, Connecticut, in 1890, receiving the degree of A. B. He attended the law department of the National University, D. C., and in 1902 received from this institution the degree of LL. B. The degree of LL. M. was conferred upon him the following year. He was admitted to practice in the District of Columbia Supreme Court, and in 1900 was admitted to the Supreme Court of the United States.
NOME AND SEWARD PENINSULA, 1905

JAMES C. GAFFNEY

J. C. Gaffney is a merchant of Nome, and a leading dealer in high grade clothing and gentlemen's furnishings. He was born at Storm Lake, Iowa, in June, 1875. Twenty years of his life were spent in North Dakota. He was educated in the public schools and in the University of North Dakota. He is the son of T. W. Gaffney, a well-known lawyer of Seattle.

His first business experience was in the drug line which he learned and followed for four years and a half. Subsequently he became associated with the general merchandise business of Grand Forks, North Dakota, and has followed mercantile pursuits ever since. He came to Nome in the spring of 1900 as manager

of a mercantile institution. In September, 1903, he bought out the business, and is now one of the prominent merchants of the city.
November 27, 1902, he and Miss Marguerite McPherren were married in Nome.
NOME AND SEWARD PENINSULA, 1905

JERRY GALVIN

In 1898 Galvin started for Dawson. He acquired a bench claim off Upper Discovery on Dominion Creek, and mined it successfully until the latter part of the season of 1899, when he sold it and came down the Yukon on the last boat, arriving in Nome in October. His first experience after arriving in Nome was on Sledge Island where he and a party of prospectors were marooned for twelve days.

Jerry Galvin who arrived in Nome from Dawson late in the season of 1899, was one of the first prospectors to go to the Kougarok District, a comparatively undeveloped district of the Nome country. White men had been as far inland as Mary's Igloo, but beyond this the country was unknown. Jerry Galvin and George Ostrom were the first white men to enter this unknown region. Piloted by an Eskimo who told them he knew where gold could be found, they went up the Kuzitrip to Idaho Bar, where prospecting revealed colors in the ruby sand. They were the first white men to visit the mouth of the Kougarok River. They went up the Kougarok as far as the mouth of Windy Creek, but did not go farther because above Windy Creek there was no fuel.

The winter season of 1899-1900 was the mildest in the recent history of the country. They prospected all winter in the Kougarok country, except for trips to Nome to obtain supplies(200 miles by the coast trail). He found pay-streak which was yielded as much as $225 the pan, and he has since discovered other pay-streaks.

Jerry Galvin is a native of Wisconsin, and was born in Eau Claire April 22, 1869. The family moved to Michigan, and he was educated in the public schools of that state. He began life for himself at the age of sixteen in railroad work on the Soo line, beginning as a freight brakeman, and going through the list of promotion for efficient service, until he was a passenger conductor. In this last capacity he worked for the Northern Pacific for twelve years. After he was promoted to freight conductor on the Duluth, Superior and Western Road, he had charge of the construction train on his division.

NOME AND SEWARD PENINSULA, 1905

GEORGE W. GARSIDE

George W. Garside was born at Manchester, England August 18, 1847. A year later his parents brought him to the United States, landing at New Orleans. In 1849 they joined the vast army, which that year crossed the plains and invaded California. The family settled at Santa Clara near San Francisco and there the boy grew up. He attended the Santa Clara College, being educated for a mining profession. His first employment was at the great Comstock mine as a civil and mining engineer where he remained from 1869 to 1884. While in that position he gained valuable practical knowledge in mining.

He reached Juneau in 1884 and his knowledge of mines and mining made him an important factor in the district from the very first, as his education had been along the lines of geology, mineralogy and metallurgy.

In 1875 Mr. Garside was married to Miss Ella M. Mann. To this union there was one son who now holds an important position on the Southern Pacific Railroad. After the death of his wife, Mr. Garside was married in 1890 to Miss Bessie Dver Hill, who bore him two sons and two daughters. The family has resided continuously in Juneau.

ALASKA MONTHLY MAGAZINE, Oct-Nov. 1907

JAMES R. GAUDIN

In July 1897, James Gaudin left Victoria, B.C., on S.S. Thistle with a crew of men and supplies, machinery and equipment including a

saw mill to build a steamer at Teslin Lake.
Disembarking from the ocean vessel at Wrangell, they moved their outfit up the Stikine River in Telegraph Creek, and during the fall, winter and spring were arduously engaged in dragging their equipment overland 150 miles to Teslin Lake. This project was known as the F.N. York Company.

At Teslin Lake they constructed the steamer, Anglian, first of the '98 fleet to be built in the North from native spruce and started for Dawson City down the Teslin River (then called the Hontalinqua) about June 20, 1898.

The steamer Anglian joined the fleet of the newly organized Canadian Development Co., which was purchased in 1901 by the British Yukon Navigation Co. (River Division of the White Pass & Yukon Railroad) and operated for several seasons. The steamer was dismantled in 1931 at Whitehorse shipyard.

Jim Gaudin was promoted to position of Chief Engineer in 1902 and in 1914 became Superintendent Engineer in charge of the mechanical department and personnel of the company. Mr. Gaudin personally did all the daughting, blue-printing and supervising for the various construction projects of the company.

James Gaudin served the River Division of the White Pass & Yukon Railroad for 54 years, retiring September 30, 1952.
     ALASKA WEEKLY, October 24, 1952

C. C. GEORGESON
Dr. C.C. Georgeson was born in Denmark in 1851. From his youth he was interested in agriculture and made a study of the agricultural problems of his native land before coming to this country. On his arrival in America he entered the Michigan State College from which he was graduated and later was grated the degree of Doctor of Science. For two years he was assistant editor of the RURAL NEW YORKER, after which he became professor of agriculture and horticulture at the State

College of Texas.

His work had attracted the attention of Japan and he accepted the position of professor of agronomy at the Imperial College of Agriculture at Tokyo, where he remained seven years. On returning to the states he accepted the chair of agriculture at Kansas State College and it was from here that the federal government sent him to Denmark to study dairying in that county.

On May 12, 1898, Dr. Georgeson arrived at Sitka to determine the agricultural potential of Alaska. His instructions were broad and his facilities and budget extremely limited. However, for the next thirty years he carried on the work and gave the world an entirely new picture of the agricultural possibilities of the territory.

In 1927 he retired and made Seattle his residence. Dr. Georgeson died in Seattle, April 1, 1931. He is survived by his widow, Margaret T. Georgeson, two daughters, Mrs. Lee Bennett, Miss Dagmar Georgeson, and a son, V.L. Georgeson.

ALASKA WEEKLY, April 3, 1931

DAVID GILCHRIST

Mr. Gilchrist is a native of Canada, but the son of an American citizen, and was born in County Grey, January 7, 1870. When thirteen years old he worked in a logging camp, and took his place among men in a thirty-five mile drive of logs on the river. He went to Winnipeg, and hauled wood with cattle; was there during the stirring days of the Reil Rebellion. He drove stage, and finally went west with a carload of horses, Vancouver being the destination. In this part of the country he worked in logging camps, but shingle bolts and farmed.

In the spring of 1892 he started from Seattle to Alaska, and arrived in Juneau July 3. Since that date he has been an Alaskan. He worked at teaming for the Nowell Gold Mining Company, and then bought a team and began a freighting business. May 7, 1896 he left Juneau with three white men and seven Indians for Lake Tarkena, 375 miles distant over the Dalton Trail. The object of this trip was to build rafts and prepare for the shipment of a herd of cattle to St. Michael. Returning from this trip, he was left by the Indian guides because their guides were afraid of being attacked by the Stikeen Indians. But Mr. Gilchrist got back to Juneau and assisted in driving thirty-seven head of cattle to Lake Tarkena. The expedition continued its journey from Lake Tarkena on rafts. The rafts were wrecked in the rapids of Tarkena River, and the party lost all their personal effects, but continued with the stock overland to Fort Selkirk. Again rafts were constructed, the cattle were killed and the meat was put aboard, and the expedition started down the Yukon to Dawson. Dawson was then a new camp, and a ready market was found for the meat, which was sold at fifty cents a pound. He mined a little in Dawson that winter, and early the next spring made the trip overland to Dyea without tent or stove.

Mr. Gilchrist came to Nome in the spring of 1900, and landed on the beach with only $2.50. He went to work, bought a team as soon as he had enough money, engaged in the freighting business, which prospered, and in the spring of 1904 he was elected to the office of city councilman. February 22, 1902, he married Miss Nettie Widness. They have one child, a daughter.

NOME AND SEWARD PENINSULA, 1905

WILLIAM ADDISON GILMORE

William Addison Gilmore is a native of Oakland, Cal., and was thirty-five years old January 19 of this year, 1905. When he was one year old his parents moved to Portland, Ore., and thence to Vancouver, Wash., where he lived until twenty years of age. After graduating from Monmouth College in 1891, he began the reading of law, and three years later went to Chicago and entered the law department of the Northwestern University, and was a student in this institution for two years. In 1897 he was graduated from the law department of Lake Forest University, receiving the degree of LL. B. He returned to the Northwest, and in 1897 opened an office and began the practice of his profession in Seattle. In 1898 he was appointed secretary of the Republican State Central Committee of Washington.

The following year he formed a partnership with P. V. Davis, but the prospects of the Northern gold fields caused him to join the great stampede to Nome. During the first season in Nome he was retained by the Good Hope Mining Company of Chicago, and the Swedish Mission in suits over Anvil Creek claims, in which he was successful and for which he received large fees. He has since been attorney in a number of prominent suits in the Federal Court of this division of Alaska.

He is a prominent member of the Arctic Brotherhood, and at this writing is Arctic Chief of Camp Nome, No. 9. He is also an Eagle, being a member of Aerie No. 1, of Seattle. He belongs to the Woodmen of the World, and Modern Woodmen of America, and retains his membership in the Seattle Athletic Club.

November 6, 1891, he married Miss Carrie I. Thompson, of Tacoma. The fruit of the union is a daughter, Dorothy Belle, born in 1903.

NOME AND SEWARD PENINSULA, 1905

J. C. GILPATRICK

J. C. Gilpatrick was born in the State of Maine At Lisbon, 68 years ago. He came to Alaska in 1887 and located first at Kodiak He is a miner and prospector but has put in much of his time since coming north seal hunting and guiding hunting parties. He is married and has a home in Seward. Mr. and Mrs. Gilpatrick have no children. He owns valuable mining property in the Seward mining district from which he has taken considerable free gold.

Mr. Gilpatrick went to Dawson in 1898, and on down to Fortymile in 1899. He went to Nome in 1901. He has resided in Seward for the last five years.   **PATHFINDER, July 1920**

ALBERT JAMES GODDARD

A.J. Goddard was born in Muscatine County, Ohio; graduated from the Norton Normal and Scientific Academy, and is an Alumni of Iowa Agricultural College. After graduation, he clerked in the crockery store of G.W. Dillaway at Muscatine for two years. He then traveled as a salesman for McDonald Bros. Crockery Co. of Minneapolis for two years. Deciding to locate in the West, he came to Seattle, arriving in 1888, and with his brother he founded the Pacific Iron Works, which was the only foundry and machine shop in Seattle and for years the business supplied material to the shingle and lumber mills,. After the fire in Seattle, Mr. Goddard supplied fire hydrants for the city and designed and made the posts for the city's cluster lights. In 1892, Mr. Goddard was elected to the city council, in which position he served for eight years. In 1894, Mr. Goddard was elected to the legislature and was instrumental in securing the present tract for and the permanent location of the University in Seattle. Mr. goddard has been president of the following well-known concerns, which have had an important part in stabilizing and building the city: the Pacific Iron Works, A.J. Goddard & Co., Bankers, North Side State Bank, and Consumers Publishing Co., and general manager of the Upper Yukon co. A.J. Goddard, in 1897 and 1898, took two steamers and a sawmill over the Chilkoot and White Pass trails, and operated the steamers A.J. Goddard and F.H. Kilbourne on the upper rivers and lakes, the latter steamer being the first to go to the strike at Atlin in 1898. Returning to Seattle, Mr. Goddard was elected to the city council in 1908 and for ten years he helped mould the destines of the city. Of late years, he has erected many of the best apartment houses and residences in the city. He was the first president of the Order of Alaska and Yukon Pioneers, and is now the historian of that order. During the years Capt. Goddard spent in the North, he secured a pictorial record of the

events of the Klondike stampede, depicting the trails and hardships encountered on the trail.
ALASKA WEEKLY, October 25, 1929

F. L GODDARD

Born in Massachusetts almost seventy years ago, Dr. Goddard graduated from Long Island Medical College in 1887. He took post-graduate work in Germany and England and eventually came out west and located at Tacoma, Washington, where he married Miss Mary Clunas and their union was blessed with two children, a boy and girl. Later he accepted the appointment as Superintendent of the Washington State Hospital at Stellacoom which he held during two administrations.

In 1905 Dr. Goddard arrived in the Territory. With his family he decided to make his headquarters in Juneau and enjoyed an excellent practice in that city as well as in Douglas. For a time he was company physician for the Treadwell and later moved to Sitka where he purchased the Sitka Hot Springs which he developed and where he made his home for many years.

Dr. Goddard's professional standing was of the highest. He served as president of the first Territorial Board of Medical Examiners and was twice president of the Territorial Medical Association. Throughout his years of practice he was a Fellow of the American Medical Association.

Dr. Goddard died in Sitka, Alaska January 1932. He is survived by his wife, a son, E.M. Goddard of Juneau, a daughter, Mrs. Don Wright of Bellingham and two grandchildren. ALASKA WEEKLY, January 22, 1932

MARY HOWES GODDARD

Mrs. Goddard, whose maiden name was Howes, was born in Buckland, Mass., in 1823. She was educated in the same state graduating from Mt. Holyoke Seminary under mary Lyons in 1846. Mrs. Mills, until recently President of Mills College, Oakland, Calif., was a class mate. Miss Howes spent a number of years teaching in Alabama and later in Philadelphia.

During the Civil War she was with Dorothea Dix aiding in the work of caring for the sick and wounded. She heard Mr. Lincoln deliver his noted speech at Gettysburg. After the war she was married to P.M. Goddard in the albert E. Barnes Church, Philadelphia, of which they were both members. Later they moved to Brooklyn where they were members of Dr. Beecher's church. In 1888 they came to Tacoma, Wash., where they resided until three years ago since which time they have lived with her son, Dr. F.L. Goddard, who owns the Sitka Hot Springs at Sanitarium about twelve miles from Sitka.

Mrs. Mary W. Goddard died at Sanitarium, Alaska, on Thursday March 31, 1910.

THLINGET, April 1910

WALTER GOODWIN

Walter Goodwin was born in 1872, the son of the late Col. J. M. Goodwin, for over thirty years mining editor of the SALT LAKE CITY TRIBUNE. Soon after graduation from college as a civil engineer, Mr. Goodwin went to Skagway and assumed a position on the engineering staff of the White Pass & Yukon railroad. At that time, he was one of the original locators of the famous Engineer gold mine in the Atlin district. From Skagway, Goodwin went to Valdez, where for a number of years he was with a railroad proposition there. Still later, he went to Nome, where he represented the Alaska Road Commission for many years, when the late General Wilds P. Richardson was at the head of the commission. He surveyed and built the road from Seward over Rainy Pass into the Iditarod district. Soon after America entered the world War, was assigned as chief engineer of the work of building railroads and storage depots at Columbus, Ohio. A few years after the armistice, he was locating engineer for the scenic Mulholland Highway in California. For a number of years past, he was employed by the Washington State Highway Department and at the time of his death was its chief maintenance engineer.

Mr. Goodwin died June 1929 in Seattle,

Washington. He is survived by a widow, Mrs. Mary N. Goodwin, two sons, Sherwood and Leland; a brother, Frank L. Goodwin of Tacoma; and a sister Mrs. A.C. Goss of Unalaska. A cousin, Mrs. Joseph Wilson married a brother of the late President Wilson.
ALASKA WEEKLY, June 7, 1929

ALBERT C. GOSS
Albert C. Goss was born in Moretown, Vermont in September 1871. He went to Alaska in 1896 and entered in the employ of the Alaska Commercial Company. He was stationed at Kodiak until 1911, when that station was sold to the R.C. Erskine interests. He then went to Unalaska to take charge of the A.C. Company station there, and later purchased the company's far-west stations at Attu and Atka islands, in the Aleutian group. About this time, he joined Samuel Applegate in the blue fox farming industry and later bought out the extensive Applegate holdings in Southwestern Alaska. He owned a power boat, the EUNACE, in his commercial, trading and fox farming enterprises and had built up a profitable business.
Albert C. Goss died in Seattle, December 18, 1928. He is survived by his wife, Clara Goodwin Goss; a son, Cecil Goss; and a brother, Dr. Roland Goss of Vermont.
ALASKA WEEKLY, December 21, 1928

ARNOLD S. GRAHAM
Arnold Graham was 71 years old and was born in Adel, Ia. coming with his parents over the old Oregon Trail to Oregon in 1865. He had his first experience as a fisherman on the Columbia River at the age of 13 years and had engaged in fisheries operations from Requa, Calif. to the Nushagak area in Alaska. He joined the gold rush to the Klondike in 1897, and engaged in freighting operations between Skagway and the Chilkoot Pass. Later he was also engaged in the logging business industry for a number of years.
Arnold Graham was general superintendent

for Libby, McNeill & Libby at the canneries of that company in Bristol Bay for the past twenty years and before that was connected with the J.C. Smiley cannery at Blaine and the Key City Packing Company at Port Townsend.

Mr. Graham died in Seattle, Washington in November 1932. He is survived by his widow, Mrs. Georgia Thorne Graham of Seattle; two brothers, Tilden and Silvo; three sisters, Mrs. Inez Warren, Mrs. Louise Kent and Mrs. Mabel Bush; and two nephews, Guy V. Graham and Walter G. Graham all of Oregon.

ALASKA WEEKLY, December 2, 1932

WHIT M. GRANT

Whit Grant is a man 35 years of age; an able lawyer. He came to Davenport in '68 when a youth from his native state of Alabama, on the invitation of his uncle, Judge James Grant, and entered Griswold college as a student. After leaving that institution as a graduate in 1872, he entered the law department of the state university, graduating with high honors in the class of '73. He entered upon the practice of his profession, and before long was appointed attorney for the C.M. & St. P. He went into partnership with his uncle in '78--the firm being Grant & Grant. He has been quite successful in his practice, having been admitted to practice before the United States Supreme Court in '81 and conducted many cases involving large interests in the federal courts in the states of Kansas, Nebraska, Arkansas, Illinois, Iowa, and Missouri. He has served as alderman, as city as city attorney, and as state senator with great credit. He is a brother of ex-Governor Grant, of Colorado and of W.W. Grant, one of the eminent physicans and surgeons of the state.

In September of 1887, he was appointed United States Attorney for the District of Alaska.

ALASKAN, November 12, 1887

GEORGE A. GREEN

Captain Green was born in Quebec, Ontario

in 1880. He came to Seattle in 1894 and in 1899 the lure of the North called him and he headed for the Klondike, going over the White Pass from Skagway to the Yukon. He engaged in river navigation, operating the steamer RELIANCE on the Yukon and was master of that vessel and others on the rivers of the Interior for many years.

During the last seven years he had been operating on the Lower Kuskokwim River with the Alaska River Navigation Co. of which he was the president and general manager. He maintained his residence in Seattle sailing North each spring and returning in the fall after the close of river navigation and his home ton Queen Anne Hill.

Captain Green died in Seattle, Washington, February 7, 1933. He is survived by his widow, Mrs. Katherine Green; two sons, Jack and Jerry; his mother, Mrs. E. Green; and a sister, Mrs. E.J. Hurley, all of Seattle; two brothers, Dan Green of Hot Springs, Alaska, and Captain J.W. Green of the United States Army, stationed in the Philippines.

ALASKA WEEKLY, February 10, 1933

NATHANIEL GREENE

Mr. Greene was born in Bridgeport, Connecticut, May 13, 1855, and went to Alaska in 1893, locating in Juneau, where he was connected with the Nowell mining operations as an accountant. For eight years he was city clerk of the capital city and also served the town in other public positions. Having resided in Juneau for seventeen years during the early settlement of that part of the territory, he became acquainted with men in most of the camps of Alaska.

In 1910 Mr. Greene went to Cordova as accountant for the Cordova Power Company, which later became the present Alaska Public Utilities and for years was also the secretary-treasurer of that corporation. He was city clerk and magistrate for many years, and for four years was president of the Cordova School Board; served for three years as Bank Examiner of the Third division, was president of the Cordova Republican Club and a charter member of Igloo No. 19, Pioneers of Alaska.

On account of ill health Mr. Greene left Cordova in May, 1924, for San Francisco where he continued to reside up to the time of his death.

Nathaniel Greene died in San Francisco, January 23, 1926. He was nearly 76 years of age, and is survived by his wife and daughter, Dorothy, now Mrs. J.J. Rankin of San Francisco, and a brother Charles, librarian at Oakland.

ALASKA WEEKLY, February 12, 1926

JAMES W. GREENSLATE

James W. was born in Springfield Illinois, December 3, 1856. He came to Ketchikan May 21st, 1893. He went with the rush to Dawson and the Yukon country. After spending some time Inside, he came back to Ketchikan.

He prospected on the Unuk River, making several trips in that section. Prospecting and trapping is his favorite pastime, although he has become a proficient troller, having an up-to-date boat, which he calls his summer home.

PATHFINDER, June 1920

KATHERINE D. SIMMONS GRIFFIN

Katherine D. Griffin, whose maiden name was Simmons, was born in Weston, Mo., November 26, 1867. She and Mr. Griffin first met in Kansas City, Mo., and they were married in Minneapolis in 1890. They made their home in Butte, Mont., until 1899 and went from here to San Francisco, from which latter place Mr. Griffin came north in 1901, going to Nome, St. Michael and then to Dawson. He returned to the states a year later and brought Mrs. Griffin north, coming up the river from St. Michael to Dawson, where they made their home until 1905. In 1905 they moved to Chena where Mr. Griffin previously had become interested in a general outfitting business with several partners.

By 1907 he had bought out his partners. Branches of the store were established at Ruby and in the Iditarod district.

Mrs. Griffin resided at Chena with her husband until the business was sold in 1915. They then moved to Seattle. They returned to Alaska and went into the fishing business at Halibut Cove and later at Three Saints Bay. Mrs Griffin was with her husband in the westward district, and moved with him to Kodiak in 1922.

Katherine Griffin died in Seward, Alaska, August 20, 1930. The only close relatives of the deceased are her husband and a brother, Charles Simmons, who came north in June, 1929, and who has made his home in Kodiak.

ALASKA WEEKLY, September 12, 1930

GEORGE B. GRIGSBY

George Grigsby was born in Sioux Falls, South Dakota, December 2, 1874. He received his education at the University of South Dakota. He was admitted to the bar in 1896, and opened a law office in his native state.

During the war with Spain, he received a commission as First Lieutenant, in his father's command.

George Grigsby, attorney-at-law, now engaged in the practice in the city of Ketchikan, went to Nome, Alaska in 1902 to join his father, Col. Melville Grigsby, since deceased, who had been appointed United States district attorney for the Second Judicial Division. The young lawyer took a position as an assistant district attorney on his father's staff and remained in that position for a period of six years, when he was elevated to the position of U.S. district attorney serving until 1910. Then he took up private practice in the city of Nome. In 1914 he was elected mayor of Nome, and in 1916 he was elected attorney general of the Territory. Upon assuming this office, Mr. Grigsby removed to Juneau, the capital. In 1919 he was elected delegate to congress from Alaska to fill the unexpired term of the late Delegate Sulzer.

Mr. Grigsby is 53 years of age. He has resided in Alaska since he went there in 1902.

ALASKA WEEKLY, August 17, 1928
NOME AND SEWARD PENINSULA, 1905

ANDREW GROSVOLD

Andrew Grosvold was born February 9, 1863 in Norway. Mr. Grosvold went to Alaska in 1885, arriving at Sand Point on February 13.

During his first summer there, Mr. Grosvold fished. The following year he joined a cod-fishing vessel and in 1887 he was at Karluk But it was in 1888 when he first actually returned to Sand Point for good. In that year he started a fishing station of his own. In 1890 he shifted the station to Sanak Island.

In 1892 Mr. Grosvold joined the scores of sea otter hunters; skins were plentiful then and brought from $150 to $200 each. Fox, bear and wolves abounded in great numbers. In those days he is recalled as having said he saw as many as 48 bears in one day.

In 1899 he sailed his own boat to Nome with a number of prospectors aboard; there he located the famous Lena and Mattie claims on the head of Dexter. In 1900 he sold out to C.D. Lane for $200,000, after which he made his first trip to the States since 1888.

The following year saw him engaging in blue fox raising, on several of the Shumagin Islands, and from that time he continued in this line along with his mercantile and water transportation business. In 1902 he bought out Sydne & Hough at Sand Point.

Andrew Grosvold died in Seward, Alaska, February 2, 1933. Surviving Mr. Grosvold is his wife and children at Sand Point; a daughter, Mrs. A.H. Mellick of Seattle.

ALASKA WEEKLY, February 17, 1933

ROYAL ARCH GUNNISON

Royal Arch Gunnison came to Alaska in 1904 as a United States District Judge for the First Division in which capacity he served for four years, through appointment from President Roosevelt. After the expiration of his term of office he opened a law office here, and has been actively engaged in the practice of that profession ever since that time.

Judge Gunnison was a native of Binghamton,

N.Y., where he was born June 23, 1873. He graduated from Cornell University, and worked as a newspaper reporter at Elmira, N.Y., where he later began the practice of law. He was appointed referee in bankruptcy at Elmira and was serving in that capacity when President Roosevelt appointed him District Judge, with his headquarters at Juneau. He succeeded Judge Melville O. Brown.

He was appointed Federal Food Administrator for Alaska shortly after the outbreak of the war and has been serving in that capacity since.

Royal Gunnison married Miss Cob--(?) of Binghamton, New York. This union produced a son, Royal Gunnison, Jr. Judge Gunnison died in Juneau, Alaska, June 15, 1918.

DAILY ALASKAN, June 17, 1918

GORDON HALL

Gordon Hall, who is now counsel for and a director of the Wild Goose Mining and Trading Company, has been identified with the mining interests and litigation of Alaska since the fall of 1898.

Mr. Hall was born at Piqua, Ohio, December 18, 1870. Mr. Hall's early education was obtained in public schools at Ann Arbor and Marquette, Michigan. He went to college at Trinity, Hartford, Conn., and was graduated from there in the year 1892, with the degree of Bachelor of Science. From Trinity he went to Harvard, and after a three years course at the Harvard University Law School, was graduated with the degree of Bachelor of Laws. Shortly after receiving his sheepskin he became junior member of a law firm in San Bernardino, California.

In the spring of 1897 he went to San Francisco and opened a law office in the Mills Building, and rapidly built up a lucrative law practice. In the summer of 1899 he was employed by the interests that were afterward known as the Golovin Bay and Norton Sound Mining Companies to go to Alaska to perfect and clear up the titles to properties owned by them in the Nome and Council City regions.

Mr. Hall is now the holder of valuable properties in Alaska, in addition to enjoying an extensive law practice at San Francisco.

On February 23, 1904, at San Francisco, California, he married Miss Alice Conway Bolton, daughter of Colonel Edwin B. Bolton, Tenth Infantry, U. S. A.

Mr. Hall is a member of several fraternal and social organizations, including the Bohemian and University Clubs of San Francisco.
NOME AND SEWARD PENINSULA, 1905

ISAAC HAMBURGER

Isaac Hamburger, was born in Brooklyn, N.Y., in September, 1860. After attending the public schools of New York, he attended and graduated from college. From the time of his graduation from college until his death, "Ike," was he was affectionately called by his hosts of friends, always followed the general business of stenographic work, and he was everywhere known as one of the very best in that work. Along in 1886 he went to Montana, where he spent twenty years, with the exception of one year spent in San Francisco.

Practically all of Mr. Hamburger's work was either in court reporting or as private secretary to high officials. When Senator Carter was elected to Congress from Montana in 1889, Ike went to Washington as his private secretary, and clerk of the Committee on Mines and Mining. he worked with Senator Carter when the senator was Republican National Committee chairman during the presidential campaign of 1892. Previous to going to Washington Mr. Hamburger was court reporter in the district court at Helena, with Judge William H. Hunt, now one of the judges of tea Circuit Court of Appeals at San Francisco. He again served as private secretary for Senator Carter from 1885 to 1901 and from 1905 to 1907. During the latter year Mr. Hamburger was married, and after his first son was born in 1907, he and his family located in Tacoma. In 1909 they moved to Alaska, Mr. Hamburger coming as secretary to Judge Cushman. They lived in Juneau for a year after which they moved to Valdez, where they resided until the summer of 1922, at which time he gave up his position as court reporter and moved onto a farm near Paradise, Butte County, California. At Valdez he worked with Federal District Judges Cushman, Overfield, Brown and E.E. Ritchie.

Mr. Hamburger remained on his California farm for only about a year, when he came to Tacoma to accept the position as private secretary to Judge Cushman and reporter of his court. It was while the family were on a shopping trip in Seattle that he met his death. He was killed by a stray bullet which a city policeman had fired.

Mr. Hamburger left a wife, Mrs. Elsie B. Hamburger, and four children, Lewis, Nancy, Elsie, and Helen. The family resides on the farm near Paradise, California.

PATHFINDER, February 1924

GEORGE HARKRADER

George Harkrader was born in Warren county, Ohio, May 29, 1847. He came to Juneau in April 1881 from Sitka, when he went to Fort Wrangell, and from there to Cassiar country. After his arrival in Juneau he took up a quartz claim in the Silver Bow basin and a hillside placer claim. These were located where the Juneau-Alaska or Little Treadwell is now. He was a partner of Henry Coons and Dan Campbell for six years and they took out of their placer in that time over $75,000. Mr Harkrader was one of the original owners in the Nevada Creek district, and also had quartz property on Admiralty Island. He spent a considerable amount of money in the development of a coal property on Chatham Straits near Killisnoo, which he still owns. It is considered valuable. He is one of the pioneers of this mining district.

ALASKA MONTHLY MAGAZINE, Oct-Nov. 1907

WILLIAM HARRIS

William Harris was a nephew of Richard

Harris, who, with his partner, Joe Juneau, were the original settlers of what is now the city of Juneau. After remaining here for several years, Richard Harris went to Montana in 1882 on a visit to his brother, and on his return he was accompanied by his nephew, William. The latter worked at Treadwell for a number of years, visited and worked in many of the Interior camps and in Nome. Leaving Alaska early in the present century, he went to the Outside, and for several years was chief of police of Leadville, Colorado. But the lure of the North was too strong to resist and he returned to Juneau about the year 1908 and again went to work at treadwell. It was in the year 1911 or 1912 that Emery Valentine, mayor of Juneau, appointed William Harris chief of police of the city.

As evidence of the bravery of Harris, Mr. Valentine relates that when a boy of 16 and when accompanying his parents by wagon train from Missouri to Montana, the father and son went out one morning to gather up their horses, which had wandered some distance from the camp, and that while so doing they were fired on by Indians in ambush, and elder harris being shot through the breast, from which wound he died a years later. Others in the camp heard the shooting, and when they arrived on the scene young William had killed three of the attackers and was gallantly standing off a dozen or so more.

After serving Juneau for two years as chief of police, Harris resumed his employment at Treadwell, remaining there until the Alaska Juneau began operations, where he has been employed ever since and until overtaken by his final sickness, which came on him nearly three months ago, since which time he had been in St. Ann's Hospital, where he passed away the last week of February, 1928. He is survived by his wife and two nephews, John and Richard Harris, all of Juneau.

ALASKA WEEKLY, February 24, 1928

MARY E. HART

Mrs. Mary E. Hart, the lady manager for Alaska's exhibit, and hostess of the Alaska building at St. Louis, during the Louisiana Purchase Exposition, is the first woman to be honored by appointment from Alaska to an official position. She is an able journalist and represented the State of California at the Columbian Exposition of 1893 in charge of its historical exhibit.

During early organization days of the PACIFIC MONTHLY, she was editor and proprietor of that progressive magazine. Continuously since that time, she had been engaged in literary work, and on becoming a resident of Nome, Alaska, was elected President of the most northerly Woman's Club in the world, and the Secretary of the Alaska Academy of Sciences. Mrs. Hart is a life member of the Pacific Coast Woman's Press Association.

ALASKA MAGAZINE, April 1905

CHARLES DARWIN HASKINS

Mr. Haskins is a native of New Hampshire, but spent his boyhood days in Vermont. He was born October 9, 1853. At the age of thirteen he was a telegraph operator in the country office of Vermont, and a year later filled a position in the telegraph office of the City of Bangor. Concluding that he wanted to be a sailor he shipped before the mast and sailed in a number of vessels engaged in the coast trade. Tiring of a sailor's life he started to learn the watch making trade, but he never forgot his first love. As a small boy at school he excelled in physics, and possessing an ingenious mind it was natural for him to drift back to the vocation that he began to learn when eleven years old. Before he was twenty he was foreman of the Western Union Telegraph factory in New York, and in his twenty-second year he was superintendent of the factory which employed 180 men. He remained with this company until they were succeeded by the Western Electric Company, April, 1879. This company was succeeded by the Bell Telephone

Company, and Mr. Haskins was associated with the mechanical and manufacturing department of this company until 1889, when he was taken into the law department of the company as chief expert. During his long service with these companies he made eleven trips to Europe to establish electrical factories at St. Petersburg, Berlin, Paris, Antwerp and London. During his association with electrical companies, comprising the greater part of his life, hundreds of electrical inventions have been submitted to him.

C. D. Haskins went to Nome in 1902. During the season, he worked on a claim on Gold Run and cleaned up the munificent sum of $32.40. But this did not check the development of the gold fever. His experience and observation told him there was gold in this region; the question to solve was the method of extracting it. He came to Nome again in the summer of 1903, and his experience this season convinced him that a ditch should be constructed that would supply water to all the mineral ground of this region. He accordingly organized the Haskins Ditch and Mining Co. (Ltd.), with a capital of $2,000,000, and raised the money necessary to build a ditch eight miles long from Canyon Creek to Gold Run.

NOME AND SEWARD PENINSULA, 1905

T.W. HAWKINS

T.W. Hawkins, of the mercantile firm of Brown & Hawkins Corporation, of Seward, Alaska, has been in the Northland continuously since 1898, at which time he set out from his home in Virginia to join in the great stampede to the Klondike. Later, he went down the Yukon River to Nome, and was in that camp a couple of years, and in 1902 went to Valdez. It was here that the firm of Brown & Hawkins was formed. In 1903, the steamer Santa Ana took the first continent of railroad engineers and men to Resurrection Bay to start construction on the Alaska Central Railroad. Mr. Hawkins joined the steamer at Valdez and was among the argonauts who founded the beautiful city of

Seward on a site that was then a wilderness. Soon after he landed, Mr. Hawkins established a branch store of his firm, starting business in a tent structure. From the beginning business was good, and the firm decided to concentrate its activities in that growing little city. Other mercantile establishments came, survived for a time and then departed, but the pioneer firm of Brown & Hawkins weathered all financial storms incident to the building up of a business in a city on the frontier in a region of unknown and undeveloped resources. Today, the Brown & Hawkins Corporation operate one of the great mercantile concerns of the Northland.
ALASKA WEEKLY, November 23, 1928

GEORGE C. HAZELET

Mr. Hazelet went to Valdez, Alaska in 1898, at the head of an exploration company. The party located placer holdings in the Copper River valley. Returning to Valdez, he had charge of the first construction work on the Copper River & Northwestern railroad, which was to have been built from Valdez to Kennecott, where the great Bonanza copper mine is located. Later, the company changed its plans, in favor of the Copper river route, in lieu of passing through Thompson's Pass, and Mr. Hazelet founded the Cordova Townsite Company, after selecting the townsite that was to be the coast terminus of the proposed railway line. From the beginning, he had been the president and general manager of this townsite company. In addition, he was vice president of the Cordova bank, general manager of the Chilkat Oil company, with oil lands in the Katalla district and was interested in the Cordova-Fairbanks Auto Transportation company. He was also concerned in other business activities in the town he founded and which he lived to see grow into a thriving community.

George Calvin Hazelet, aged 65 years, died in Cordova, Alaska, Thursday, August 5, 1926.
ALASKA WEEKLY, August 13, 1926

PROF. WILL HENRY

The development of the Solomon River mines and the rapidly increasing population last year in consequence thereof, made the appointment of a U. A. Commissioner for this district advisable. The Judge of the District Court selected Will Henry for this position, the appointment dating from June 15, 1904. Prof. Henry is an educator with thirty years experience in educational work. He filled the position of principal of Nome District Schools during the term of 1902-'03. He is a specialist in philology and mathematics, two branches of learning to which he has given much time and thought. During a residence of many years in Colorado he spent his vacations in the mines, studying practical mineralogy, and acquired an expert's knowledge of ores. It was this fact that led to his employment by a capitalist to visit Nome in 1900.

Prof. Henry is a native of Ohio, and was born April 25, 1855. His family moved to Colorado during the Civil War. He was educated at Oberlin College, and began the work of a teacher early in life. In May, 1897, he and Miss Anna S. Skerrett were married at Cripple Creek. Mrs. Henry is a niece of Admiral Skerrett, of the United States Navy.

NOME AND SEWARD PENINSULA, 1905

S. C. HENTON

S.C. Henton is the United States commissioner of the Port Clarence Mining District, with headquarters at Teller on Port Clarence Bay. He was appointed to this position in October, 1901. The Port Clarence precinct and recording district is the largest recording district of Seward Peninsula, extending from Port Clarence Bay to the Arctic Ocean and Kotzebue Sound on the north, Bering Strait and Bering Sea on the west and south, and Sawtooth range of mountains on the east.

Judge Henton is a native of Iowa, but was reared and educated in Indiana. In 1886 he moved to the Pacific Coast and began the practice of law in 1890. He was United States commissioner for the State of Washington for a period of several years, filling this position until 1898.

NOME AND SEWARD PENINSULA, 1905

CHARLES E. HERRON

Candidate for Republican National Committeeman, Charles E. Herron was born in 1867 at Grayson, Carter County, Kentucky. Mr. Herron is married and the father of three children, the eldest now attending the University of Washington, having served overseas with the United States army, the two younger, a boy and a girl, were born at Nome Alaska.

Mr. Herron came to Alaska in 1898, landing in Skagway. He has resided in Alaska continuously since that time. He is the owner of two Alaska daily newspapers, the Alaska Capital and the Anchorage Times. During his residence in Alaska he has engaged in the mining and fishing industries.

ALASKA DAILY CAPITAL, April 23, 1920

WILLIAM H. HESSE

Some eight years ago Mr. Hesse became interested financially in mining matters in Alaska and continues in the business today. He is accounted one of the pioneers of the Seward Peninsula in Alaska, where he has large interests in the gold placer grounds, and tin and quicksilver deposits, with an office in Nome.

William Hesse, father of our subject, was born in 1834, in Crivitz, Prussia, where he was reared and educated. At the age of eighteen, in 1852, in company with his father and the family, he went to the United States, and for a short time made his home in Rochester, New York. From Rochester the family removed to Milwaukee, Wisconsin, and there he met his future wife, Miss Clara Vehring, a lady of German nativity, and who, when sixteen years old, went to America with an uncle, she being an orphan. Mr. Hesse died in Neenah, Wisconsin, in 1885, and his wife followed him

Wisconsin, in 1885, and his wife followed him to the grave in 1893.

William H. Hesse was born in Menasha, Wisconsin, November 2, 1860, and received his elementary education in the public schools in Neenah, supplemented with a course at the University of Notre Dame, Indiana. At the age of twenty-one he entered into partnership with his father in the hotel business, as managers of the Neenah Hotel. On the death of the senior Hesse, in 1885, the son continued the business until 1893, when he disposed of his interest.

In the meantime Mr. Hesse discovered the existence of white quartz quarries near Wausau, Marathon County, Wisconsin, and conceived the idea that this might be made a valuable adjunct to the resources of the Badger State. He had given considerable attention to geology and mining. With specimens of the Marathon County quartz in his possession, he returned to Neenah from a visit and began experimenting. He soon discovered that quartz, pulverized, could not only be utilized in the manufacture of a fine quality of sandpaper, and for other purposes, but that it made one of the best water filter beds possible. He established a factory in a small way in Neenah, and soon won a reputation with his product that induced the people of Wausau to offer him sufficient inducements to remove his plant to that city, where he engaged in the business on a large scale. The correctness of his judgment is testified to by the fact that the Badger Quartz Mill is among the more important industries of the Wisconsin Valley today, its output being shipped in carload lots to all parts of the country.

Mr. Hesse has always taken a deep interest in public matters, whether they concerned the prosperity of his home city, the state, or the nation. In his political affiliations he is a Democrat. He has served his party as a member of both county and congressional committees, and as a delegate to state, county and city conventions. He served the city of Neenah for three years as a member of the common council, and as mayor for one term, 1891 to 1892.

At the present time (1905), Mr. Hesse is serving the people as the president of the Board of Libraries of Winnebago County. He has been a member of the school board for several years.

In 1887 Mr. Hesse married Miss Flora May Dunham, a native of Ohio. They have one child, Monica A. Hesse.

NOME AND SEWARD PENINSULA, 1905

E. COKE HILL

Judge Hill was born and raised in the State of Oregon. His father, William Lair Hill, a prominent lawyer of Oregon, Washington and California, compiled the first codes of Oregon and Washington.

Judge Hill came to Alaska in 1900, residing in Nome where he practiced law until 1911. During that time he was assistant United States Attorney under Melvin Grigsby. In 1911 he went to the Fourth division, practicing law in Iditarod and Ruby, servicing as a special assistant to the united States Attorney for five years and was U.s. Commissioner at Ruby and Fairbanks.

It was at this time that Judge Hill took the mail contracts pioneering the present mail route from Nenana to Flat city, and earned a reputation as a dog-musher in the Interior. In 1924, Judge Hill left Alaska for San Francisco where he practiced law. In March of 1927, he was appointed federal judge in Alaska for the Third division(Valdez).

ALASKA WEEKLY, April 1, 1927

DR. EDMUND E. HILL

Dr. Edmund E. Hill came here with the big rush of 1900 and has been a respected resident of Nome ever since. In the early days of the camp, when the town was without government, Dr. Hill, as the presiding officer of the board of directors of the Chamber of Commerce, took the initiative in ridding the town of the undesirable element. A sufficient amount of money was raised and the disreputables were rounded up and deported on the last boat that left at the close of navigation. Later he was a prime mover in the organization of what is known as the "Second Consent Government," which was organized by the merchants and property owners of the city and which continued in the management of affairs until the incorporation of the city of Nome in 1901. The Doctor was health officer and city physician during that period and gave his services gratuitously.

He is a native of San Francisco, California, and was born November 21, 1868. He was graduated from the Cooper Medical College in the class of '95, and prior to coming to Nome held several important official positions in San Francisco. He has a predilection for politics, and when the second election for the incorporation of Nome was held the Doctor took a leading part in the fight for incorporation, which was carried by an overwhelming majority. To his efforts is due in a great measure the incorporation of Nome. He has served in the common council of Nome, and as chairman of the finance and building committee, supervised the construction of the City Hall and the Dry Creek Bridge. The Belmont Cemetery and the abolition of the obnoxious dog license tax, are credited to his diligent work. He has twice been health officer of Nome.

Dr. Hill is a practicing physician and the proprietor of the Cut Rate Drug Store in Front Street. He is also interested in a number of mines near Nome.

NOME AND SEWARD PENINSULA, 1905

MAX R. HIRSCHBERG

He was born in Columbus, Ohio, March 25, 1877, and educated in the Columbus and Youngstown high schools. The family moved to New York in 1893 and Max obtained a print shop. He obtained employment in the Incandescent Electric Light Company of New York where he gained a practical knowledge of the electrical business. Attracted by the Klondike strike he started for Dawson in 1897. When he arrived at Juneau the season was growing late and the Dyea Pass was blockaded. He and his party remained in Juneau until the following spring.

In the spring of 1898 they started across the pass a short time before the disastrous snow-slide at Sheep Camp. They escaped the slide but their entire outfit of 5,500 pounds was covered by the avalanche, only fifty pounds of which was recovered. They packed this remnant of the outfit to the summit where it was stolen. His associates turned back, but he continued the journey to Dawson to find employment in the camp. With meager means he started a road-house. He prospected on Dominion and Sulphur Creeks. He left Dawson for Nome March 9, traveling on a bicycle.

When he arrived at Shaktolik the ice in the river was breaking. In attempting to cross the Shaktolik River he fell into the water and came near drowning. He lost his watch, and his poke containing $1,500 in dust. At this season of the year the snow and sunshine make the light very intense, and before Mr. Hirschberg had gone far he became snow blind. During two days, suffering great agony as he wandered over the country, he fortunately stumbled onto a tent and found assistance. After two weeks recuperating, he resumed the journey and wheeled into Solomon. At this camp he had the misfortune to break the chain of his bicycle, so he rigged up a sail and attached it to the wheel and sailed over the ice to Cape Nome. In the following winter Mr. Hirschberg rode on a wheel from Dawson to White Horse.

He arrived in Nome May 2, 1900 and found employment as a cook on an Anvil Creek claim. During the season he found some float quartz which he traced to the head of Nome River and located the ledge. That fall he went back to the states and organized the Arctic Mining and Trading Company in Youngstown, Ohio. Returning to the Nome country in 1901 he started a store in Teller and began to acquire likely looking mining property. He began quietly to buy and bond mining claims on Sunset Creek, and by the fall of 1903 had the entire creek, comprising 104 claims, under bond. He also acquired a large number of tin claims at Cape Prince of Wales and in the vicinity of Ear Mountain. He returned to the states this season, and made arrangements to take up the bonds on the Sunset property and undertake the work of development. In the spring of 1904 he returned to Seward Peninsula with a outfit to build a ditch from Agiapuk River, which will furnish the water for mining the Sunset property. The steamship Charles Nelson was chartered in San Francisco to transport the outfit and supplies to Teller. Eighteen miles of ditch was completed during the season of 1904, and two hydraulic elevators and several giants will begin the work of washing the gravels of Sunset Creek this springs, 1905.

While he was in the states in the winter of 1903-'04, he took a course in tin assaying in Columbia College, and subsequently visited the tin mines of Cornwall. Mr. Hirschberg has great faith in the future of the tin properties of Northwestern Alaska.

NOME AND SEWARD PENINSULA, 1905

ANDREA NILSSON HOFSTAD

Andrea Nilsson was born in Bergen, Norway, April 26, 1867. In 1886 she came to Portland, Oregon, to make her home with a sister who lived there. A few years later she met Edwin Hofstad, deputy collector of customs at Juneau, who had come to Portland on a business trip. The two were married in 1896 and lived in Juneau for several months until Mr. Hofstad was transferred to Wrangell. Their first child, Thor Hofstad, was born in the Wrangell customs house. A third transfer sent the family to Sitka for a time. Returning to Wrangell in 1898, and has been the family resident ever since.

Andrea Nilsson Hofstad died in Wrangell, Alaska, October 1932.

WRANGELL SENTINEL, October 14, 1932

CHARLES G. HORSFALL

Charles G. Horsfall was born in Derbyshire, England, July 5, 1859. He immigrated to America in 1869, and settled in Brooklyn. His father subsequently purchased a flouring mill on Long Island, where he was initiated in the first rudiments of his vocation as miller and engineer.

C. G. Horsfall resided in New York until 1892, when he moved to Salt Lake City to install roller machinery in the plant of the Inland Crystal Salt Co., at Saltair, Utah, retaining his position as superintendent, until 1900, when he resigned in order to become a member of the Utah-Alaska Mining Co., and joined that memorable rush to Nome.

March 14, 1902, Mr. Horsfall began the construction of the Nome River bridge. This was the fourth bridge constructed at this place, the three others succumbing to the storms and ice a few weeks after completion. Mr. Horsfall strongly maintained that it was possible to erect a bridge at a reasonable cost that would withstand the elements. His judgment, based on experience in dock and bridge building in New York, has been verified by the structure that spans Nome River.

Mr. Horsfall and his wife are well and favorably known in this part of the Northland. They were married in Nome, having met for the first time in the Northern mining camp in 1900.

NOME AND SEWARD PENINSULA, 1905

E. C. HOWARD

E.C. Howard was born in Superior, Wisconsin, August 8, 1861. He spent most of his early manhood at Duluth, Minn., where he established the first department store.

Later, Mr. Howard moved to Butte, Montana where he was western representative of Armour company, Chicago meat packers. His territory embraced Montana, Idaho, Washington, and Wyoming.

Leaving Montana, Mr. Howard made his first trip to Alaska in 1908. He made his home in Ketchikan, then a hamlet. He saw the possibilities of the fur industry and for many years was the Alaska representative of an eastern fur house. He then opened a fur business in Ketchikan.

E.C.Howard died in Ketchikan, Alaska, August 15, 1926. He is survived by his sister and two brothers: Ida Howard Gilbert of Pasadena, California; Ben F. Howard of Riverton, Monitoba; and Jay Cook Howard of Duluth, Minnesota.

ALASKA WEEKLY, August 26, 1926

GEORGE A. HOWE

Born, Hallowell, Maine, 1848. Came to San Francisco by rail, 1869. There until 1886 when for ten years he made trips to Alaska on sealing and trading schooners. Came to Cook Inlet and established a trading post at Shutna River near Tyonic. Went to Old Knik spring of 1895 and established trading post. Was there two years. Started back to San Francisco but while at Juneau was called to Seattle to Join expedition of Major Glenn over Portage Pass to the Cook Inlet country, his mission being to search for pass to Cook Inlet for a railroad. Thirty soldiers were in the party. Was with Glen for three months over ground where Anchorage now is, and other points on Cook Inlet. Went back to Juneau and brought Prof Georgeson to Kenai to survey government far land. Then went with him to Kodiak for same purpose, finishing work in 1898. Then went to Seattle and took U.S. Com. Wiggins to Rampart season of 1899. Took first thawing machine to that country. Mined on Hunter creek. From there to Nome, spring of 1900. There two years and then went back to Juneau, from which point he operated in different lines until 1915 when he came to Anchorage and has resided in Anchorage ever since.

PATHFINDER, November 1919

NELS OLSON HULTBERG

N.O. Hultberg is one of the earliest pioneers of Seward Peninsula. He was sent by the Swedish Missionary Society to Golovin Bay in 1893, the object of this trip being to establish an industrial school for natives.

He had not been here long before he learned that the country was mineralized and contained gold. As early as 1895 natives brought him gold prospects from Nome River, which was then known by the native name of Iarcharvik.

In August 1897, P.H. Anderson arrived at Golovin, having been sent out by the Swedish Missionary Society as missionary to this station. This gave Mr. Hultberg a chance to get away from the work in which he had been engaged, and to devote his time to prospecting. Having heard a report of a gold strike on Sinuk, River, four other prospectors went on an expedition with him up the coast to investigate the report which he had received from natives.

The expedition sailed in a small craft, but a storm arising before they reached their destination, they were forced to make a landing in the mouth of Snake River. During their detention at this place they prospected on Dry Creek, finding colors. On Anvil Creek, Mr. Hultberg obtained a pan of gravel in which he got sixty-eight colors. Subsequently he left the party and went up the creek and took another pan of gravel from which he obtained 169 colors. This was the best prospect that he had ever seen from this part of the country.

They resumed their trip. On the way to Golovin, they encountered a very severe storm which prevented them from going ashore. They were lying out on the sea three days and four nights, without any shelter, in a small open boat and short of provisions. On their arrival at Golovin, Mr. Hultberg was so exhausted that he did not dare to return to what he considered the greatest discovery he had made on the various prospecting trips. Hultberg was compelled to go to the states on account of poor health. He returned to Nome in the spring of 1899, landing at Nome the 18th day of June, without funds. Shortly after his arrival he was one of the first victims of the typhoid fever epidemic raging during the season of

1899.

In 1900 he organized a party and started to go across country from Norton Sound to this stream; becoming ill while on the way, he had to abandon the trip. Mr. Hultberg has been more fortunate during the past two years in his ventures in Alaska. Among other enterprises which he has promoted and successfully financed is the McDermott Ditch in the Solomon River country.

Mr. Hultberg is a native of Southern Sweden, and was born March 24, 1965. His father was a manufacturer of farming implements, and after receiving a public school education his on learned the trade of a wood and iron worker. He left Sweden in 1887, and went direct to Pullman, Illinois, where he was employed for a period of several years by the Pullman Car Company.

Mr. Hultberg and Miss Hannah Holm were married at Unalakleet July 8, 1894, but Missionary Karlson. It is the first white marriage solemnized in Northwestern Alaska. Miss Holm, who was a resident of Galesberg, Illinois, and whom he met before he went to Alaska, was brave enough to take the long journey to the Swedish Mission on Golovin Bay. They have four children. The oldest, Albia Abita, was born in Alaska. The other children are Hilmar Amnon, Charles Olof and Hazel Opherima. Besides his Alaska interests, Mr. Hultberg has a colonization enterprise in Turlock, California, this place being his winter home.

NOME AND SEWARD PENINSULA, 1905

ROBERT HART HUMBER

R. H. Humber holds the position of superintendent of the mail route between Nome and Unalakleet. Every winter since 1900, he has carried mail in Northwestern Alaska. In four winter seasons and through every phase of winter weather he has traveled with dog teams a total distance of near 17,000 miles. He has had many experiences on the trail, several perilous adventures, but has escaped unharmed

and without even a serious frostbite. December
15, 1902, he fell through the ice of Norton
Sound. Fortunately his arm caught on firm ice
and he got out quickly, but not before he was
water soaked from the waist down. It was 45°
below zero that day. The distance to Isaac's
Point was fifteen miles, and he knew that he
must accomplish this journey or freeze. His
water soaked garments froze instantly. He ran
the entire fifteen miles, and arrived at the
road-house in a little more than two hours
after meeting with the accident. The violent
exercise prevented freezing, but his feet
became very numb. He carried an ax with him,
and with the handle he beat his feet to keep up
the circulation, and he was ready the next day
to start back with the mail.

Mr. Humber was born in Lincoln
County, Kansas, November 19, 1871. He is of
Southern ancestry and was educated at the
Louisville Military Academy. His boyhood days
were spent in Montana, and in 1887 he was
appointed assistant postmaster under George W.
Carlton of the Deer Lodge Postoffice.
Subsequently he was associated with the British
Columbia Smelting and Refining Company at
Rossland. He was among the first men to go
over the trail to Dawson in 1897. He
prospected in the Klondike country, in the
Forty-Mile country and in other parts of the
Northwest until the spring of 1900. He came
down the Yukon in a small boat immediately
after the break up of the ice. On account of
his postoffice experience he obtained a
position in the Nome Postoffice, and had charge
of the money order department, and every winter
since has been a sub-mail contractor.

NOME AND SEWARD PENINSULA, 1905

JOSEPHINE HUMPHREY

Josephine Humphrey was born in Sterling,
Illinois, January 5, 1865, and came with her
parents to Towanda, Pennsylvania, when three
months old. There she grew to girlhood and was
married to Julius A. Mason, son of a Civil War
officer and childhood friend, October 1, 1891.

To them was born three sons, Julius, Eugene and Joseph.

Mrs. Mason pioneered in the truest sense of the word, the family having taken a homestead and a trade and manufacturing site on Wrangell Narrows. They lived there seven years until the illness of Mr. Mason necessitated a return to Wrangell, where he died in 1913.

Residence in Wrangell has been continuous except for visits Outside. Mrs. Mason and her son Julius, who has been with the Alaska Packers for many years and spends his summers at Alitak, Kodiak Island, and his wife and small son occupy the family home. The second son, Eugene is with the Cook Inlet Packing Company, Seldovia. He is also married and has a young daughter.

WRANGELL SENTINEL, April 8, 1932

OMAR J. HUMPHREY

Omar Humphrey was born in Yarmouth, Maine, in 1856, and educated at Kent's Hill Seminary, Readfield, Maine. He went to sea when only fourteen years of age, and has seen almost continuous service until 1900.

Captain Omar J. Humphrey has been identified with the development of Alaska for more than twenty years, coming north in 1884 for the Karluk Packing Company. In 1889 he was appointed superintendent for the Pacific Steam Whaling Company, and during that year he began construction on several canneries. These canneries and equipment represented an expenditure of nearly one million dollars. In 1898 the interests of the Pacific Steam Whaling Company demanded the organization of regular steamship service, and Captain Humphrey was appointed manager of the fleet of steam and sailing vessels.

In 1901 Captain Humphrey began operating steamships on his own account. He made St. Michael his headquarters, and dispatched steamships from Seattle to St. Michael, connecting with his river steamers supplying interior points. He operated the first steamship line out of Seattle for Southwestern,

Alaska.

The season of 1904 marked the close of Captain Humphrey's independent transportation operations. During 1905 he was agent for the Alaska Commercial Company, operating steamers to Northwestern Alaska.

In 1906 Omar J. Humphrey was elected delegate to Congress from the third district.

Selling his interests in the north to the Northern Commercial Co, he became agent for the Alaska Commercial company with offices in Seattle. In 1906 Mr. Humphrey incorporated and was president of the Alaska Coast Co., operating a line of steamers to Alaska. He was chairman of the trustees of the Shipmaster's Association of the United States, and was a trustee of the Washington Trust company from the time of its incorporation until its consolidation with the Dexter Horton National Bank.

He continued to be actively engaged in shipping and commercial enterprises until this country became involved in the late war at which time he tendered his services to his country. He was accepted and made lieutenant commander of the United States Naval Reserves and his first assignment was as master of the then new 7,500-ton steel steamship BREMERTON, a product of the Seattle Construction and Dry Dock company of Seattle. He remained in the service, as commander of the BREMERTON and other steamers; carrying men and supplies to the shores of France, and dodging submarines, until the close of the war. He then went in command of a steamer owned by the Steel Corporation making regular trips around the world, and it was while in this service the he rescued the passengers and crew of a sinking British vessel in the Indian Ocean, and in recognition of which the British government gave the captain a very beautiful silver cup. He continued in this service until a few years ago, when he had reached the age limit and retired from active duty.

He spend summers at the Humphrey ranch in Northern California; the autumns he loves to

spend at the old homestead at Yarmouth, Maine, while the winters he spends under the sunny skies of Southern California.
  ALASKA WEEKLY, September 20, 1929
  ALASKA MAGAZINE, January 1906

HARRIET ELIZABETH FROST HUNT
  Harriet Elizabeth Frost was born at Tumwater, near Olympia in the then territory of Washington, the end of the "Oregon Trail." Except for a few years in California, her early life was spent in Washington. Her parents, Andrew Jackson Frost and Mary Frost were among the earliest pioneers of Washington, her father crossed the plains with his parents in 1844, and her mother in 1854.
  She was married in Pierce County, Washington in 1880 to Forest J. Hunt. They had five children, three girls and two boys. The oldest boy, Elmer, died at the age of nine, and the other son, Dale Ward, passed away in Alaska in 1923, a victim of influenza. He was buried on his 38th birthday at Ketchikan, Alaska. The three daughters are married and live in Ketchikan.
  In March of 1898, Mr. Hunt left for Wrangell, Alaska to seek work, leaving Harriet and the four children on the farm in Gig Harbor, Washington. Mrs. Hunt and the children joined Forest in May 7, 1898, and on the day she arrived, began baking bread to supplement the family income.
  Mrs. Hunt soon extended her business by taking over a small restaurant called the Blue Front--and was particularly known for her lemon pies.
  In the fall of 1899 Mrs. Hunt took the children to Tacoma, Washington for schooling during the winter. At the time there was a flurry of excitement over some rich quartz strikes near Ketchikan.
  Mr. Hunt decided to move to Ketchikan after the arrival of Mrs. Hunt and the children, leaving her to close out the stock later, which she did and arrived in Ketchikan in June 1900 from Wrangell.

Ketchikan was incorporated that year, a school board elected, teacher employed, and a library association formed, Mrs. Hunt being chairman of the first meeting. She is still an active member of the Board. This was the source of our present public library.

Having purchased a portrait camera from Fred Garlyon of Wrangell, Mrs. Hunt took up the study of photography and soon opened the first photography gallery in Ketchikan, which she conducted for several years in connection with Mr. Hunt's store.

Mrs. Hunt has been very active in all civil work; was a charter member and first Worthy Matron of Aurora Chapter No. 3, Order of Eastern Star in Ketchikan of which she has now been made a life member. In 1928 Mrs. Hunt was appointed by action of the National Republican Convention at Kansas City, National Republican Committeewoman for Alaska, the first time that Alaska women have been recognized in this manner.

She has been persistent and forceful in her efforts to secure Alaskan institutions for the care of the insane, indigents, and all dependents upon public need, within the Territory.

Mrs. Hunt was the working member of a committee which executed and published the first illustrated booklet of Ketchikan and vicinity ever published. The illustrations were almost all from her own photos.
STROLLER'S WEEKLY, April 1, 1932

P. S. HUNT

P.S. Hunt was born in Michigan and when a small boy moved to Kalamazoo. The date of his birth, April 24, 1866. He received his business education in Kalamazoo and lived there until he was 18 years of age. On March 29, 1887 he was married in Grand Rapids, Michigan to Miss Rose Frazer of Ashtabula, Ohio. The young couple soon left for California and located at San Jose, where they lived eight years. Later they went to Sacramento, and from there Mr. Hunt came to Alaska in 1898, leaving the family, a wife and two sons, at home. He settled in Valdez and the family followed in 1907. He followed his vocation that of a photographer, until 1915 when he was appointed official photographer of the Alaskan Engineering Commission. He then made his home in Anchorage and attended to his official duties.

On October 14, 1917 he was suddenly stricken while attending to his work in Seward, and fell unconscious on the street, dying.
PATHFINDER, December 1919

THOMAS H. HUNT

Thomas Hunt was born at Port Huron, Michigan, on the 4th day of September, 1857, and first went to school in his home town. Later he went up into the Wisconsin lumber regions and after some years' service became a lumber inspector and shipper. Several years later he was in Duluth, Minn., and from there went down the Mississippi in the logging business. Mr. Hunt came to Alaska in the year 1898, landing in Valdez among the first ones. He has prospected over a large portion of the Valdez district and owns some property, but of later has been serving as crier in the District Court.

Mr. Hunt has held many positions of trust in the town and at present is serving his second term as Town Clerk.
PATHFINDER, May 1920

CHIEF ISAAC

Born some 85 years ago along the Yukon
ALASKA DAILY EMPIRE, September 28, 1922
River(?), Isaac was elected chief as a young man, and through many years of trail before and after the coming of the whiteman, proved his worthiness for the honor and trust imposed in him by his people.

Tall, slender, sinewy and muscular, he was of superior physical proportions, and time also proved him as well endowed mentally. His friendliness to the whites, dating back to the days of the Russian occupation of the Yukon and

Alaska, and his influence with other Indians, went far toward smoothing the way for prospectors, traders, trappers, missionaries, and others who pioneered the Northland. Those who knew Chief Isaac well agree that, had he been a white man with opportunities for education, combined with his natural ability and personality, he would have proved to be an extraordinary figure in most any walk of life.

The chief was a devout member of the Church of England. He was a faithful attendant at services in the church at Moosehide.

Chief Isaac died in Moosehide, Yukon Territory in April 1932. He is survived by two sons and two daughters.

ALASKA WEEKLY, April 15, 1932

JIMMY JACKSON

Capt. Jimmy Jackson, full blood Alaska Indian was born at Taku 54 years ago, son of Chief Onaklosh.

Jimmy Jackson was trained for his life in the Interior as mail carrier and conqueror of hardship when a boy in the Cassiar country, where he worked for Sylvester, afterward a Wrangell sawmill man. After three years of mining there he worked in the Sylvester sawmill for two years, and then returned to the Cassiar for the Hudson's Bay Company.

From there he came to Juneau and secured a contract with the United States government as a mail carrier.

Jimmy Jackson first earned fame in this section and the Interior of Sourdough Days for a round trip from Juneau to Circle City, a distance of more than 1,000 miles, by way of Taku and the Yukon River, in mid-winter, with the mail. He started from Juneau with four companions and a dog team.

Before he had reached his destination, Jimmy Jackson had thrown away everything except the mail and something to eat. He camped in the open in January weather without blankets. Finally the dogs began giving out and that meant that he had to take the mail on his back. He killed the last dog before he had met anyone

and was eating that when he reached his
destination. He was liberally rewarded at
Circle City, where a purse was raised for him.
The big companies each donated $150 and
individual miners and prospectors contributed
to the fund. They presented him with a dog
team and sled, food, and blankets for the
return trip.

Jimmy was in the Interior, still carrying
mail, when the Klondike was struck. He was
there when Captain Turnbull started up the
Yukon for the present site of Whitehorse with
the river steamer GOLDEN STAR, and Jimmy was
shipped as pilot. He has been a pilot ever
since. For the last 14 years he has been
employed by Taylor and Drury, and he says with
pride this is the first season he has failed to
stay with his ship until she was put away for
the winter. He lives in Whitehorse, Yukon
Territory.

ALASKA DAILY EMPIRE, September 28, 1922

M. R. JAMIESON

Mr. Jamieson was born in Australia in
1866. He arrived in Dawson in 1898. From
Dawson he went to Atlin, B.C. where at one time
he was a owner of the Engineer gold mine. He
located in Stewart, B.C. during the first boom
and was proprietor of the Northern Hotel, which
was burned in 1914. He afterwards conducted
the Copper Travern at Skeena Crossing south of
Hazelton, and in 1919 he again returned to the
Portland Canal camp, where he established the
Hyder Hotel in Hyder, Alaska.

For the past year he had been associated
with Arthur J. Brown in the Portland Canal
Brokerage Company, in Vancouver, B.C.

M. R. Jamieson died in Stewart, B.C.,
September 9, 1928.

ALASKA WEEKLY, Sept. 21, 1928

GEORGE JAMME

George Jamme, mining engineer, with
offices in Seattle, first went to Alaska in the
spring of 1899, at the instance of the Cook
Inlet Coal Fields Company, a Philadelphia

concern that had taken over coal deposits in the Kachemak Bay region. His work was to outline a general plan for the development of the holdings, etc. He built the town of Homer, constructed a large wharf there and began construction of the eight-mile railway from the town to the coal fields. While there, he had occasion to visit the west shore of the inlet and seized the opportunity make an examination of the oil possibilities from Iliamna Bay to Tyonek. These latter are now well-known.

Mr. Jamme passed the two summers of 1902 and 1903 on the Aleutian Islands, making a reconnaissance of the coal fields about Herendeen and Chignic Bays and the intervening country. He also spent several weeks looking over the oil structures in the vicinity of Coal Bay. In 1904 he made an examination of the coal deposits of the Matanuska Valley, and believes that he was the third white man to have been beyond Granite Creek, in that region, and the trail he blazed on his way to the Chickaloon is the line now used by the Alaska Railroad. Later, he passed several weeks in the Controller Bay region.

Mr. Jamme spent the summer of 1905 in the Mckenzie River basin. He went by canoe from Fort McMurray, on the Athabasca, to the head of the delta of the Mackenzie, covering the oil fields adjacent to the waterways. Here he located sites for five wells, all of which have since been drilled and proven. Part of the season of 1906 he spent near Yakutat and on the Alsek river, the remaining portion near Sitka, and at the head of Portland Canal. He passed the winter of 1906-07 in Controller Bay examining ice conditions and the possible relation to terminal facilities.

Mr. Jamme gave his entire time during 1908-09 to the A.Y.P. Exposition, in which he was the chairman of the mines committee. Mr. Jamme has been in Alaska many times since the Exposition, both in a professional capacity and on personal business.

ALASKA WEEKLY, January 10, 1930

ANDREW JENSEN

Born in Lugumkloster, Denmark, November 7, 1850, Jensen left that country when he was 17, came to America and settled in Dubuque, Iowa. On March 20, 1876 at Mason City, Iowa, he married Ingeborg Schmidt, whom he had prevailed upon to leave her home in Brede, Denmark, and come to the united States. The young couple made their home at Chapin Town for three years, and in February 1879(?) came to Dakota territory and homesteaded in the Red River valley seven miles south of what was called Third Siding, now known as Buffalo, N.D., where they made their home for 34 years until they moved to Fargo in 1913.

The lure of the northlands found a willing subject in Andrew Jensen at the age when most men have passed the adventurous period. At 48 he was farming his homestead in Buffalo, but news of the Klondike fortunes inspired him to try his luck, and in the spring of 1898 he left the Buffalo farm with his sons and started for Edmonton. At Athabasca landing he and his companions fitted out for the voyage down the Mackenzie River to Fort McPherson over McDougal pass and down the Porcupine to Fort Yukon.

Mr. Jensen had already staked his claim on Anvil Creek in 1899 when the swarms of gold seekers converged on Nome. He and two partners opened up and mined the lower half of No. 5 on Anvil Creek in the summer of 1899 and 1900 they having secured a lay on the same from H.C. Hultberg.

After returning to North Dakota from Alaska, Mr. Jensen remained at Buffalo with his family until they moved to Fargo, where he continued the development of the grain fields, finding time to take an active part in community life. He was interested in politics and in the early days in Dakota held numerous township and county offices.

Andrew Jensen died in Fargo, North Dakota, August 7, 1933. The children surviving Mr. Jensen are John Frederick, of Minneapolis; Thomas D. of Nome; Katherine, Moscow, Idaho; Harry, Tower City, N.D.; Mrs. Peter L.

Peterson, Arnegard, N.D.; Minnie and Ida, Fargo.

ALASKA WEEKLY, October 13, 1933

CARL M. JOHANSON

Carl M. Johanson, vice-president of the Northern Bank & Trust Co., was born in Southern Sweden in 1867 and at the age of thirteen he came to the United States, locating with his parents at Omaha, Nebraska. His education is credited to Williams College, Mass., and to the Cornell University Law School. Johanson's was not a family of means, and his expenses at college were met with means provided by his own energy, principally by writing for newspapers and magazines. For four years Johanson played on the Football team at Williams; while at Cornell he captained the varsity eleven for two years.

He was admitted to the bar in Utica, N.Y., in 1892, and readmitted in Minn. in 1894, where he enjoyed a large practice. He was a man of energy with a desire, too, for adventure; and when the rush went to the Klondike in '97, as he tells it himself: "I got the gold fever and had to go. That is all there is to it."

By way of the Skagway trail Mr. Johanson reached Dawson on October 8, 1897, later locating claims at Bear Creek and fortymile. In 1899 he removed to Eagle City, where he organized and operated a saw mill. He is credited with having built the first frame building in Alaska, north of the sixty-fifth parallel of latitude, and his record as a builder exceeds that of any other man in the Northland. Over fifty structures are standing, today, to the credit of his work.

He was appointed district attorney, which office he held for a short time, when in 1899 he was appointed United States commissioner for the Eagle precinct.

In 1903 he went to Fairbanks, where he organized the Tanana Development Co., which later became the Tanana Mill Co., by which were consolidated the three saw mills then at

Fairbanks. In 1904 Mr. Johanson moved his mill from Eagle City to Cleary Creek, where it is now operated independently of the Tanana Mill Co.'s interests.

In 1905 Mr. Johanson left Fairbanks and became manager of the Gold Bar Lumber Co. in Pierce County, Washington, of which corporation he is still the vice-president.

Mr. Johanson, associated with J.G. Price, J.E. Chilberg, I.H. Moore, Tom Larson and other Alaskans, organized the Northern Bank & Trust Co., in which he is now the active vice-president.

ALASKA-YUKON MAGAZINE, October 1907

ALMA JOHNSON

Alma Johnson was born sixty years ago in Sweden near the northern boundary of Norway, but came to the united States with her parents when a child. At Marquette, Michigan when a young girl, she met John G. Smith, who went west on a prospecting trip in the Cascades and later went in to the little city of Seattle to prepare a home for his bride-to-be. She joined him there in 1891 and they were married din their own home, on the site of which now stands Armory Hall near the waterfront.

the next year Mrs. Smith remained in Seattle while her husband went on a sailing boat to the new mining camp at Juneau. In 1894 they broke up their Seattle home and Mrs. Smith became one of the handful of pioneer women who had joined their husbands in Juneau, In 1897 Mr. Smith went ahead to Dawson and two years later Mrs. Smith with her little daughter made the hard trip into Dawson.

The Smiths mined successfully near Dawson and the young wife loved the thrill of the Northern camp and made light of the frontier hardships. When the Nome rush was on, Mr. Smith drove a dogteam from Dawson to Nome arriving there early in April. Mrs. Smith looked after the final cleanup on their ground and with the coming of summer, when it was impossible to get passage on the Yukon river steamer, she journeyed by rowboat with her little daughter and her husband's brother as far as Circle City where she secured accommodation in a tiny tent set up on a scow in tow of a river boat, and in that fashion made the trip across Alaska to Nome.

At Hastings Creek about ten miles south of Nome, Mr. Smith built a log house which Mrs. Smith conducted as a roadhouse while her husband was away on prospecting trips. Here their son was born, the second white child born in the Nome district. In 1905, Mr. Smith having acquired a sizeable fortune, sold his holdings and the family moved to Seattle.

Prospecting trips and mining ventures in Alaska were conducted through later years while still maintaining the Seattle home.

Six years ago Mr. and Mrs. Smith and their son established a large fox farm at Vank Island, just out of Wrangell. Mrs. Smith never lost her love of mining adventure. She was a woman of unbounded energy and indomitable courage. When ill health came she met it in the pioneer spirit which had dominated her life and refused to allow it to curtail her activities in her home and garden, or her interest in the mineral resources of this district.

Mrs. Smith died September 15, 1938. She is survived by her husband and son at Wrangell, two daughters, Mrs. Earl Blenheim and Mrs. Julius Fisher of Seattle, relatives in Michigan and Minnesota, and numerous friends throughout the North.

WRANGELL SENTINEL, September 22, 1933

CHARLES JOHNSON

Charles Johnson was born in Drummin, Norway, May 17, 1862(?). In early manhood he emigrated to Honolulu, where, at the age of 20, he was married to Christina Erickson. They came to the united States in 1886, landing at San Francisco and coming from there direct to Port Townsend. They homesteaded at Blyn in the early days of their residence in this section, later moving back to Port Townsend to make their home. Mr. Johnson followed various occupations during his early residence here and in 1889 was hauling water in Port Townsend.

At the very beginning of the gold rush Mr. Johnson went to Alaska. His trip on the Dyea trail over Chilkoot Pass in 1897 was replete with adventure, all of which he carefully chronicled in a diary which is now in possession of his family. He mined gold at Dawson and Circle City for several years and then returned to Port Townsend.

Here he was in business for some time. Later, he owned and operated several bowling alleys. He moved to Port Angeles for some time, operating bowling alleys in that city in 1922 and 1923. At that time he returned to Port Townsend and retired from active business. He purchased the Haller Building in that city.

Mrs. Johnson died May 9, 1925.

Mr. Johnson passed earlier this week in Port Townsend. He is survived by four children and a brother, Edward Johnson, who lived in the east. The children are: Walter Johnson, first assistant engineer with the Alaska railroad; Charles Johnson of Juneau; Mrs. Alice McInnis of Quilcene; and Mrs. William Rideout of Port Townsend.

ALASKA WEEKLY, January 30, 1931

CHARLES SUMNER JOHNSON

Judge C. S. Johnson has been a resident of Alaska for sixteen years. He came from Nebraska to Sitka in 1889 as United States Attorney for the district. In 1897 President McKinley appointed him to the office of Judge of the District Court of Alaska, a position which he filled until the spring of 1900, when he resigned to engage in the practice of law at Nome. Judge Johnson's earliest recollections are associated with a log cabin on an Iowa prairie where he was born August 31, 1854. He is of Scotch ancestry, and his father was one of the pioneers of Ohio. C. S. Johnson's boyhood days were spent in Iowa. He attended the public schools of Clarinda, a town in Page County. When he was fifteen years old he was thrown upon his own resources to obtain the education which he so much desired. He learned the printer's trade, and earned enough money at the case to attend the Iowa State College. In 1877 he was graduated from the law department of the University of Iowa, and the same year he moved to Wahoo, Nebraska, and began the practice of law with N. H. Bell, under the firm name of Bell & Johnson. He was married September 18, 1879. Mrs. Johnson is the daughter of Major J. B. Davis, of Wahoo, Neb. In 1882 Judge Johnson was elected to the Nebraska Legislature from Saunders County. Three years later he moved to Nelson, Neb., and served two terms as Prosecuting Attorney of Nuckols County. In 1889, and before the expiration of his second term of office, he received the appointment of U. S. Attorney for Alaska. He went to Sitka, where he lived until the expiration of his term of office; and it is a noteworthy fact that he is the only District Attorney for Alaska who ever served a full term. After the expiration of his term of office he practiced law in Juneau until 1897, when he received the appointment of Judge of the Federal Court for the District of Alaska. His resignation in 1900 was because of the inadequate salary attached to the office, $3,000 a year.

In 1899 the growth of the mining camps in the Yukon Valley and the discovery of gold at Nome created the necessity for a session of the District Court in a number of places in this part of the district. Accordingly, Judge Johnson started on a circuit that required him to make a trip of 7,000 miles. The itinerary was as follows: To Dawson via White Pass, down the Yukon to Eagle, Circle, Rampart and St. Michael, terms of court being held in each place; thence to Nome, where the first session of the District Court was held; thence to Unalaska, Unga and Kodiak, a revenue cutter being provided by the Government for this part of the trip; and thence to Sitka. This journey occupied a period of three months, and is undoubtedly one of the longest circuits ever made by a court. At that time Judge Johnson's jurisdiction extended over a territory near 600,000 square miles in extent, and the only means of expeditious travel were vessels on navigable streams.

When Judge Johnson arrived in Nome in August, he found a spacious tent for the accommodation of the court. The rainy season was making a record, and the tent was not impervious to the constant downpour, but leaked bountifully. Mud in the streets of Nome was from a foot to two feet in depth, and a part of the vestment of the Judge when he convened court were a slicker and a pair of gum boots.

Judge Johnson's interpretation of the law has been comparatively free of mistakes, as only two of his decisions have been reversed by the Supreme Court.

NOME AND SEWARD PENINSULA, 1905

JOHN JOHNSON

John Johnson was born in Vermland, Sweden, August 17, 1874. He is a farmer's son, and was educated in the public schools of his native land. He learned the carpenter's trade, and immigrating to the United States in 1892, worked at his trade six years in Chicago.

In 1898 he went to Alaska, and became a miner. He stayed in Rampart a year, and worked a lay on No. 5 Little Minook. The result of his first mining venture was not successful. News of the Nome Strike reached Rampart during the winter, and in the spring of '99 he left these diggings for the new camp, arriving at Nome in July. Securing employment from the Pioneer Mining Company.

In the latter part of November he went to the Norton Bay country on a prospecting trip. This was an unprofitable expedition, in which there were hardships and a narrow escape from death. On New Year's day, while crossing Norton Sound, his team went through the ice, but he got the dogs out. Returning to the Nome region in March he prospected on Solomon River, where he had staked claims the previous year. In the summer of 1900 he worked for the Pioneer Mining Company, and had charge of their cleanups on Snow Gulch, Mountain and Rock Creeks.

In the fall of 1900 he and Axel Olson were outfitted to the Fairhaven District. They prospected tributaries of the Inmachuk and other streams of the Arctic slope. They named several streams of this region, among them Excelsior, Polar Bear, Mystery and Moonlight.

Going into this country, they cached some of their provisions on the Noxapaga River, and they did not leave the Arctic region until their supplies were pretty near "peluk," believing that a day's journey would take them to their cache. When they started on the return trip one of the worst blizzards of this country swept over the snowy wastes of the trackless region. The first night out they could not make a fire and they crawled into their sleeping bags to escape freezing. The next day was worse, but they traveled, and at night found a landmark by which they knew they were on Good Hope River. They had journeyed over a part of a circuit, and were farther away from the cache than when they started. There was no abatement of the blizzard. For two days they lived on unsalted beans. On the fifth day, almost famished and nearly exhausted, they arrived at their cache, and found it empty. A pariah of the trail had robbed it. The next day they met some Eskimo, who supplied them with fish.

Mr. Johnson and his partner were reported lost, and when they arrived in Nome a search party had been organized. Mr. Johnson was ill for a week, and concluded that he never would start on another trip of this kind. But a week after his recovery he was on the trail again, bound for the same region. Returning to Nome late in the season, he learned of the Candle Creek strike. This discovery of gold was made when he was prospecting only five miles away. He returned to Candle Creek, and in the following winter went to Nome to obtain merchandise for Magnus Kjelsberg, which was hauled to Candle Creek over the snow.

Mr. Johnson lived at Candle City until August, 1902, when he arranged for a trip to

Kobuk River. Crossing Escholtz Bay to get a boat, he encountered a servere storm and was blown out to sea. He and a companion were out twenty-four hours. Thge mast of their boat was broken and swept away by the strom, but the wind subsiding, they succeeded in pulling to the shore at the mouth of Alder Creek. He built a cabin 400 miles above the mouth of the Kobuk. In November he heard of the strike on Shungnak, a tributary of the Kobuk, sixty miles below his camp, and immediately went to the new diggings. Overtaken by illness, he was compelled to return to Nome in April. This trip of 500 miles was made in nine days, and seventy miles of the journey was traveled on snow shoes without resting. After undergoing an operation for appendicitis, he went to California.

Returning in the spring of 1904, he worked for the Pioneer Mining Company, and in the fall secured from the company a lease on the Portland Bench, near Little Creek. Taking Nels Peterson and Carl Anderson as partners, the work of sinking holes to bedrock on this claim was begun. Six shafts were sunk before pay was found. In sixty days a dump was taken out from which $413,000 was cleaned up.

NOME AND SEWARD PENINSULA, 1905

CAPTAIN E. W. JOHNSTON

Captain Johnston has been identified with the lighterage business in Alaska since the first stampede to the Klondike in 1897. When the news of the gold discovery on the upper Yukon reached the outside, Captain Johnston was a resident of Seattle and was engaged in building lighters, operating a stone quarry and conducting a general freighting business on the Sound. He immediately saw the business opportunity of lightering freight and landing passengers from steamers at Skagway, and was the first man to engage in this business at that place. The smallest lighter that he took from Seattle had a carrying capacity of 400 tons.

Captain Johnston conducted this business

during the seasons of '97 and '98. He worked almost incessantly. He made money and made friends. Probably there is no man in the North who knows more of the Klondikers than Captain Johnston.

The Nome gold discovery and the development of these gold fields in 1899 convinced Captain Johnston that there would be another business opportunity in his line of work on the waterfront of Nome. He immediately set to work constructing a lighterage plant to take to Nome in the spring of 1900. Every year since that memorable season he has been in Nome, and has handled a great many thousand tons of freight that have been shipped into this country. From the beginning of his work at Nome he saw the necessity of a harbor to provide better facilities for discharging cargoes and to provide a safe anchorage during storms for the small craft of the sea. He was able to secure the organization of a company which subscribed the necessary funds and gave him the contract to perform the work. He is making a Nome harbor this season.

Captain Johnston was born in Chicago November 30, 1860. He is a son of Dr. Johnston, a well-known citizen and pioneer who settled in the "Windy City" in 1834. Captain Johnston is self-educated. When a small boy he was sent to school, but had the misfortune in the very early part of his scholastic opportunities to be challenged by the bully of the school. He gave the bully an unmerciful thrashing and the paternal rebuke caused the independent youngster to leave home. He began life for himself by catching minnows and selling them to the fishermen for ten cents the dozen. He got a berth on a sloop sailing on Lake Michigan and worked for a year at a salary of two dollars and fifty cents a month. When he was sixteen years old he and his elder brother bought the schooner El Painter and sailed her on the lake. At the age of twenty he was in command of the lumber schooner Dan I. Davis. He sailed the lakes for many years.

In 1886 he went to Seattle and engaged in

the hardware business for two years prior to resuming the line of work on Puget Sound with which he has been familiar from his early boyhood.
    NOME AND SEWARD PENINSULA, 1905

CHARLES D. JONES
  Charles D. Jones, United States marshal for the Second judicial division of Alaska, with headquarters at Nome, metropolis of that division, went to the Northwestern Alaska placer gold camp in the spring of 1900. That has been his residence since that early date. When he first went to Nome Mr. Jones devoted his time to mining on the creeks and on the beaches.
  He was re-appointed to the marshalship by President Coolidge June 30, 1925, and this term expired June 30, 1930. He is holding office until his successor is appointed, and is a candidate to succeed himself. He is a married man, and both himself and wife are in Seattle at this writing.
    ALASKA WEEKLY, July 18, 1930

J. P. JORGENSON
  Mr. Jorgenson arrived in Juneau on the steamer Idaho from San Francisco November 12, 1885, and at once engaged in the carpenter trade and during the next two or three years worked on many of the better class buildings then under construction. In 1888 he entered into business for himself as a contractor and builder putting up his first building between the Loavre and Germania. He continued in this line of work until 1893.
  He went into the Yukon country to try his fortune, but six months experience up there induced him to return to Juneau, and on his arrival here he leased one year a building belonging to ex-Governor John G. Brady. When the lease expired he bought the property and built his present structure. The front building was 50 x 60; back of this he built a warehouse and a planing mill. This mill was equipped with modern machinery for the

manufacture of sash doors etc. In the year 1892 he built a sawmill near Gastineau channel, which has furnished the lumber not only for Juneau, but for many of the mines and canneries in this part of the country. This saw mill has contributed much toward the success of Juneau. Mr. Jorgenson estimates that his mill contributes $6,000 each month to Juneau's economy.

Mr. Jorgenson was married in San Francisco January 17, 1896 to Miss L. Deborah Henselwood of West Liberty, Iowa.

ALASKA MONTHLY MAGAZINE, Oct-Nov. 1907

GEORGE W. JOSEPH

Senator Joseph was born on Joseph Creek, in Modoc county, California, in 1872 of Scotch-Irish parentage. After finishing high school in his native town, he went to Portland, where he lived until the gold excitement in the Klondike and in Alaska in 1897 attracted him to the scene. He departed for the Yukon camp, going in by way of St. Michael, late in the fall of 1897. The steamer on which he took passage was frozen in at the mouth of Little Minook Creek, and the whole expedition on the steamer passed the winter of 1897-98 prospecting and mining.

Mr. Joseph secured a placer claim, No. 7 above discovery on Little Manook Creek. After the spring cleanup, Mr. Joseph went on to Dawson and spent the summer prospecting on the Klondike River. He returned the fall of 1898 to Portland, and engaged in the practice of law. Later he was the Republican candidate for governor of the state.

Mr. Joseph died June 16, 1930 near Astoria, Oregon. He is survived by his widow, Mrs. Bertha L. Snell Joseph, and a son, George W. Joseph, Jr.

ALASKA WEEKLY, July 4, 1930

ANTHONY E. KARNES

Anthony E. Karnes was born in Kansas in 1888.

He worked his way through Washburn

College, after which he was in school work for six years, when he joined the Army and served with the A.E.F as a machine gunner; he took part in two drives, the St. Mihiel and Meuse-Argonne, and was wounded in action a few days before the close of the war.

After returning from France, he spent a year in Ponca City, Oklahoma, as Principal of the high school, then went to Boise, Idaho, where he was principal. While in Boise he was president of the Boise Teachers Club. From Boise he went to Twin Falls, Idaho, as Principal of the High School. While at the latter place, he was President of the Southern Idaho Teachers' Association, comprising eight counties, and was also Secretary of the Idaho High School Declamatory Association.

In the fall of 1923 he was elected as Physics teacher and assistant football coach of the Piedmont High School in Piedmont, California, and while there, took summer school and night school work at the University, where he received his master of arts degree in education in April, 1924. He continued his studies there the following year when he went to Tomales, California where he was principal of the high school until he was elected as superintendent at Ketchikan in 1927. Since coming to Alaska, he has served two years as Director of the National Education Association for Alaska and attended the conventions of this organization in 1930 and 1931. At the Columbus, Ohio convention in 1930 he gave an address on Alaska.

WRANGELL SENTINEL, October 7, 1932

ANDREW P. KASHEVAROFF

Alaska's history, in many respects, is the history of Russian Father A. P. Kashevaroff and his people. For the past 100 years his people have been identified with Alaska.

Phillip A. Kashevaroff, the grandfather of Andrew came to Sitka about the year 1820 as an instructor for the Colonial school. He died at Sitka October 22, 1843, aged 64. Rev. Kashevaroff's Father, Peter, was born in Sitka,

June 8, 1829 and died Jan. 1877 at Kodiak. One aunt, Anna, was born Oct. 19, 1831 and another Alexandra May 11, 1834. Two uncles--Alexis was born Sept. 9, 1839 and Phillip, Nov. 19, 1844.

His mother's brother, Illarion J. Archimandritoff was the Senior captain of the Russian American Company's merchant marine fleet in Alaska. Later, he was made governor of the Eastern Siberia. He was supposed to have left a fortune, and Father Kashevaroff still has some paper roubles for souveniers from the estate.

He had three sisters, Namely: Jeditulia Victoria, B.C. married to Captain William George who brought the first American trading vessel to Alaska for the Hutchinson Kole Co., the successors to the Russian American Fur Company. From 1868 to 1900 Captain George was on the Alaska run, being the pilot for the Pacific Coast Steamship Co. for 40 years. He was considered one of the best navigators of the Northern waters. Mary, Rev. Kashevaroff's second sister was the wife of the late Father Mitropolsky, priest of the Russian church stationed in Alaska. Barbara, his third sister is now living with her niece, the wife of the Archpriest Rev. Peter Ropoff in New York City.

Two brothers Peter and Nicholas, both ordained priests are living in the westward. One at St. George and the other at Kodiak.

The transfer of Alaska from Russia to the United States was made Oct. 18, 1867. Father Kashevaroff was born four years previous at Kodiak. His wife, formerly Martha Bolshanin, was born at Sitka in 1874, and the two married in Sitka in 1893.

All the children of the two were born and educated in Alaska. Cyril was born in Nutchek, Prince William Sound, Aug. 16, 1894. At the break of the World's war he was entering the California university. He, with other young men, enlisted among the first. Cyril served two years in the army as corporal.

Mary, was born at Kodiak July 5, 1900; Nadja at Sitka Feb. 6, 1902; Lydia at Sitka June 26, 1904. Natalia at Sitka Nov. 6, 1908, and Xenia at Juneau Aug. 28, 1913.

Father Kashevaroff was educated in San Francisco both in American and Russian schools. While young he returned to Alaska to take up the educational work among the natives. He served in the capacity at Sitka, Killisnoo, Nutchek and Kodiak.

He was ordained to the priesthood in Sitka in 1904, and
appointed Superintendent of the Theological Seminary at Sitka and the superintendent of the Russian Churches in Alaska. He was raised to the rank of Archpriest in 1916. After the organization of the Russian Church in Alaska he served two summers as U.S. Deputy collector and inspector at Nakat. In winter he acted as the assistant weather observer under Mr. M.B. Summers. He was appointed the Librarian of the Historical Library in October 1919 and the curator of the Historical Museum in 1920

The physical as well as the moral courage of Father Kashevaroff has been tested many times. When he was at Nutchek fighting the liquor traffic among the natives he was threatened with physical violence. He has organized mission schools and temperance societies among the natives in many places.
JUNEAU SUNDAY CAPITAL, Feb. 19, 1922

KAZIS KAY

At the age of 17, Judge Kay had acquired a high school education and was placed on his own resources, but while making a start as a coal-breaker boy, he lost no time in taking advantage of our night school opportunities, and finally qualified himself for the completion of his law course. He received the decree of Bachelor of Laws, and was admitted to practice by the Supreme Court of the United States.

Upon leaving home to make his way in the world, Judge Kay first secured work in the coal fields, and pressing steadily onward as mason's helper, miner, newspaper reporter, soldier in the U.S. Army(Spanish-American War), linguist, qualified by the U.S. civil service commission in six languages, he attained the position of chief inspector of U.S. Immigration for Alaska.

In 1902 he was assigned to the chief inspector, a position for the Territory of Alaska. He made his headquarters in Sitka, then the capital, and later established himself in Ketchikan.

In 1912 Judge Kay resigned from the service in order to become a candidate for delegate to Congress, but being defeated for office he left in 1913 for Seattle where he practiced law.

On December 21, 1926, he made his appearance in the Superior Court here and had his name officially changed to "Kay."

Presently, he is serving on the Superior court for King County, Washington. Judge Kay is married and has four children: a daughter, Julia; a son Kazis Jr.; and two additional sons, names unknown.

ALASKA WEEKLY, September 18, 1931
September 2, 1932

J. W. KEEN

James W. Keen was born in Devonshire, England, April 1, 1842. His father, Thomas F. Keen was a native of Scotland and was born at sea in 1802 while his father, Col. Thomas E. Keen, was returning from the war in Egypt. His mother was Mary Ann Fisher, also a native of Scotland. He came of a long-lived family, having an uncle who died at the age of 115, while his aunt, Lady Jessie Pelly, died at 102.

When a boy of 16, he left London September 3, 1858 on the Hudson's Bay Company's bark-rigged steamer LABOUCHERE for Victoria, B.C. arriving there February 2, 1859. During his apprenticeship which expired in 1863, he traded with the Indians through the inland waters of British Columbia and Alaska.

This boyhood experience was of importance to the united States government in later years. In the Alaska boundary dispute the British asserted that the Hudson's Bay Company had flown the British flag on the soils of alaska for years. They were sparring for possession of Lynn Canal. Capt. C. L. Hooper of the United States revenue cutter service, said it was not true and that Pilot Keen could give the facts.

George Evans, a retired naval officer, was sent to Seattle and got Keen's affidavit that the Hudson's Bay Company had done all its trading exclusively from the vessel and not from shore. The Indians allowed no trespassing.

In 1864 he shipped on the NORTHERN LIGHT, carrying the mail from Port Townsend to Dungeness, Port Angeles and Victoria, and in 1865 started the first ferry from Seattle to Port Blakeley with the sloop KATE ALEXANDER.

During the summer of 1865 he was engaged in prospecting for codfish up as far as Kodiak Island. After the transfer of the territory in 1868, he started out on a fur-sealing expedition. The latter was evidently not a successful venture for he returned on the steamer Constantine. Subsequent to this, several successful trading trips were made to Chilcaht for Messrs. Whitford & Stores of Sitka. The following winter he went as pilot on board the U.S.S. Saginaw, under Capt. Richard W. Meade, continuing in the same position as long as the Saginaw remained in Alaskan waters.

While acting as pilot on board the Saginaw he did duty as interpreter also, having managed to acquire an extensive knowledge of the Thlinket language during his numerous trading trips.

In the summer of 1869 Capt. Keene acted as pilot on board the revenue cutter Lincoln from Sitka to San Francisco and transferred in 1871 from the Lincoln to the revenue cutter Reliance. He was attached to the latter until she was sold in San Francisco in the fall of 1874. Then he was variously employed until May 1875. Subsequently acted as pilot on board the Wolcott and afterwards in 1870 acted as pilot on board the U.S.S. Alaska to Sitka from Victoria.

In the fall of 1880 he was employed as

master on board the now historic little steamer Favorite, owned by the N.W.T. Co. After completing his contract with the latter company, which embraced a four months trip through Alaskan waters, he returned to Washington Territory. On this trip the foundation for the subsequent development of the great oil and fish works at Killisnoo was laid. In 1882 he superintended the construction of the missionary steamer Evangel.

He left Washington to take charge of the steam schooner Leo on her last trip up here under a charter of Dr. Sheldon Jackson, general agent of education in Alaska.

Capt. Keen marked seventy-five buoys and lights on the inside passage to Alaska, which the government placed at his suggestion as aids to navigation.

Keen was known to the Indians as "Sacatekeyish," "Father of the Beaver."

Captain Keen held the oldest navigator's license on record. His first license was taken out seventy-one years ago in Sitka, Alaska. His last renewal was in 1927.

In 1903 he reentered the government service permanently as Pilot and was retired in 1915 by a special act of Congress.

Captain Keen was married in Port Townsend to Annie S. Gage of Montreal, who died in 1910. Later he married Ann Clare, who survives him. He also is survived by three children, Mrs. a.E. LeBallister, Mrs. John M. Spargur, and Crosby E. Keen.

    ALASKAN, December 4, 1886
    ALASKA WEEKLY, September 22, 1933

J. C. KELLUM

Judge J.C. Kellum was born at Westport, Jackson County, Mo. He graduated from Harvard University in 1873, taking the degrees of A.M. and B.L. He practiced law in Kansas City, Mo., about twelve years, then moved to Arizona in 1887, where he continued his practice until 1898, when he went to Dawson. While in Dawson he was associated with Wade, Clark & Wilson, the leading law firm of that place. He removed to Circle in 1900, and finally took up his residence in Fairbanks in the winder of 1902-03. He has ever since that time been a member of the firm of Claypool, Kellum & Cowles, having just recently retired from active practice. He has a great many holdings in the leading industries of Fairbanks, among which are the Tanana Bottling Works, the Tanana Valley Railroad and the Tanana Electric Company. He is also heavily interested in real estate, and is one of the pioneer mining men of the Tanana Valley.

Among the richest of his mining claims is No. 6 below on the right limit of Cleary Creek. He owns the lower 400 feet, and during the years of 1905-07 his lay men took over $600,000 from this piece of ground.

Judge Kellum owns one-quarter interest in the Homestake and Golden Association claims on Little Eldorado Creek, besides minor interests in claims throughout the Tanana Valley. He has been engaged in the mining business over ten years, having been interested in several claims near Dawson, prior to his entering the Tanana Valley.

Judge Kellum, with his wife, resides in Fairbanks. Their only son is at present a student in the University of Washington, at Seattle.

ALASKA-YUKON MAGAZINE, January 1909

WILLIAM A. KELLY

William A. Kelly, the subject of the brief sketch was born near Punxsutawney, Jefferson County, Pennsylvania, in October A.D. 1850(?).

He was reared on a farm and did all the work incident to farm life. At the age of seventeen he left home to do for himself with no capital save a suit of homespun and his mother's benedictions. His early educational advantages had been meager and he now determined to earn some money and educate himself.

He first hired out to a farmer at $12.50 per month; next he clerked in a store at $15 per month; then he attended an academy in the summer and taught school each winter until he completed the academic course; he then attended a Normal school and graduated in the scientific course.

In the spring of 1885 he came to Alaska as government teacher and took charge of the Industrial Training school at Sitka, resigning in 1891. In 1892 President Harrison appointed him United States commissioner for Alaska to reside at Fort Wrangel, serving four years. He was also commissioned by the bureau of education superintendent of government schools for south eastern Alaska which position he still holds.

ALASKA MINING RECORD, January 1897

JOHN A. KEMP

Mr. Kemp, who was born in Gold Hill, California, moved to Arcata at an early age and received his education there, and lived there until he was past 21 years of age, when he left for Alaska about the year 1878. He went first to Letun Bay between Sitka and Yakutut, where he remained for a number of years in mining. He made two trips back to the states in the early '90's, but returning the second time, he found his mining claims jumped, so he went to Juneau and remained there until the great gold strike was made in the Klondike in 1898. Immediately closing out his interests in Juneau, he left first for Dawson, and later went on to Forty Mile River.

Here he mined for several years on Jack Wade Creek, a tributary of Forty Mile River, then in 1907 he purchased two stores, one at Jack Wade Creek, and the other at Steel Creek, a town built on the creek by that name, also a tributary of Forty Mile River. He operated the store at Steel Creek. He was engaged in mining, merchandising, and he also conducted a roadhouse for much of the time. He was United States Commissioner from 1910 to 1916 and postmaster.

He left Alaska in 1932 and returned to California, his native state.

ALASKA WEEKLY, April 22, 1932

FRANK M. KEMPFER

Frank Kempfer was born in Minnesota in 1870, and started out in life as a printer's devil in Minneapolis, Minn. in 1885. In 1900 he went west to Montana and since that early date has followed prospecting and mining. He went to Valdez in 1910, where he has since remained. It was Mr. Kempfer who financed the Pathfinder Magazine in 1920 to help develop Alaska. Mr. Kempfer is familiar with the mining possibilities of the Valdez district, as his time there has been taken up with prospecting, contracting and construction work for mining companies and the Alaska Road Commission. For the past ten years he has developed a large amount of ore at the Ethel mine and is the president and general manager of the Ethel Mining Company.

ALASKA WEEKLY, September 21, 1928

JOHN HENRY KILBUCK

John Kilbuck was born on the Indian reservation in Kansas in the year 1862. He is a lineal descendant of the Chieftain Gelemend, Chief of the Delawares. His father was then government interpreter. Until eight years of age he was raised on the reservation where the Rev. Joseph Romig was Moravian missionary. Dr. Romig was father of Dr. J.H. Romig of Seward, and Edith Margaret Romig. When a lad of eight years John Kilbuck was sent to Nazareth Hall, a church military school in Pennsylvania. From this he graduated and entered the Moravian College and Theological Seminary in Bethlehem, Penn. He graduated in the classical course and then took up the theological course being ordained a minister in 1885. Coming west to visit his parents he met Miss Edith M. Romig, teacher at the reservation where he and she were once playmates together, her father being a missionary. Mr. Kilbuck was then under appointment to go to the Kuskokwim river, Alaska, as missionary. Ere long it was announced that Miss Romig was to be the bride of this self-suffering man and in 1886 they were wed and sailed for Alaska where they founded with Rev. Weinland the first Moravian mission in Alaska and what is now known as Bethel Mission. Here he served in church work for twelve years and went home on a visit thinking not to return to Alaska, but his work called him back and he returned to government service to Wainwright near Point Barrow. There he remained for two years, going from there to Douglas for the government school there. He then returned to the states for a winter, and then returned to Alaska where for the past ten years he has been stationed assisting with the Kuskokwim mission where he was superintendent of schools and reindeer for the Central Coast district in Alaska.

Rev. Kilbuck was one of the most versatile linguists in the Territory speaking the Eskimo and Yukon dialects fluently, and at the time of his death was writing a history of his people and their legends.

Rev. Kilbuck died in Kuskokwim country recently.

CORDOVA DAILY TIMES, March 15, 1922

S. T. KINCAID

S.T. Kincaid was engaged in the sheep raising industry in Idaho when gold was discovered in the Klondike. He left Seattle on August 5, 1897, and arrived at Dawson, Y.T., on January 30, 1898. In the Klondike, he mined on Adams Hill, in the White Channel. With the discovery of gold in the Fairbanks district, on the Alaska side of the line, Kincaid joined the stampede from Dawson to the new camp. Still later, in 1910, he joined the rush to the Iditarod district. While exploring in the Kaiguh mountains, he discovered a rich galena property, which he developed. he made two shipments of the ore to the smelter from the mine. Then silver values began to decline, making it necessary to suspend operations. Mr. Kincaid was appointed a deputy United States marshal of the Fourth division, April 1, 1920, and has held this post for the past four years and six months. He is in charge of the marshal's office at Flat, in the Iditarod district.

ALASKA WEEKLY, November 7, 1930

HORACE P. KING

At the Nome municipal election in April, 1904, H. P. King received the highest number of votes cast for any of the candidates for the office of councilman, and when the new council organized Mr. King was unanimously elected mayor of Nome. Mr. King was not a stranger to politics when he was elected to the Nome council, as he had served two terms in the legislature of Nebraska, filled the office of county commissioner, was president of the council in Friend, Nebraska, for several years, and was president of the school board of his district for a period of nine years.

Mr. King was born in Brooklyn, New York, Nay 26, 1847. His father was in the mercantile business. He moved to Warrensburg, New York, and engaged in business at that place until the subject of this sketch was eleven years old, when the family went west and located on a farm near Monroe County, Wisconsin. This change of residence and vocation was made on account of the failing health of the father. Here H. P. King lived until he was nineteen. As the country was new and without educational advantages, the young man did not have the opportunity to go to school. Up to the time of leaving Warrensburg he attended the public school of that place, and after his father's death he returned to Warrensburg and attended the Warrensburg Academy for one year. Returning from school he continued to reside in Wisconsin until 1870, when he went to Nebraska, locating in Seward County where he followed farming, subsequently settling in Friend, Saline County, and engaging in the mercantile business. He has represented both of these counties in the state legislature.

Mr. King came to Nome in 1899, and returned to the states in the fall of 1900. He came back to Nome in the spring of 1901, and in 1901 he went to Kewalik. Candle Creek had just been discovered, and Mr. King secured two lays from Blankenship on property that appeared to be very promising. One of these lays he traded for a grocery store on the Sandspit in Nome, and returning to Nome he conducted a grocery business on the Sandspit until after he was elected to the common council, when he moved his place of business to Front Street.

January 1, 1872, Mr. King and Miss Jennie Cunningham were married in Nebraska. Four children were born to them, two of whom, a son and daughter survive. H. Porter King, his son, a young man of 26 years, came to Nome in 1903, bringing his wife, and is associated with his father in business. The daughter, Maude, is the wife of Herbert McIntyre of Omaha, Nebraska. Her mother resides with her.
NOME AND SEWARD PENINSULA, 1905

ROBERT ALLEN KINZIE

Robert Kinzie was born at Fort Independence, Boston Harbor, Mass., on the fifteenth day of January, 1874. He is the son of General and Mrs. David H. Kinzie, whose ancestors were the first settlers of Chicago. His early education was received in the public and private schools of Utah and California. In 1893 he entered the University of California and after graduating worked in the mines of California, Idaho, Mexico and British Columbia. He was then assistant to Ross E. Browne, and subsequently to F.W. Bradley, leaving the latter service to accept a position as general manager of the Jesus Maria Mines Co., with head office at Parral, Chihuahua, Mexico. From there he went to Alaska as assistant superintendent of the Treadwell group of mines. He was married in Nov. 1901, to Miss Veronica Kennedy of San Francisco. In 1904 he assumed the superintendency of the Treadwell Mines.
ALASKA-YUKON MAGAZINE, September 1907

MAGNUS KJELSBERG

In 1897 the United States Government hired sixty-seven Laplanders, Finns and Norwegians to take care of the reindeer in Alaska. Magnus Kjelsberg was a member of this expedition, having been employed in the capacity of foreman of the herders. He is the son of a merchant of Kaafjord, Norway, a town supported in a large measure by the industry of cooper mining. He was Born October 1, 1876, and received his early education from private tutors, subsequently attending school at Bergen. He had not attained his twenty-first year when he left home.

The trip from Haines Mission was one of great hardships. The expedition started in March, but before it got 200 miles on its journey half of the deer were dead. The rations for the trip proved inadequate and as the death of so many deer made it possible to dispense with the services of a number of herders several members of the expedition were sent back to Haines to go by steamer to St. Michael and thence to the reindeer station at Unalakleet. Mr. Kjelsberg was a member of this party.

Mr. Kjelsberg formed a partnership with Jafet Lindeberg, another young man from Norway, who had come to the country in search of gold. By the agreement Kjelsberg was to remain in the employ of the Government, and his salary was to be used to buy supplies for the use of Lindeberg in prospecting.

Mr. Kjelsberg was at Unalakleet when he heard of the great strike on Anvil Creek. He immediately went overland to Golovin and started with Missionary Anderson, driving deer teams across the country to Nome. At Cape Nome they met Lindeberg, Lindblom, Brynteson, Kittilsen and Price, who had $1,800 in gold dust which they had rocked out in a few days.

The entire party returned to Golovin Bay where most of the winter was spent making preparations for the next season's work. Supplies were obtained at St. Michael and freighted over the ice to Nome. In the early spring before the snow disappeared Mr. Kjelsberg whipsawed lumber out of driftwood found on the beach. This lumber was used to make sluice-boxes. In June Mr. Kjelsberg established a camp at the mouth of Quartz Gulch at No. 6 Anvil Creek. Snow Gulch seemed to offer a better opportunity for expeditious work, and he determined to move his camp. He and his brother carried the sluice-boxes on their backs over the hill a distance of three miles to Snow Gulch, each man carrying one of the heavy boxes at a trip.

Mr. Kjelsberg has operated in the Nome country since the discovery of gold on Anvil Creek. In the winter of 1899-1900 he visited his old home in Norway and traveled over Europe. He is a stockholder and director in the Pioneer Mining Company, and has invested in real estate in Oakland and San Jose, California. He is married, and he and Mrs. Kjelsberg spend the winters at their home in Oakland.

NOME AND SEWARD PENINSULA, 1905

LYMAN E. KNAPP

Lyman Knapp was a member of the class of 1862. He received an A.B.A.M., Phi Beta Kappa, was a D.U., and was given an honorary degree of LL.D by Whitman, Oregon, College in 1892. He was in the Civil War. He was in three battles, Gettysburg, Spottsylvania Courthouse and Petersburg. At Petersburg, he was leader of the 17th Regiment in the final charge of the assault, breaking through the Confederate line while suffering three severe wounds. For his heroism and gallantry in action he was brevetted as Lieutenant Colonel by President Lincoln.

At the close of the war he resigned his commission and returned to Middlebury to become editor of the MIDDLEBURY REGISTER, a position he held from 1865 to 1878. In the years he served in that capacity, he studied law and was admitted to the bar. During the years of 1879 to 1889, he was a Probate Judge and served in the legislature.

While serving as Probate Judge, he was picked by President Harrison to be governor of Alaska, serving from 1889 to 1893. When he returned to the States in 1893, he lived in Seattle where he died in 1904.

ADDISON COUNTY INDEPENDENT(Ver.), June 10, 1960

EARLE W. KNIGHT

He was born in Ann Arbor, Mich., Dec. 11, 1887, and came to Washington in 1904. He had lived in Everett before coming to Seattle.

Mr. Knight achieved renown chiefly as an editorial writer. His editorials and especially his column, "As I See It," which appeared weekly in this newspaper were read by all who were sincerely concerned with, or actively involved in, the Alaskan scene. It was in this endeavor that he made his life's work into a profession--in the fine meaning of the word. Politically, Mr. Knight was of Republican persuasion. He was a bitter foe of the New and Fair Deal philosophy of government. Entrenched mediocrity in high government positions, graft, corruption, irresponsible labor leadership, Communism in any and all its manifestations--and especially government policy as reflected by the Gruening administration in Alaska--these were anathema to him.

And he said so--fearlessly and without equivocation. Mr. Knight's editorial comment was in the best journalistic tradition-- brilliant, incisive, analytical--and reflected a personal and passionate devotion to the interests of Alaska and the Pacific Northwest.

THE ALASKA WEEKLY under Mr. Knight's aegis, concerned itself chiefly with political economic and social policies in their broad mission of this newspaper was to let every Alaskan know what other Alaskans were doing, thinking about, and planning in the way of promoting the good of their respective communities, districts and the Territory as a whole.

Mr. Knight became associated with THE ALASKA WEEKLY in 1923. He was also the publisher of the FUR JOURNAL, and formerly headed the Montgomery Printing Co., a job printing firm.

Mr. Knight also gave much of himself to

civic and social affairs. He was one of the founders of the Washington State Press Club, life member and honorary president. He was a member of the Seattle Chamber of Commerce's Alaska committed, and had traveled extensively in an effort to promote business and trade between Seattle and the Territory. Also, he was a member of the Rainier Club, the Washington Athletic Club and the Arctic Club.

Mr. Knight, editor and publisher of THE ALASKA WEEKLY the past 29 years, died suddenly of a heart attack at his Seattle home Sunday, August 3. He was 64 years old.

Mr. Knight is survived by his wife, Elizabeth; two daughters, Mrs. Elsa Knight Thompson, Seattle, and Mrs. Jeanne Paterson, Washington, D.C.; a son, James Knight, Seattle; two brothers, Walter, who will continue with THE ALASKA WEEKLY, and Raymond Knight; and a sister, Mrs. Heloise Wardell, all of Seattle.

ALASKA WEEKLY, August 8, 1952

GEORGE J. KOSTROMETINOFF (COLONEL)

Colonel George J. Kostrometinoff is one of the very few Caucasian residents of Sitka who bears the distinction of calling that beautiful city his birthplace. He was born on July 18th, 1854, of Russian parents, becoming an American citizen by virtue of the treaty between the United States and Russia ceding Alaska to the United States.

His education was received in the Russian Colonial school at Sitka and in the American schools of the same place. His father was general agent for the Russian-American Company at Kodiak; and his uncle, J.S. Kostrometinoff, representing the Russian government negotiated the sale of Ft. Ross in California to Jno. A. Sutter.

Having a thorough knowledge of Russian, English and the native dialects, Mr. Kostrometinoff at an early age rendered valuable assistance to the government in the capacity of interpreter. As interpreter he accompanied the expeditions to the territory above the Lynn Canal where, through him, testimony was gathered from the Chilkat and other Indian tribes in the matter of adjusting the Canadian boundary questions. He was appointed District Court Interpreter and Deputy United States Marshal, and in the capacity of the latter, his office brought him frequently to Portland with prisoners.

He was married in San Francisco in 1886, his bride being the daughter of the priest then officiating in the Russian Orthodox church in that city. He returned to Sitka where he has since made his home. He was appointed Lieutenant Colonel of the organized Militia of the District of Alaska; and on the staff of Governor Lyman E. Knapp, he attended the Columbian Exposition in Chicago in 1893.

Colonel Kostrometinoff is a devout worker in the Church, and has been warden in the Russian Orthodox Church at Sitka for many years. In recognition of his faithful and devout work he was presented with a handsome silver cup by the Emperor Nicholas II; and he bears the honor of wearing the decoration of the order of St. Daniel I.

ALASKA-YUKON MAGAZINE, October 1907

GEORGE KYRAGE

George Kyrage was born in Greece in 1853. There is no record of his early life.

In 1878 he was hired as a steward on the United States ship VADALIA. At that time the VADALIA was on a foreign tour.

Reaching Boston in January 1879, he transferred to the WACHUSETT which sailed up the Pacific Coast.

The WACHUSETT cruised in Alaskan waters for six months and then went to San Francisco. Kyrage left the ship there and returned to Alaska, resolved to seek his fortune in the new land of gold. This was in 1882. His first venture was a restaurant and bar in Sitka, and later he worked for the Northwest Company nearly five years. In 1888 he came to Juneau, and his first employment was with Olds of the Occidental, where he became cook for the best part of a year, and then took a position in the

Central House, then run by W.F. Reed, where he remained until the latter's death in 1892, when he started in business for himself as proprietor of that place, which he ran five years, and then changed to the Arctic and later to the popular Juneau Hotel, which he has conducted for the last two years.

ALASKA MONTHLY MAGAZINE, Oct-Nov., 1907

J. H. LANDER

Mr. Lander was born in Illinois in 1859, but ran away from the family where he had been placed on account of poverty in his own home, at the age of 14, and went to Texas, where he soon became a cowboy. He followed the life of the plains for several years. At 16 he was foreman of a ranch and at 20 was cattle inspector and represented Texas at the Dodge City, Kansas yards. His judgment of cattle was so dependable that when he was only 22 years old he was hired by large cattle interests to buy herds in Oregon.

While still a comparatively young man he was made stock inspector for the state of Montana and afterwards the more difficult job of stock inspector at the Chicago stockyards. He knew over 7,000 brands and to whom the cattle belonged carrying them.

His life in the early West was full of adventure and perils. Once when Little Wolf and his band of Indian braves were on the war path they attacked the ranch where Lander was employed and killed the entire force except Lander, who was out on the range herding cattle at the time. Taking a hand in the Indian War in 1879, he served as scout under Gen. Thomberg and won distinction for his bravery. He knew intimately many of the famous frontiersmen of the early West, including Buffalo Bill, Wild Bill Hickok, Billy the Kid, Jim Dahlman, Gen. Custer, Billy the Bear, John Chisholm and others.

Of all his Western experiences Lander liked best to talk of his association with Theodore Roosevelt. As captain of the Miles City No. 6 roundup in 1886 Lander was thrown in

daily contact with Roosevelt, who was one of
the 300 cowboys serving under him during the
three months' roundup.
    Lander went o Alaska(date unknown) and
mined at Willow Creek. He lived near Wasilla,
Alaska for many years.
    J. H. Lander died at Lapeer, Michigan,
July (?) 1930. He is survived by one son,
Richard E. of Bay City; a daughter, Mrs.
Gordon Jones of San Francisco; and a sister,
Mrs. M. L. Parks of Harvard, Nebraska.
            ALASKA WEEKLY, July 18, 1930

CHARLES D. LANE
    Charles D. Lane was born in Palmyra,
Marion County, Missouri, November 15, 1840.
His parents were Virginians of Scotch descent.
His father was a miller and a staunch old
Democrat of the Jackson type. in 1852 Mr. Lane
crossed the plains with his father. The family
settled in Stockton, California, and engaged in
farming and stock raising. Although only a boy
of twelve, Mr. lane began the work of gold
mining the first winter he resided in
California. In the fifty odd years that have
elapsed since then he has worked at mining in
every phase, and is familiar with the use of
all kinds of mining machinery, from the rocker
to the best improved and most modern apparatus.
His experience has covered every feature of
gold placer and quartz mining. For a period of
his life he drove an ox team, and he is now
proud of the fact that he was one of the best
ox drivers in the West.
    His first experience in quartz miming was
acquired in Nevada where he obtained a quartz
property in 1867 and operated it for several
years; but the venture was not a success.
After that mine, he worked for wages as foreman
in a quartz mine at Battle Mountain. He drove
ox teams in Nevada and farmed in Idaho. His
first successful mining was on Snake River in
Idaho. He afterward operated by hydraulic
methods the Big Flat Mine of Del Norte County,
California.
    He was fifty years old when he made the

strike in the now famous Utica mine at Angels, California. This great quartz property had been exploited to a depth of ninety feet, but a great deal more work was necessary to be done to prove its values. After three years of unprofitable work his associated became uneasy and wanted to dispose of their interests. Notwithstanding the adverse condition, Mr. Lane never lost faith in the property. He succeeded in inducing San Francisco capitalists to buy out his partners and supply the money that was necessary to continue the development work. The Utica Mine has produced $17,000,000 and is still a valuable property.

The Fortuna Mine of Arizona is another valuable property which Mr. lane has developed. This mine has produced $3,000,000. Mr. Lane became interested in Alaska in 1898, at the time of the Kotzebue Sound excitement., and outfitted an expedition to go to this country. He accompanied the expedition and spent a part of the summer of 1898 in this region, and then returned to San Francisco. When the Anvil Creek discovery was made, Charles Lane returned to the Seward Peninsula.

Realizing at the outset the necessity of a large amount of money to develop his plans, he organized the Wild Goose Mining and Trading Company with a capital of $1,000,000. The money that was taken out of the ground was expended for improvements which consisted of facilities for mining work, and in the acquirement of additional property. Many miles of ditches were constructed, a great pumping plant to force the water from Snake River to the summit of Anvil Mountain was erected, and two railroads were built, one from Nome to Anvil Creek and the other from Council City to No. 15 Ophir Creek. At the close of the season of 1904 the company paid all of its outstanding indebtedness and declared a dividend of thirty per cent.

NOME AND SEWARD PENINSULA, 1905

TOM T. LANE

T. T. Lane is the elder son of Charles D.

Lane. He was born in Stanislaus County, California, May 3, 1869, and educated at Santa Clara College. When he was six or seven years old his father was placer mining in Idaho, and with plate and quicksilver the boy did some mining for himself, learning to clean the plates and retort the gold. When he was attending school his vacations were spent on a hydraulic mine operated by his father in Del Norte County, California. He learned the business of mining and has been operating both placer and quartz mines for himself ever since he was twenty years old. His early operations were in California and Mexico, but he has been identified with the Nome country since the beginning of active work in this region.

Mr. Lane did not go to Nome until 1900 on account of his interests in Mexico. He took charge of the interests of the Wild Goose Company during his father's enforced absence in California. It was during this period that he bought the Mattie, Lena, Edna and Rosalind for the Company. Mr. Lane will operate extensively on Dahl, Arctic and Homestake Creeks. In 1901 Mr. Lane bought the Maudeline, Diadem and the Little Jim fraction, adjoining the Mattie claim on the left limit of Anvil, and has successfully operated these properties.

T. T. Lane developed the first quartz mine in Seward Peninsula. In 1902 he acquired a quartz ledge on Hurrah, a tributary of Solomon River.

Mr. Lane's residence is in San Francisco. He is a member of the Bohemian and San Francisco Clubs of that city. He belongs to the Masons, Elks, Workmen and Native Sons.
NOME AND SEWARD PENINSULA, 1905

FRANK S. LANG
Frank Lang was born in Austria, October 4, 1855, and went to America when only thirteen years old. He is the second son of a family of twelve children. On his arrival in this country he started to learn the tin smith's trade in Mannetowock, Wisconsin. His salary at the beginning was two dollars a week, but it

was only a short time until he was earning journeyman's wages, two dollars the day.

He went to Chicago in 1870, arriving in that city one month before the devastating fire. After the fire the rebuilding of the city created a strong demand for the kind of labor he was able to furnish, and being an excellent and a rapid workman he made money fast. He left Chicago in 1876, going to the lake Superior country, and thence to the Black Hills, arriving in Deadwood May 10, 1877. He built the first road from Grayville to Spearfish. From the Black hills he drifted back to Iowa, and from Iowa he went to Nebraska where he farmed. In the spring of 1880 he was back again in Montana. In 1893 he established a hardware business in Helena.

In the spring of 1900 he left his business in Montana and came to Nome, bringing with him the tools of his trade and the materials for the establishment of a tin shop in the new mining camp.

Mr. Lang has an inventive mind, and several of his inventions are very useful commodities, possessing a commercial value. The Nome country is treeless. A stunted growth of willows is the only available fuel for the prospector and miner of the interior. Mr. Lang has invented a stove to burn this kind of fuel, and its popularity is attested by the tremendous demand for it. He has a sharp eye for business, and during his career in Nome has bought thirteen different stocks of goods, most of them from stores going out of business. He has established a branch store in Fairbanks, the new town in the promising mining region of the Tanana. Mr. Lang is the owner of the Federal Jail property in Nome.

It has been a long time since Mr. Lang left his native land, but every year since he was fifteen years old he has sent money home. June 4, 1884, Mr. Land was married in Montana to Miss Julia Carter. Mrs. Lang still resides in Helena.

NOME AND SEWARD PENINSULA, 1905

WILLIAM H. LANG

W. H. Lang is at the head of one of the large ditch enterprises of Seward Peninsula. He is the general manager of the Flambeau Ditch and Mining Company, which is constructing a thirty-mile ditch from the Flambeau River to Hastings Creek.

Mr. Lang is a native of Rock County, Wisconsin, and was born September 25, 1856. He was educated in the public schools of Dau Claire. When he was a young man he and his brother formed the Line Construction Company. The business of this company was constructing and building, and its field of work was in Northern Wisconsin. Several electric light plants were constructed by the company. Another feature of the company's work was the building of lumbermen's log driving dams. Mr. Lang followed this character of work until 1897 when he started for the Klondike by way of White Pass. He spent two years on the Yukon in the business of mining. He returned home in 1899, and in the following spring went to Nome on the Robert Dollar. During his first two years in the Nome country he mined on Hungry, Oregon and Bourbon Creeks. In 1903 he organized the Flambeau Ditch and Mining Company and has been associated with the enterprise as general manager ever since.

Mr. Lang was married in 1878 in Minneapolis, Minn. Mrs. Lang was formerly Celia Kelly. They have two children, Will and Cora, both of whom have reached maturity, the latter being the wife of W. J. Heiser. The family resides in Portland, Oregon.

NOME AND SEWARD PENINSULA, 1905

LEON A. LARIMORE

Leon A. Larimore was born in St. Louis in 1869. His father was John W. Larimore, a wheat and grain merchant who controlled, at one time, the elevator system of St. Louis. His mother was Miss Carlisle, the sister of Judge S. S. Carlisle, of Seattle, and James L. Carlisle, postmaster of St. Louis.

He received his early education in St.

Louis and afterwards attended college in Tennessee. When he completed his education he entered a bank in St. Louis and served as clerk, but soon after, receiving a political appointment, he made politics his profession until struck with the gold fever in 1898.

He then went as far north as St. Michael, where, hearing rumors of a strike having been made in the Nome district, he went to that region and located a number of claims. He and his partners constituted what has since been known as the Nome-Sinook Mining Co., and staked the territory now occupied by the town of Nome. Since that time he has been engaged, with varied success, almost continuously in mining.

In 1901 he married Miss Jessie Gambrill, of St. Louis.

NOME AND SEWARD PENINSULA, 1905

JOHN D. LEEDY

J. D. Leedy arrived in Nome on the steamer Garonne in the spring of 1899, and the steamer Garonne was the first vessel to arrive at Nome from the states. Among the inhabitants who had spent the winter in Nome was a brother of Mr. Leedy.

Mr. Leedy had acquired considerable experience as a miner in the Black Hills and in British Columbia, and he immediately devoted himself to the work of acquiring mining property by lease or appropriation. During this year and the years that followed he prospected and mined with varying success. He staked the first quartz claim ever staked on the peninsula. He was employed by the Alaska Banking and Safe Deposit Company as an expert to investigate properties offered as collateral for loans. Mr. Leedy has the record of never having advised a loan by which the company lost a dollar.

J. D. Leedy was born in Fredericktown, Knox County, Ohio, February 4, 1865. His father was a lumber manufacturer, who moved to Trenton, Missouri, when the son was an infant. When he was eleven years old J. D. Leedy went to the Black Hills. In addition to the public school education he has been a student in the State School of Mines in Rapid City, S. D. He began the work of mining at an early age, striking his first drill when he was fourteen years old. He left the Black Hills country in 1889 and went to Seattle, and ever since that date he has mined in British Columbia, Washington and Alaska.

Mr. Leedy married Nellie G. Norton in Nome, September 16, 1899.

NOME AND SEWARD PENINSULA, 1905

HENRY BELFIELD LEFEVRE

Judge Henry Belfield LeFevre was born on April 8, 1857 in Milwaukee. He was the grandson of the Rev. Clement Fall LeFevre, prominent in the history of the state of Wisconsin. and the son of George LeFevre and the former Emma Beal, daughter of the Lieutenant Governor of Wisconsin in the 1850s.

As a child, during the Franco-Prussian war, he spent five years in Europe with his mother, vacationing there for her health. At that time, he learned to speak French and Spanish fluently, which later led many of his acquaintances in the Territory to believe he was French, although he was in reality English.

After the death of his father in 1871, Henry LeFevre went from Wisconsin to Lone Rock in Eastern Oregon, where he engaged in raising stock and served in several clerical capacities. There he also began the study of law, specializing in probate work. He was in one of the first classes of the University of Notre Dame.

He practiced law for several years in Wisconsin, later in Kalama, Washington and along the Columbia River district. In Hepner, Oregon, he entered the newspaper business and became editor of the Gazette, later taking over the Citizen in Puyallup, Washington.

He was married in Puyallup on April 5, 1891 and had one daughter, Ruth Elizabeth. He came to Alaska alone in 1895 and worked for the Treadwell Mine.

He was then in Dyea and Skagway for about

17 years, being associated in the latter place with John W. Troy in publishing the Skagway Alaskan. His mother joined him about that time and lived with him in Alaska until her death some time ago.

He also spent several years in promoting the Engineer Mine on Tagish Arm in the Atlin district, where he prospered. He was admitted to the bar in Skagway and became United States Commissioner there.

About 1915 he came to Juneau to attend the second session of the Territorial Legislature, having been defeated for office as a candidate on the Republican ticket.

He served in Juneau also as United States Commissioner and went into the practice of law.

Judge H. V. LeFevre died in Juneau, Alaska March 31, 1942. He was 85 years of age.
DAILY ALASKA EMPIRE, March 31, 1942

HARRY LELAND

Harry Leland joined the stampede to the Klondike in 1898(?). His first stop was Skagway, then a booming, bustling embryo city. Here Mr. Leland took a position in Moody's newly-formed bank, and when he accumulated sufficient funds, he continued his journey to Dawson City. In the fall of 1899, he joined the stampede to Nome. In 1900 he went to Kougarok district, where he prospected for something over a year. He was in Nome in the fall of 1901; and took a position with the Wild Goose Mining Company and was sent to the Council City operation of a company. Here he remained with the company until the fall of 1909, when he returned to Seattle. In the spring of 1911, he went to the Iditarod. Here he prospected for awhile and accepted employment with the Riley dragline scraper operating on Otter Creek. Then the Ruby camp was struck and he prospected in that area for a year and a half. In the spring of 1915, he was back in Ruby again, where he took a position with the Yukon Gold Company. Mr. Leland was with the company until the dredging operations were completed. He came out over the trail in December, 1918, to Seattle, his old home city, and in May, 1919, he made an association with Lamping & Company, general insurance agents, with offices in the Colman building, where he has remained since. He makes his home with his wife and family in South Alki, West Seattle. Mr. Leland possesses his very fine singing voice, and this accomplishment made him in demand in all the northern camps in which he lived.

ALASKA WEEKLY, May 30, 1930

A. T. LEWIS

A.T. Lewis (born 1846), who is senior member of the Portland law firm of Lewis, Lewis and Finnegan, has not visited the territory since 1886 and told the Chronicle that little is to be recognized today of the Ketchikan of 40 years ago.

At that time there were only a few houses, a saltery and fishing was about the only other industry, although there were a few prospectors in the district.

Mr. Lewis came north in the early eighties as a missionary. He was later appointed clerk of court and during the term of office served by John Kinkead acted as governor for a few months while Mr. Kinkead was ill. Mr. Lewis also served the Territory in the capacity of Indian agent and says that he is under the impression that he was the first judge appointed in the territory. He swore in the fist jury ever empaneled in Alaska.

For a time Lewis was associated in the practice of law with A.P. Swineford, who became the second governor of Alaska and who served in that capacity for a period of years. Lewis left Alaska in 1886.

ALASKA WEEKLY, July 16, 1926

CAPTAIN DANIEL B. LIBBY

Captain D. B. Libby first went to Alaska in 1866 and had charge of a part of the construction work of the Western Union Telegraph Company, which at that time was attempting to erect a telegraph line across Canada and Alaska to connect with a Siberian line by a cable across Bering Strait.

He is a native of Maine, and was born February 3, 1844. He served as a soldier in the Union Army, and after the war went to Pike's Peak. While in Alaska in the employ of the Western Union Telegraph Company he had charge of a division of the line construction. He spent the winter in 1866 and 1867 in a camp on Grantley Harbor named Libbysville. After he returned from Alaska he was ticket agent for the Southern Pacific Railroad Company, in San Francisco, for fifteen years. Failing health compelled him to resign this position, and he went to Mendocino County, California, where he fully recovered. His second journey to the Northland was made in 1897. He left San Francisco August 18, sailing on the steamer North Fork. He was accompanied by his brother-in-law, Louis Melsing. He spent two winters in the Fish River Country. At the present time he is at the head of a prospecting expedition in the unexplored country of the Kuskokwim Valley.

Louise Melsing, of San Francisco, and Captain Libby were married in 1882. They have two children, Daniel B., Jr., and Adeline E. The son is now a young man of eighteen years and an assayer.

NOME AND SEWARD PENINSULA, 1905

ERIK. O. LINDBLOM

Erik O. Lindblom is the son of a school teacher. He was born in Dalarne, Sweden, June 27, 1857. When a young man he learned the trade of tailor, and gratified a nomadic instinct by traveling over a large part of Europe. He went to America in 1886, and was following his trade in Oakland, California, at the time of the Kotzebue excitement. April 27, 1898, he shipped before the mast on the bark ALASKA commanded by Captain B. Cogan, carrying passengers and their outfits to the new gold fields. The vessel encountered ice in Bering Sea, and it was not deemed safe to enter the Arctic Ocean until the season was farther advanced. While at Indian Point on the Siberian coast, Mr. Lindblom learned from whalers that no discovery of gold in paying quantity had been made in the Kotzebue Sound country. The reports of the whalers were very discouraging.

While anchored in Grantley Harbor, a part of the crew was sent ashore for fresh water. Mr. Lindblom was one of the sailors in the detail and he had made up his mind to quit the ship. He knew that there was a mission and a trading station on Golovin Bay, which could be reached by crossing the country a hundred miles or more. But he had no conception of the difficulties in the way, the streams which were now at flood and which had to be crossed, the slow progress one makes traveling over the country, and besides this he was without food. The third day out he encountered a prospector on one of the streams but the prospector's food supply was nearly exhausted. and he could not supply Lindblom with food for the trip. He was forced to return to Grantley Harbor.

When he got within sight of the harbor he saw the bark ALASKA still riding at anchor. It was evident that a part of the crew was searching for him. This was a critical situation from which he escaped by the aid of an Eskimo. Promarshuk, a chief, an oomalik among the Kavariagmutes, with his family, dogs and wares, was starting on a trading expedition to Golovin Bay. He took the sailor into his boat made of walrus skins and covered him with pelts to hide him. Promarshuk's oomiak sailed within a few rods of the ALASKA, and passed unmolested out of the harbor. In July they landed at Dexter's trading station on Golovin Bay.

In September he joined a group of prospectors that outfitted a scow with a sail and a keel and sailed in this vessel on a hundred-mile sea voyage. They skirted the coast, making slow progress, as the weather was stormy and the rain incessant. September 15 they arrived at the mouth of Snake River. On September 22 they made discoveries and locations on Anvil Creek, and subsequently prospected on Snow Gulch, Glacier, Rock, Mountain, and Dry Creeks.

By this time winter was encroaching, but notwithstanding the freezing ground, the prospectors constructed a crude rocker and worked assiduously with it and with pan and shovel. In three hours panning on snow Gulch Lindblom, Lindeberg, and Brynteson obtained gold valued at $166. Within a few days the party extracted more than $1,500 of gold dust.

Mr. Lindblom is the owner of a valuable quartz mine in Mexico, and has varied property interests. He is also operating in the Kotzebue country, where he owns some promising property.

During the winter season Mr. Lindblom lives in Oakland, Cal. He is fond of automobiling, and being able to indulge in luxuries, owns a valuable machine.
NOME AND SEWARD PENINSULA, 1905

JAFET LINDEBERG

Jafet Lindeberg, president of the Pioneer Mining Company and prominent mine owner and operator of Seward Peninsula, has the distinction of being one of the three men who first discovered gold on Anvil Creek and Now Gulch. This discovery made in September, 1898, was the inception of active mining operations in Northwestern Alaska. At the time that Mr. Lindeberg, in company with Erik O. Lindblom and J. E. Brynteson, made the famous strike he was a mere youth. He was born in Norway September, 1874, and was just 24 years old when the discovery was made which not only turned the current of his life but changed the course of the lives of thousands of others.

The partners, known as the Pioneer Mining Company, mined a large quantity of gold in 1899 and 1900. In 19801 the Pioneer Mining Company was incorporated, and Mr. Lindeberg was elected president and general manager.

Mr. Lindeberg owns the electric light and power works at Nome, and he and his three early associates constructed and own the Moonlight

Springs Water Works which supply Nome with pure water and provide the town with protection in the event of fire. The Nome Electric Light plant is the first one established in Northwestern Alaska.

Mr. Lindeberg is married. Mrs. Lindeberg is a member of an old and prominent family of California. Their winter home is the Palace Hotel, San Francisco.

NOME AND SEWARD PENINSULA, 1905

E. R. LINTON

Dr. E.R. Linton was born in Toledo, Iowa, September 22, 1871. He received a public school education and when sixteen years old left for Colorado. He has been dependent upon his own resources ever since his early boyhood. He studied dentistry in the University of Denver, and practiced his profession six years in that city. He left Denver in 1900 for Nome, and established a dental office in the northern mining camp. He went out in the fall of that year and did not return until 1902. During the interim he was in Oregon. Upon his return he fitted up the finest dental offices in Nome.

NOME AND SEWARD PENINSULA, 1905

GUDBRAND J. LOMEN

Gudbrand J. Lomen was born of Norwegian parents on a farm near Decorah, Iowa, January 28, 1854. He attended the common schools of the state, Luther College, and in 1875 was graduated by the State University of Iowa with the degree of LL. B. Two years later he was elected to the office of Clerk of the District Court of Houston County, Minn., and held this office for a period of eight years. Removing to St. Paul, he established an office and began the practice of law. In 1889 he was the Republican candidate for Municipal Judge of St. Paul, but was defeated with the rest of his ticket. He represented the first ward in the House of Representatives during the session of 1891, and took an active part in Minnesota politics, serving on county and congressional committees.

G. J. Lomen and Julie E. M. Joys were married in Manistee, Mich., May 27, 1878.

He came to Nome with the rush in 1900, and was engaged in the practice of his profession until Sept. 1, 1903, when he accepted the office of deputy clerk of the U. S. District Court, at Nome. While practicing law in Nome Mr. Lomen acquired a number of valuable mining interests. He has been an attorney in a number of important cases before the District Court in Nome, notably as the representative of the plaintiffs in the celebrated No. 14 Ophir suit in 1901.

Loman served as mayor of Nome from 1917 to 1919, was later appointed United States attorney there, and in 1921 became federal judge for that district, a position which he held until he moved to Seattle in 1932.

It was during his early days in Alaska that Judge Lomen envisioned the native herds of reindeer as an immense potential source of meat supply--a vision which led to the establishment of the Lomen Reindeer Corporation by his sons, a business which shown immense growth year by year.

Judge Lomen was a member of the Pioneers of Alaska, the Luthern Church and the Republican Party. He was knighted with the Order of Olaf by the King of Norway for his sevice to Capt. Roald Amundsen during Amundsen's explorations in the Arctic. He also had served as vice-consel of Norway in Nome.

Judge Gudbrand Lomen died in Seattle, Washington, June 12, 1934. He is survived by his widow, Mrs. Julia Lomen; five sons, George and Ralph of Seattle, Carl of Washington, D.C., and Harry and Alfred of Nome; and a daughter Mrs. F. Clinton Austin, Seattle.

NOME AND SEWARD PENINSULA, 1905
ALASKA WEEKLY, June 15, 1934

ALBERT J. LOWE

A. J. Lowe was one of the first men to arrive in Nome in the spring of 1899. He followed the ice down the Yukon, arriving in Nome in June. He was appointed special Deputy

Marshal by United States Commissioner Rawson, and took an active part in the Consent Government, being a councilman in Nome's first council, and when the federal officers in July, 1900, arrived, he was appointed to a deputyship in the marshal's office.

Mr. Lowe is a native of New York and is forty-three years old. In his younger days he was agent of the Adams Express Company in Boston. He went to Dawson over the White Pass in '97, and never has been out of the country since. His first winter was spent at Dawson and Forty-Mile. He had many interesting experiences on the Yukon, and has seen Nome in nearly every phase of growth.

When he arrived in Nome, June 27, 1900, the camp consisted of only a few tents. Later when the beach diggings were discovered he paid twenty dollars for a rocker made out of soap boxes and starch boxes. At that time there were not more than half a dozen rockers in the camp. Some that were in use were whipsawed out of drift-wood, and put together with nails drawn out of boxes. Mr. Lowe's first day's work on the beach with his rocker netted him $140. He says he has seen spots on bedrock in the beach literally covered with gold.

As a member of the Consent Government Council Mr. Lowe was on the street committee, the sanitary and the drainage streets work was under his supervision. Mr. Lowe has made an efficient federal officer. He is a brave man who never shrunk from difficult or dangerous work. As an officer under Commissioner Rawson in the early and trying days of Nome he did his share in preserving peace, maintaining order and enforcing the law.

NOME AND SEWARD PENINSULA, 1905

FRED LYNCH

Fred Lynch was born in Cork, Ireland, August 24, 1835. His parents emigrated first to New Orleans in 1840 and then to Kentucky, where Mr. Lynch spent his early youth. He served with the Confederate forces during the War of the Rebellion, and started for the west shortly after Lee's surrender.

Little is know of his experienced in the west, except that he was with the Pony Express.

Drifting north ahead of the flood of settlers who swept the west shortly after the close of the war, Mr. Lynch made his way to the Caribou country where he engaged in mining. At some time in his adventurous career he was the guest of Peter Ogden, the Hudson's Bay factor in charge of Fort St. James.

Fred Lynch landed in Wrangell in 1873 about the time of the first gold excitement in the Cassiar. He followed the lure of mining for a time, and then organized a transportation service on the Stikine river, using the great cedar war canoes of the Wrangell Indians, and the natives themselves for the crew. During his career as a riverman Mr. Lynch transported thousands of dollars in gold dust without loss to a shipper.

Early in the '80s, soon after the first steamboat appeared on the Stikine, Mr. Lynch abandoned his river venture and settled in Wrangell. He operated the first salmon salteries in Alaska, located in Karta bay, near Kassan, about the year 1882, and disposed of it to return to Wrangell where he entered the hotel business. In later years he was associated with J.G. Grant in the Wrangell hotel and made his home with the Grant family the latter years of his life.

Fred Lynch died in December 1931. He is survived by six children, Mrs. J.D. Grant of Wrangell, Mrs. John Cool and Mrs. Ted Daily of Ketchikan, and Charles, Michael and Edward Lynch of Wrangell.

ALASKA WEEKLY, December 11, 1931

M. H. LYNCH

Mr. Lynch came to Alaska in the 1880s. For thirteen years he was with Treadwell Mining Company in the Commissary Department. He came to Anchorage when it was a tent city down in the valley, landing here on the 22nd day of April, 1915. He is in the Real Estate and Insurance business in Anchorage and owns considerable property in the city. He is also member of the City Council.

PATHFINDER, November 1919

JOHN LYONS

John Lyons was born in Bendigo, a mining town in Australia. After a few years in Australia the family returned to Ireland; remained there only a few years; and then set out for America, locating in Walla Walla, Wash. His father, Thomas Lyons and Uncle, Patrick Lyons, pioneered in the wheat-raising industry. From the Walla Walla high school John Lyons went to the Santa Clara college in California, graduating from that institution with a business course. Later he studied law in Oregon University at Salem.

In 1898 the Klondike stampede was at its height, and John Lyons then a young attorney, headed for Alaska. In Juneau, he took a position as bookkeeper for the Treadwell Gold Mining Company. The U.S. Bureau of Education hired him to take charge of the 1900 Alaska census. This position took him over much of the then little known territory. This work completed, Federal Judge M.C. Brown of Juneau appointed Mr. Lyons as the United States commissioner for the newly created Valdez district. That was in 1901.

John Lyons served as United States commissioner for the largest recording district in Alaska for nearly eight years. His district extended from Yakutaga Bay to Bristol Bay, Western Alaska, taking in the islands of Southwestern Alaska and the Copper River and Cook Inlet valley. He resigned this office in 1908 and entered into a law partnership with Judge Fred M. Brown. This partnership was severed in 1913, when Judge Brown was appointed federal judge for the Third division. Mr. Lyons and E.E. Ritchie then formed a law partnership with offices in Valdez. In 1917 Mr. Lyons decided to move south to Seattle.

Since living in Seattle, Mr. Lyons had been engaged in the practice of law in the Alaska Building.

John Lyons died in Seattle, Washington, November 22, 1930.
>ALASKA WEEKLY, November 28, 1930

FRANCIS BISHOP MacDONALD
Mrs. Francis Bishop was a teacher for several years in the Nome public school. She was born in North Dakota in 1888, but at a very early age her parents removed to Hillsdale, Michigan, where her early years were spent. She was a graduate of the University of Michigan and at the time of her death was 38 years old.

Mrs. MacDonald was postmistress at Candle for two years and also had charge of the Alaska Telephone Co. office at that place.

Mr. MacDonald is a pioneer of the Northland, born at Glengarry, Ontario. He was among the advance guard of stampeders to Dawson, arriving there in 1897, from whence he came to Nome, going to Candle when that camp was in its infancy and remaining a permanent citizen for the past 25 years. Mr. MacDonald is U.S.Commissioner at Candle.

Francis Bishop MacDonald died at Candle April 16, 1926 in child birth. She is survived by her husband and a two-year and six-month girl, Mary Francis MacDonald. Her sister, Miss Margaret Bishop, school teacher at Deering for the past two years; a father, mother and brothers residing at Hillsdale, Michigan; and a brother, Dr. T.P Bishop.
>ALASKA WEEKLY, July 2, 1926

W. H. MACKEY
W. H. Mackey was born in Butler County, Pennsylvania, in 1856. After the war his father moved to Warrenburg, Missouri, where young Mackey was educated. He studied law and was admitted to the bar. He went to Helena, Montana, where he entered the mining business. He was the first one to open up the Montana sapphires as well as a number of placer mines. He came to Seattle to 1889, and the following spring went into Alaska, going into most of the camps of the Northland. Finally in 1894, he

settled at Homer, Cook Inlet, in developing coal properties there. His company built seven and one-half miles of railroad track, and two locomotives and ten cars and a dock. Then the conservation wave hit Alaska, and the government withdrew all the company's coal lands. Then Mackey went to the Kenai River, to open a placer prospect. His boat, on which he was transporting his big outfit, struck a rock and went to the bottom, he barely escaping with his life. Mr. Mackey is now interested in the mining industry on the east side of the Cascade range, being concerned in Fortune Creek. He thinks that district, both in placer and hardrock, will prove one of the best in the state of Washington.

ALASKA WEEKLY, June 14, 1929

THOMAS A. MARQUAM

Tom Marquam came to the territory in 1897 as assistant to Joseph W. Ivey, then collector of customs for Alaska, and for a time made his headquarters at Juneau. He was later transferred to Skagway. When Fairbanks was struck he went into the Interior and for a time edited the FAIRBANKS TIMES. Deciding to return to the practice of law he opened up offices.

Tom Marquam came from prominent Oregon pioneer stock. His father, the late P.A. Marquam, came to that territory in 1851, where he engaged in the practice of law and eventually received the appointment of federal judge. He raised a family of eleven children.

Tom, with his three brothers, attended the Bishop Scott Academy, now known as the Hill Military Academy. Tom later went to the University of Oregon as well as to Stanford University. As a young man he was a leader in athletics and amateur theatricals. He as also a commissioned officer in the national guard.

Marquam entered politics in the Tanana valley. In 1926 he was delegate to congress from Alaska.

Some time later Tom Marquam left the territory for Washington, D.C., where he made his headquarters until last March, when he moved to New York City.

Thomas A. Marquam died in New York City, November 23, 1931. He is survived by his wife; a brother, Gus Marquam; and five sisters, Mrs. thomas Prince, Mrs. McLaughlin, Mrs. Dr. Chas. E. Hill, and Mrs. Dr. C.C. Newcastle, all of Portland, and Mrs. A. K. Velton of Port Orchard, Washington.

ALASKA WEEKLY, December 4, 1931

EDWARD MARSDEN

Marsden was born in 1869 in the old Canadian village of Metlakatla. His father and mother, both dead, were Sam and Elizabeth Marsden, special workers for the late Father Duncan who founded Metlakatla. In 1888, Father Duncan took young Marsden and began to train him for the ministry.

Marsden was sent to the Carlisle school for three months and sent from there to Ohio to Marletta college which he attended five years, and next was sent to Lane Seminary and after four years graduated. From Marletta college he received the bachelor of arts degree.

He was sent to Saxman in 1897 where he organized the Presbyterian church. He also built there a sawmill which operated for a number of years. Later he established the Presbyterian mission in Ketchikan.

Rev. Mr. Marsden was an active industrialist as well as a minister. He built and operated the first Alaska steamboat which was named the Marletta and was the first native in Alaska to hold a steamboat license. He traveled all over Southeastern Alaska.

He established his headquarters in Metlakatla in 1917. The Presbyterian church there was organized in 1921 with 60 charter members and under his direction grew until it now has about 215. Rev. Mr. Marsden drew the plans for the church there and superintended its building.

Rev. Edward Marsden died in Ketchikan, Alaska, May 6, 1932. He is survived by his wife and son, John Marsden, and daughter, Mrs. Ted Benson. WRANGELL SENTINEL, May 13, 1932

HERMAN G. MARTENS

He was born in San Francisco, California on September 9, 1874, and educated in the public schools of San Francisco. He began mercantile life when he was seventeen years old with the well known San Francisco house, Tilman & Bendel. He was with this firm for ten years, beginning at the bottom and working himself up to a leading position in the firm.

In 1901 he was elected secretary of the Ames Mercantile Company, and in the fall of 1902 he came north and took charge of the company's extensive business in Nome.

NOME AND SEWARD PENINSULA, 1905

GEORGE S. MAYNARD

George S. Maynard of Nome, Alaska, is the editor and publisher of the Nome Nugget, and he is a typical northern newspaper man. He took over the Nugget along in 1909 and has been the sole publisher proprietor and editor of that publication since that early day. But George Maynard is more than an editor and publisher; he is a linotype operator, a pressman and a commercial printer. The Nome Nugget was established in 1900 by Major J. F. A. Strong, when Nome was a big mining camp.

In addition to doing about all the work on the Nugget, Mr. Maynard has been active in the civic life of Nome. He has served as mayor of the town for a half a dozen terms and has been one of the main-stays of the Commercial Club of the city. George Maynard, still in his teens, joined the stampede to the Klondike in 1898, and was employed as a printer on the Dawson newspapers for a couple of years. During the winter of 1899-1900, he mushed down the Yukon to Nome. That little city on the shore of Bering Sea was the end of the trail for him. Mrs. Maynard, whom he married in Nome, is passing the winter in Seattle.

ALASKA WEEKLY, December 14, 1928

ANGUS McBRIDE

Angus McBride was born and reared on a farm six miles north of Beden, St. Louis

County, Mo.; got his early education at private school, at the neighborhood public school, and later at Blackburn University, Illinois. He returned home from the university and worked on the farm for a few years. Tiring of the slow method of making a fortune, he moved to the West, and engaged in the real estate, abstract and loan business in Eureka, Kansas. He examined land and made real estate loans for one of the large loan companies and with very good success until the panic struck that section and everything "went up in smoke."

In 1890 he moved to California "to begin life over." Not having any capital, trade or profession, he studied stenography and got a position in the law office of Mr. Arthur Rodgers in San Francisco. He remained in that city until 1895 when he secured a position in the office of the Southern Pacific Company at Tucson, Arizona, and was with that company four years. He was also employed as clerk of the Agricultural Experiment Station at the University of Arizona for a short time.

In 1900 he came to Nome, and spent the first summer prospecting, and the following winter was given a position by Mr. Borchsenius as clerk in the office of the Clerk of the United States District Court, which position he has held through the various judicial administrations.

NOME AND SEWARD PENINSULA, 1905

J. C. MCBRIDE

Mr. McBride has resided in Alaska for 35 years, and most of that time has been spent in Juneau. Born in California, he was early in life connected with one of the leading mining concerns of that State. He was first in the assay office at Virginia City, later assistant assayer for the Utica Mining Company when it was operating the largest mine in the State. He next shifted to the purchasing office in San Francisco as purchasing agent.

It was while there that he became interested in the Sumdum Mining co. and he came north in 1898 to aid in the development of property at Sumdum. After five years there, he came to Juneau and for three years he prospected and scouted various localities in this vicinity.

In 1906 he purchased C.W. Young & Company in Juneau, one of the largest general hardware stores north of Seattle, and was its President and General Manager until 1922 when it was sold.

Although always interested in politics, he had never sought office until 1920, when he became a candidate for and was elected Republican National Committeeman for Alaska. He held that office for more than four years. He continued to serve however, as National Committeeman until 1926. In 1922 he was appointed Collector of Customs by then President Harding. In addition to this commission, he has held commissions under two other Republican Chief Executives. He was appointed Postmaster at Sumdum by President Roosevelt, and Alaska Commissioner for the Alaska-Yukon Expedition in 1909 by President Taft.

ALASKA WEEKLY, July 21, 1933

E. J. MCCORMICK

Mr. McCormick was born in Strokestown, Rosscommon county, Ireland. He came to America when 21 years of age and worked at his trade as a tailor. While following this vocation, he went to Kansas City, Mo., where he took a position as a fitter and cutter with the dry goods firm of Bleen, Moore & Emery. He remained there many years. Just after the Seattle fire, he came to Seattle and later went to Portland, Oregon. Here he opened a hotel and restaurant and had built up a business when the Klondike was found.

In 1897 McCormick sold out his Portland business and went to the Klondike. He arrived in Dawson in September. He soon had a restaurant under way, open day and night. A hotel--the Portland--was build and operated by him, in connection with his restaurant.

After nine years in Dawson, McCormick

moved to the Imperial Valley in California. He located in Calexico where he went into the hotel and restaurant business. Later he moved to Holtsville, California and established a hotel and restaurant there.

E.J. McCormick died in March 1928 at his home in Holtsville. He is survived by a son, Ernest McCormick, who lives in Holtsville; by three married daughters, Mrs. Brimstone, wife of the late George Brimstone, noted athlete and for many years sheriff of Dawson, who now resides in Seattle; Mrs. Harry Lawrence, who lives in Skykomish, this state; Mrs. Harry Kaufman, who lives in Los Angeles, Calif. and his brother-in-law, Ralph Boyker, pioneer Klondiker and now owner and operator of two well known Seattle hotels, the Northern and the Stevens.

ALASKA WEEKLY, March 28, 1930

JEFFREY McDERMOTT

Jeff McDermott was born in Ireland October 31, 1839, and went to America with his parents in 1852. The family located in Ohio on the Old Western Reserve twenty-four miles west of Cleveland. In 1855 the subject of this sketch went to Iowa and thence to Kansas, which was then a territory. He was a resident of "Bleeding Kansas" through the days of the slavery excitement and lived there until the spring of 1859.

At the beginning of the Pike's Peak excitement, in the days when the old prairie schooners, labelled "Pike's Peak or Bust," crossed the wide expanse of plains, then a wilderness, he became a pilgrim to the "New Golconda." He had saved up $300, and after arriving at Pike's Peak he invested in a prospect hole.

After this mining venture he went to Montana. This was in 1861. He was one of the first four men to set up a sluice-box on Pioneer Gulch. He mined on Bancock and on Alder Gulch until 1863.

In 1864 Mr. McDermott started back to his old home, but got only as far as the Missouri

River. From Salt Lake to Atchison, Kansas, he traveled by stage, the trip requiring twenty-two days and the fare being $300. At Atchison he met an old Montana friend and they got six four-mule teams and started a freight line to Denver, 600 miles distant. In 1866 he was back in Montana again. During this year and the following year he was in the freighting business on the frontier, traveling between Salt Lake and Boise Basin; later he mined near Leesburg and worked on Silver Creek.

In 1876 he stampeded to the Black Hills, and he has since mined in Colorado, Mexico, Dawson and in the Nome country.

His first trip to the mines of the North was to the Klondike country. In this region he mined on Bonanza Creek and had charge of 39 for the N. A. T. & T. Company. He came to Nome in 1901, and having been in the mines all his life, realized and understood the great value of water. One of the first locations that he made was a water right in the Solomon River country. He was one of the first men to talk water rights and the necessity of constructing ditches. Because of the lack of adequate capital he was not able to do anything with his water right location until the season of 1904. The McDermott Ditch, the highest line ditch in this part of the country, is the result of this water right location.

Mr. McDermott is a married man and the father of three children, two boys and a girl. His family resides at Oreville, South Dakota.

ANTHONY McGETTIGAN

When the members of the Common Council of Nome, selected at the election in April, 1904, took their seats, their first official act was to unanimously elect Anthony McGettigan city clerk. Mr. McGettigan is a native of County Donegal, Ireland, and was born in the month of December, 1865. He went to America in 1889, and lived in Norristown and Phillipsburg, Pa., until 1893, engaging in the bottling business with the well known firm of J. & W. Shields, his uncles. After brief residence in Philadelphia and Chicago he went to California in the latter part of 1894 on a visit to his uncle, Col. E. McGettigan. From California he went to Butte, Montana, and worked in the Anaconda Mine, subsequently conducting a real estate business in Butte.

In April, 1897, Mr. McGettigan started for the Klondike gold fields, and has lived in the Yukon Territory and Alaska ever since then. He and his partner packed 1,500 pounds of supplies over Chilkoot Pass, and joining a party of six men, helped to whipsaw the lumber and make a scow, upon which the entire party journeyed from Lake Lindeman to Dawson. They arrived in Dawson June 19, and as wages were $1.50 an hour, Mr. McGettigan immediately went to work. He spent two winters in Dawson, prospected on the head-waters of Seventy-Mile River, and also made a trip to Forty-Mile River, Circle and Eagle. After the return from this trip, in the fall of '98, he was stricken with typhoid fever. This illness resulted from the hardships and exposure of the trip. In the winter of '97 when gold was more plentiful than food, he paid sixty-two dollars for a sack of flour, and packed it on his back fourteen-miles to camp.

In the fall of '99 he joined the stampede to Nome, arriving at the new mining camp Sept. 21. In the spring of 1900 he opened up an Anvil claim for one of the companies, and later in the season carried a pack on his back to the Kougarok country. His uncle came to Nome from San Francisco this season, and joined him in the search for gold. After returning from the Kougarok, pack horses were secured to take in supplies to permit of prospecting the ground Mr. McGettigan had staked, and considerable work was done this year and the following season on Iron Creek, a tributary of the Kruzgamepa. In 1902 a large force of men was employed for two months to open up the Iron Creek property, but the pay did not justify a continuation of operations. A claim on Twin Mountain, a tributary of Snake River, yielded better results, and during the season of 1903 he and his uncle worked the claim by hydraulic methods, realizing a satisfactory profit. During the past two winters he studied pharmacy under Arthur Dibert, the druggist.

JOHN L. McGINN

John L. McGinn came to Nome in the spring of 1900, and after his mining experiences on Saturday Creek during that summer was appointed Assistant United States Attorney, October 15, 1900. July 12, 1901, he was placed in full charge of the United States Attorney's office, and during the term of court held by Judge Wickersham in the Second Judicial Division, he went to Dutch Harbor and prosecuted and secured the conviction of Hardy the murderer, the only man ever hanged at Nome. After the appointment of a United States Attorney, he was continued in the office as a deputy, but resigned January 22, 1903. In April of that year Judge Moore appointed him as acting United States Attorney for the district. In the spring of 1903 he relinquished the position and opened an office for the practice of law. He has since been connected with some of the most important cases of the District Court at Nome.

Mr. McGinn was born in Portland, Oregon, February 26, 1871. His father came to Oregon in 1854. After receiving a public school education, Mr. McGinn took a law course in the University of Oregon, and was graduated from that institution in 1893. He was associated with his brother in the practice of law until 1898, when he went to the Philippines with the Second Oregon Regiment. He saw thirteen months of service, and was in twenty-two engagements and skirmishes. After he was mustered out he practiced law in the Philippines from June until November, returning to Portland in January, 1900. Since 1900 he has been identified with the legal profession in Nome. McGomm and Miss Elsa Searing were married in Nome April 20, 1904.

NOME AND SEWARD PENSINSULA, 1905

E.A. McINTOSH

Perhaps the Church in Alaska has had no more unique worker than Mr. E.A. McIntosh. He was a school teacher and carpenter by early training; a government teacher, missionary and doctor, from his desire to help the natives of Alaska.

In 1907, to work as a carpenter, E.A. McIntosh came to Nome. It was during the following summer that he met Mr. William T. Lopp, the Superintendent of Education for the natives of Alaska. Mr. Lopp hired him as a government teacher at the Eskimo village near Point Hope. After finishing his term of two years among the Eskimos of Pt. Hope, he was transferred to a point near the mouth of the Kuskokwim river, where he built the Government school of Kinak, and with his sister, became the first teacher. Completing his term here, he returned to California, and again went into contracting for buildings.

In 1912, Mr. McIntosh returned to Alaska to build the hospital of St. Stephens at Fort Yukon.

The hospital, once completed, Bishop Rowe asked Mr. McIntosh to undertake the charge of St. Timothy's Mission, at Tanana Crossing, where he also had on the program a new mission building. After completing St. Timothy's mission building, Mr. McIntosh resigned his position to be with his wife who had gone to California because of her health.

ALASKAN CHURCHMAN, November 1918

WILLIAM F. MCKAY

Mr. McKay was born in New Brunswick 76 years ago, and when a young man turned his footsteps westward. He took an active part in the construction of the Northern Pacific railway, particularly through the Yakima country, and later engaged in the logging business in Western Washington and about Vancouver, B.C. He eventually settled near Mt. Vernen, Wash., and there became an active figure in the political life of the Evergreen state, where he served for a long time as a

member of the Washington legislature. He
sponsored many important legislative measures,
most notable of which was the one which
resulted in the establishment of the land
grants which gave to the University of
Washington the substantial revenues which have
become one of the chief factors in assisting it
to attain the position of one of the leading
educational institutions in the Pacific
Northwest.

When yet a young man, Mr. McKay worked in
the logging business, helped to fall the firs
that stood originally upon the present site of
the heart of the city of Vancouver, B.C. In the
gold rush of '98, Mr. McKay came North and was
engaged in prospecting and mining in Alaska and
in the Klondike. He spent several years in the
Kennecott district in the Copper River region,
at the head of White River, on the Nabesna and
elsewhere in that section of Alaska. For a
number of years he also followed placer mining
in the Fortymile region and on Dominion Creek
in the Klondike, and was one of the first to
enter the now prosperous and rapidly expanding
silver-lead area known as the Mayo mining
district, in which are located Keno Hill,
Galena Hill and Sourdough Hills, now heavy
shippers of ore.

The University of Washington stands as one
of the monuments to his name, and Yukon
Territory rears one of it loftiest and most
richly mineralized peaks, namely McKay Hill, in
the heart of the new Beaver mining area as
another visible and permanent monument in his
honor.

Mr. McKay was one of the discoverer of the
hill and was the locator of valuable mining
properties on the hill.

Mr. McKay died in Mayo, Yukon Territory,
August 31, 1929. He is survived by a sister,
Barbara McKay, Burlington, Washington; by a
brother, George McKay, Burlington; and by a
sister, Kate Taylor, Seattle.

ALASKA WEEKLY, September 6, 1929

DANIEL MCLEAN

Captain Daniel McLean was born in Sydney, Cape Breton, in 1851, and commenced his marine career at that place. He afterward sailed out of New York as mate on deep-water ships, and came to the Pacific Coast about 1880, sailing over three thousand miles on the waters of Alaska and British Columbia with the seven-ton sloop, FLYAWAY, prospecting for minerals and working for some time at placer mining on what was afterward known as the Treadwell claim. He also discovered the coal mine now owned by the Alaska Commercial Company. While prospecting with his sloop, McLean was impressed with the large number of seals in that region, decided that sealing would be a good business to follow, and in the fall of 1883, with his brother Alex, took out the schooner SAN DIEGO from San Francisco, made a fair catch and sold the skins in Victoria. The following season he took out the schooner MARY ELLEN, securing 2,400 skins, 1,700 in 1885, and in 1886 broke the record with 4,268. In 1886 he brought the schooner TRIUMPH from Halifax to Victoria and the following year secured 2,500 skins. In 1888 he was ordered out of Bering Sea by the American Government. From 1889 through 1894 McLean hunted off Copper Island and along the coast of Japan.

LEWIS & DRYDEN'S MARINE HISTORY OF THE
    PACIFIC NORTHWEST, 1895

P. B. McLEOD

P. B. McLeod is identified with the shipping and transportation interests of Seward Peninsula, owning vessels and barges in the coast trade. He was born in Toronto, Canada, September 9, 1870, and received a public school education in his native city. He went to Chicago when he was fourteen years old, subsequently moving to Seattle, where he lived for ten years, and followed the business of a dry goods merchant. He sold out in 1900, and since 1901 has been connected with the shipping business of Nome.

For the past two seasons Mr. McLeod has

been the agent at Nome for the steamer Corwin.
NOME AND SEWARD PENINSULA, 1905

ALONSO P. MEAD
   Mr. Mead was born in Oakland, Michigan and came to Portland in 1891. In 1897 he and his wife established in Skagway, Alaska a missionary home and hospital for young men which they conducted for several years. They returned to Portland in 1907.
   Alonso P. Mead died in Portland, Oregon, March 22, 1918. He is survived by his wife, Mrs. Amelia Mead; a daughter Mrs. Helen Ousick of Leroy, Michigan; a son, Charles W. Mead of Skagway.
   DAILY ALASKAN (Skagway), April 4, 1918

ARIZONA CHARLIE MEADOWS
   Early-day Dawsonites will remember "Arizona" Charlie, who with his troupe, wandered into the Klondike in '98. They will remember him as a tall, broad-shouldered giant, arrayed in rich furs...Diamond studded, with his long black hair falling over his broad shoulders and his Van Dyke beard trimmed in "Buffalo Bill" fashion.
   An imposing personality was "Arizona" Charlie, who, on his arrival at Dawson, purchased a couple of steamboats from the Alaska Commercial Company which he wrecked in order to secure lumber with which to build the Grand Opera House. On the opening night of his theater he gave a wonderful banquet to forty guests and underneath each plate placed a crisp new Canadian $100 bill...It was his way to doing things.
   Realizing the value of advertising as well as the vanity of the average human person, Charlie Meadows decided to get out the first magazine record of the Klondike. This in the form of an annual which gave a complete resume of development and conditions in the great gold fields. He canvassed successful miners on the creeks whom he charged a handsome price for a brief sketch of their operations which he published with a cut of themselves.

the necessary data secured, he proceeded in San Francisco, where, through a reputable publishing firm, a most interesting magazine review of the Klondike was produced. This venture netted him many thousands of dollars.

The last twenty years of his life was spent in Arizona, where he owned a large ranch in Yuma County. He maintained a town house in Yuma, where he entertained many friends made during his worldwide trips.

Arizona Charlie Meadows died in Yuma, Arizona, December 1932. To mourn his loss he leaves a daughter and only child, Mrs. Marion M. Leiser of Home Lake Bay, Wash., and two sisters, Mrs. Mary Arnold Boswick and Mrs. Margaret Beach of San Fernando, California.

ALASKA WEEKLY, December 16, 1932

JOSHUA D. MEENACH

Joshua Meenach was born in Kentucky in 1858; came to Seattle in 1888; and this city had been the home of his family since that early date.

Mr. Meenach who was a widely known Alaska mining man, was prominent in the development of the mining industry in the Northland. He first went to Circle City, Alaska, in 1895, but remained only a few months over a year. With the discovery of gold in the Klondike, he was back again, mining on Bonanza Creek of those famous gold diggings. Later he became manager of the Reliance Mining Company of Philadelphia.

In 1900, Mr. Meenach opened up and developed the Ellamar copper mine in the Prince William Sound country, Southwestern Alaska. This property was the first important shipper of copper ore from the Northland and was a steady producer for many years.

He was the leader of an expedition into the then little known Copper River valley country in 1903 and interested John E. Andrus of New York City in the development of the Chittitu placer area, an important mining operation. Joshua Meenach died March 8, 1928 in Seattle. He is survived by his wife, Mary; by a son, Harry of Seattle; by two

daughters, Mrs. John C. Kelly of Seattle, and by Mrs. Maude Cooper of Chehalis, Washington.
ALASKA WEEKLY, March 16, 1928

MAGNUS MEISINGSETH

Magnus Meisingseth, pioneer of the Northland, stampeded to the Alsace country, Yukon territory in 1904. Soon he went to Dawson, Y.T., where he remained for some five years. Then the Fairbanks camp was in full flower, and in 1906 Meisingseth was operating on Cleary creek, one of the best of the camps, and on Chatnika Flats. He remained in Fairbanks until 1916, when he went to the Tolovana district. He stayed there until 1918, when he came south to Seattle. During the World War, he worked for the Skinner-Eddy shipyards. In 1920 he went to Hyder, Alaska, and took an active part in the construction of that town. Later, he owned and operated the Boundary Roadhouse, near the great Premier mine. Selling out the roadhouse in 1924, he made a trip to Europe, and upon his return, took over the Pioneer hotel in Ketchikan. At the present time, he is operating a curio, fur and cigar store on Heckman's dock in Ketchikan.
ALASKA WEEKLY, April 11, 1930

CONSTANTINE MELETUS

C. Meletus is one of the pioneer miners of Good Hope District. He was one of the first prospectors on Dick Creek, a tributary of Bryan Creek flowing into the Serpentine River. He staked property on this creek in 1901, and has worked on the creek every season since then, but lack of water has prevented him from operating on a scale that would yield large revenues. By using the water available which would permit of sluicing for only an hour or two each, Mr. Meletus has been able to obtain a grub-stake every season from these diggings.

Mr. Meletus was born in Vassar, near Sparta, Greece, in 1869. When he was ten years old he left home and went to Russia and Turkey. He spent five years in Russia and obtained a fair knowledge of the Russian and Rumanian languages. He has attended both English and Greek schools, and at one time could speak Italian fairly well. In 1887 he immigrated to the United States and located in Chicago. He has followed the restaurant business in Chicago, San Francisco and Seattle, and was successful in a restaurant venture at the Chicago World's Fair in 1893.

His first mining experience was in Cripple Creek. He came to Nome in the spring of 1900, and in the following season acquired the Dick Creek property, and has staid by it firm in the faith that its development would make a fortune for him. May 3, 1905, he married Miss Lyde C. Rutherford, of Revere, Mo. She accompanied him this season to Dick Creek, where Mr. Meletus is engaged in construction a ditch for the economical working of his mining property.
NOME AND SEWARD PENINSULA, 1905

WILLIAM H. METSON

William H. Metson, lawyer and financier is prominently identified with the work of developing Seward Peninsula, being president of one of the largest ditch enterprises in the country, the Miocene Ditch Company, and president of the Nome-Arctic Railway Company. In the practice of his profession Mr. Metson assisted in making the history of Nome. As attorney for the Pioneer Mining Company, in the notorious injunction and receiver law suits during the regime of Judge Noyes, leading part in that famous litigation.

Mr. Metson is a native of California. He was born in San Francisco March 16, 1864. The family moved to Nevada shortly after his birth, and most of his boyhood days were spent in Virginia City. It was here he received his early education, and developed a character typical of the West. Leaving Virginia City when sixteen years old, he went to Bodie and entered the law offices of Hon. Patrick Reddy. A few years later he accompanied Mr. Reddy to San Francisco and attended the Hastings Law School, University of California, and was graduated in the class of 1886. He continued the study of the law under Mr. Reddy. In 1900 Mr. Metson became a member of the firm of Reddy, Campbell & Metson.

Mr. Metson went to Nome in the spring of 1900 and became interested in the litigation mentioned above, and perceiving the prospects and possibilities of the country he associated himself with industrial enterprises, and is taking an active part in developing these gold fields.

Mr. Metson has served many organizations. He has been Commissioner of Yosemite Park since 1898, having been appointed by Governor Budd, a Democrat, and reappointed by Governor Gage, a Republican. He is one of the Commissioners of Golden Gate Park, San Francisco, receiving his appointment from Mayor Schmitz in January, 1905. Mr. Metson has extensive business interests in California, Nevada, Washington, and Alaska. He is a director in a number of corporations, among them the Scandinavian-American Bank in Seattle. He is a member of the Pacific Union, Bohemian, San Francisco, and Merchants Clubs of San Francisco, and is prominent in the Order of Native Sons of the Golden West.

The law firm of which Mr. Metson is a member has branch officer in Nome, Tonopah, Goldfield and Bullfrog. Mr. Metson directs these offices, most of the business of which relates to mines and mining.

NOME AND SEWARD PENINSULA, 1905

H. J. MIGNEREY

H.J. Mignerey was born in Estoban, France, August 1, 1959. He was left an orphan at the age of 6 years. At the age of 10 years, he went to work for his board. At the age of 14 years he came to the united States alone, landing in New York City with $4 in his pocket. He was unable to speak English but after a time succeeded in getting a job on a farm in New York state at $6.00 a month. Later, he got a job as delivery clerk in a grocery store in Western Massachusetts at $8.00 per month. Six years later, he formed a partnership with a young chum and purchased a run-down grocery store, for $1,000. A year and a half later, he bought out his partner, moved to larger quarters in the center of town and rapidly built up the business to a point where he had five delivery wagons to handle the trade. He sold out in 1897, and went to Alaska in April, 1898, and went over the White Pass to Lake Bennett, but soon returned to Seattle. Later, he took the boat to St. Michael and went up the Yukon to Rampart. While there he learned of the Nome strike and on December 17, 1898, he left Rampart, with four dogs and a camping outfit, headed for the outside via Dawson and Skagway, with the intention of buying a stock of goods in Seattle for merchandising in Nome. He had to pitch tent every night down the lower Yukon valley, as there were no roadhouses in those days. He bought a varied stock of goods, among which was a restaurant outfit, in Seattle, and sailed for Nome on the first steamer of 1899, the ROANOKE. Arriving at Nome, it was necessary to unload the cargoes with Eskimos and their skin boats, as the ROANOKE could not get any closer than about two miles from shore. After each passenger had gathered their belongings on the beach, Mr. Mignerey hoisted his big tent, 26 x 40 feet, hired a young man, and started to fee the crowd at $1.00 per meal. A few days later, Mignerey moved to permanent quarters on high ground. In July, 1899, Miner Bruce arrived from Siberia with a schooner load of reindeer carcasses. Mignerey bought the entire cargo and for a while controlled the fresh meat supply of Nome. Having made a good profit, Mignerey decided to go to Siberia for some more reindeer and bought the schooner JAMES G. SWAN, which had been sold by the U.S. Marshal for debt. While outfitting for the trip, a storm came up suddenly and blew the boat ashore and wrecked it. It was perhaps a fortunate thing for Mignerey, for shortly afterward he was taken down with typhoid fever. After nine weeks of sickness, he was carried on a stretch to the last boat of the season for Seattle. After recuperating, he bought an

interest in the steamer CLIFFORD SIFTON which was operated between Whitehorse and Dawson in the seasons of 1900 and 1901. It was a strong competitor to the White Pass & Yukon railways fleet of boats, operating on the same run. The CLIFFORD SIFTON was finally sold to the White Pass Company. Mr. Mignerey returned to Seattle and engaged in the wholesale potato and onion business, in which he is still engaged. ALASKA WEEKLY, September 13, 1929
NOME AND SEWARD PENINSULA, 1905

CHARLES W. MILLER
Charley Miller is one of the best known caterers and hotel men in the North, and was born in Sandusky, Ohio. His parents planned a college education, but the son ran away and began his hotel career in New York City.

Later he drifted West to Colorado and became a hotel man of Aspen. He was elected city alderman and was a candidate for the state legislature. He first located in Alaska in Seward and mined and prospected in that section. He is one of the pioneer restaurant men of Cordova and is vice president of the Western Hotel Men's Association for Alaska.
ALASKA-YUKON MAGAZINE, December 1910

H. J. MILLER
H.J. Miller, one of the leading attorneys of Fairbanks, Alaska, was born in Rockbridge County, Va., in the year 1857, but very early in life moved with his family to the State of Iowa. Here he attended the public schools until the age of eighteen, when he entered the University at Albion, Iowa, whence he graduated three years later. He went to Lawrence, Kansas, where he attended the law school from 1882 until 1884.

Mr. Miller was then admitted to the bar and practiced law in the West for a number of years. In 1897 he was sent to Dyea, Alaska, to represent the Chilkoot Railroad & Transport Company, and while there he built up a fine law practice.

After leaving Dyea he spent some time at

Atlin, B.C., where he was engaged in mining, and also spent a year at Eagle, Alaska

In 1903 Mr. Miller went to Fairbanks, where he opened up an office and has practiced law there ever since.

ALASKA-YUKON MAGAZINE, January 1909

H. J. MILLER

H.J. Miller, one of the leading attorneys of Fairbanks, Alaska, was born in Rockbridge County, Va., in the year 1857, but very early in life moved with his family to the State of Iowa. Here he attended the public schools until the age of eighteen, when he entered the University at Albion, Iowa, whence he graduated three years later. He went to Lawrence, Kansas, where he attended the law school from 1882 until 1884.

Mr. Miller was then admitted to the bar and practiced law in the West for a number of years. In 1897 he was sent to Dyea, Alaska, to represent the Chilkoot Railroad & Transport Company, and while there he built up a fine law practice.

After leaving Dyea he spent some time at Atlin, B.C., where he was engaged in mining, and also spent a year at Eagle, Alaska.

In 1903 Mr. Miller went to Fairbanks, where he opened up an office and has practiced law there ever since.

ALASKA-YUKON MAGAZINE, January 1909

JAMES M. MILLER

James M. Miller was born in 1855 at Marietta, Ohio, and came to the north in 1898 when he and his wife went to Dawson and from there to Nome where they lived for several years coming out to Juneau seventeen years ago.

Mr. Miller was manager for the Frye-Bruhn meat market in Juneau for over eight years. Three years ago he was appointed deputy United States marshal for Skagway. Mr. Miller was afterwards appointed as jailer.

Mr. Miller died March 8, 1920 in Skagway. A wife and son James, Jr. survive him. An older son, Raymond, passed away several years

ago at Juneau at the age of 14 years. He was the first white child born in Nome.
ALASKA DAILY CAPITAL, March 9, 1920

BLAKE D. MILLS

Blake D. Mills, who today owns extensive real estate interests in Seattle, was born in Port Blakely, Washington, in 1867; and when a boy his family removed to Port Discovery. His education was received in the Seattle schools. Young Mills connected himself with the Puget Mill Company, serving in various capacities in their mercantile department where he had charge of their stores at several places.

His commercial training with the Puget Mill Company was thorough; and in January, 1898, Mr. Mills joined the ever memorable stampede to Alaska, going to Dawson over the Chilkoot Pass with a shipment of merchandise, which he profitably disposed of. He returned to Seattle in the fall of the same year. In the following year he went to Eagle city, establishing a trading post for the Seattle-Yukon Transportation Co., and in 1901 he accepted the position as manager of the North Coast Trading & Transportation Co. at that place, which position he held until 1903; during which time he remained, winter and summer, at Eagle City.

In the winter of 1903, with Mr. Johanson, he organized the Tanana Development Co. and built a large saw mill at Fairbanks, Alaska. Mr. Mills took the management of this company until the spring of 1906, when there was a consolidation of mill interests and the Tanana Mill Company was formed, of which corporation he became president, holding that office today. He is a large holder of the stock in that company which owns the largest saw mill in Alaska. In 1906 Mr. Mills was elected mayor of Fairbanks.

During his residence in Fairbanks he was one of the city's most active and energetic commercial men, being the prime mover in the Tanana Chamber of Commerce, and also the organizer of the Tanana Masonic Club.

In the fall of 1906 Mr. Mills left the North, where he had so actively engaged himself for eight years. Associated with Captain Donald B. Olson, another Alaskan, in the Evans Creek Coal & Coke Co., Mr. Mills is developing the Pierce County coal properties in the region of Evans Creek, Washington. He is a director in the Trustee Company of Seattle.

ALASKA-YUKON MAGAZINE, October 1907

FRANCIS M. MONROE

Francis M. Monroe was born in Lyons, France, June 2, 1855.

In 1874 he entered the Society of Jesus, and after studies in Belgium and St. Helier was admitted into the Rocky Mountain Mission on July 2, 1885. In 1886 he came to the United States and prior to coming to Alaska, was attached to various missions in Montana.

Father Monroe came to Alaska in 1893. His first assignment was at Holy Cross Mission. In August, 1894, he was appointed to the Nulato mission. At the time of the rush to the Klondike he pastored at towns of Eagle, Forty Mile, Circle, and Tanana. He arrived in Fairbanks in 1904. It was then a bustling mining camp, and in 1906 during his pastorate he was visited by a committee of Fairbanks business men to urged him to establish a hospital. Father Monroe and the committee solicited funds and pledges from the businessmen and miners. Father Monroe prepared the plans and donned a pair of overalls and worked as one of the workmen in its construction. While in Fairbanks Father Monroe frequently made long trips by dog team to visit miners and trappers, saying Mass in remote places, baptizing children, and performing marriage ceremonies.

In 1924 Father Monroe was transferred to Wrangell as pastor of Saint Rose's parish where he served until shortly before his death in Jan. 1940.

ALASKA CATHOLIC, Jan. 13, 1940

MAJOR WILLIAM NEWTON MONROE

Major William Newton Monroe came to Nome to supervise the construction of the Wild Goose Railroad, and is the man who built the first railroad in Northwestern Alaska. After its construction he acted as superintendent of the line, and subsequently when the road was acquired by the Nome-Arctic corporation and its name changed, he was selected as manager and placed in full charge of the road.

Major Monroe is a native of Indiana, and was born June 4, 1841. He is of Southern lineage, his parents having emigrated from Kentucky to the Hoosier state. At the age of eighteen he enlisted as a soldier in the First Iowa Cavalry. For meritorious service he was promoted to first lieutenant of the Seventh Iowa Cavalry. He served his country as a soldier during a period of four years and a half, and was in a number of engagements in the Civil War, notable among them the battles of Perry Grove, Arkansas, and Springfield, Missouri. During the latter part of his service in the army he was transferred to the Western Department, and for two years fought Indians on the frontier. He was in Wyoming during the serious trouble with the Sioux.

Major Monroe was accredited with being the best drilled cavalry officer in the Department of the Platte, and has a certificate from General McCane, the commander, for his proficiency as a horseman and a swordsman. He was mustered out of service as Brevet Major, and began the work of civil life as a railroad contractor and superintendent of construction. He helped to build the Union Pacific, and in 1872 went to California, and for many years was connected with the construction department of the Southern Pacific Railroad Company. In 1884 he established the town of Monrovia in Southern California, and lived there until the spring of 1900, being engaged in the real estate business. In 1900 he came to Nome with Charles D. Lane and constructed the most northerly railroad in North America.

Major Monroe was married in Omaha,

December 25, 1864. Mrs. Monroe was formerly Mary J. Hall. The issue of this marriage is four children, Milton S., George O., Myrtle M. and Mabel H. The elder daughter is now the wife of Bruce C. Bailey, and the younger daughter is the wife of Bruce T. Dyer.

When Major Monroe was superintendent of construction on the Southern Pacific lines of the Southwest he was known among the employees by the name of "Red-Cloud." At that time his hair was red and he rode a white horse.

NOME AND SEWARD PENINSULA, 1905

JUDGE ALFRED S. MOORE

The selection of a judge for the Second Judicial Division of Alaska to succeed Arthur H. Noyes, was a matter that received more than ordinary attention from the Government at Washington, on account of the condition of affairs in the Nome judicial district. The condition in which Judge Noyes left the legal affairs of Nome, however, made it necessary for the Government to exercise care in the selection of a successor. There was a demand for a judge of ability and absolute honesty, and Alfred S. Moore, of Beaver, Pennsylvania, was selected to fill this position. He had been a lawyer in Pennsylvania since 1871, he had served three years as District Attorney of Beaver County, was president of the Law Association of the county for a period of three years; was a member of the examining board for four years; had been a trustee in Beaver College for twenty years, and was a director of the First National Bank of Beaver. His record and reputation met all the requirements, and he received the appointment of Judge of the Second Judicial Division of Alaska, in May, 1902, and entered upon his duties July 14, succeeding.

Judge Moore was born September 13, 1846; was educated in the public schools of Pennsylvania, in the old Beaver Academy and in Washington and Jefferson Colleges, and was graduated from Jefferson College with the degree of A. B., subsequently receiving the degree of A. M.

He began work as a railroad man, and during a period of twenty-five months arose from the position of baggage man to the position of conductor of a passenger train. He was only twenty-two years old when he held the position of conductor.

His railroad experience was begun on account of ill health, and on a road from St. Louis into Illinois, of which his uncle, Col. Henry S. Moore, was superintendent. Having regained his health, he returned home and studied law under Sam B. Wilson, the leader of the bar of Beaver County, and was admitted to practice law September 11, 1871. He first opened an office in Butler. After three years of practice he returned to Beaver, and in 1880 was elected district attorney of the county.

Judge Moore was one of the most successful lawyers of the Beaver bar. He never lost a single case in the Supreme Court. While practicing at Butler, oil was struck in that part of Pennsylvania, and a great deal of litigation resulted from the new industry.

Judge Moore is of Scotch-Irish descent in which there is a strain of Spanish, English and German blood. His ancestors came to America in Colonial days. He is a member of a family of lawyers, being a nephew of Chief Justice Daniel Agnew, and Robert Moore, a celebrated lawyer, was his grandfather.

NOME AND SEWARD PENINSULA, 1905

ARTHUR H. MOORE

A. H. Moore has been a resident of Nome since the spring of 1900, and has been identified with the freighting, transfer and contracting business of Seward Peninsula. He was the owner of the Gold Beach Transfer Company, doing a general freighting and transfer business, and conducting a line of stages between Nome and Council City in the winter seasons. He has also built a number of ditches in this country, among them the Cripple River Hydraulic Mining Company's Ditch the Corson Ditch, and the Golden Dawn Ditch. During the past winter he organized the Gold

Beach Development Company, of which he is superintendent. This is a St. Paul, Minn., corporation, having for its object the business of freighting, contracting and mining.

A. H. Moore is a native of Brooklyn, Me. He was born September 20, 1867, and was educated in the public schools of his native state. He belongs to a family of sailors, his father having been mast of vessels. One of his brothers was captain during several seasons, of one of the steamers of the Nome fleet. When twenty years of age the subject of this sketch shipped as a sailor before the mast. In 1888 he left home and traveled by way of Cape Horn to the Western Coast of America. He located in Port Townsend, and established a country store in the Olympic Mountains. He bought a pack train and engaged in this form of transportation business between Port Townsend and his store and the country thereabouts.

In 1897 he went up the Yukon and was employed as a mate on one of the river steamers. Mr. Moore spent a winter on Dall River, a tributary of the Yukon, and during the winter of '98-'99 he ascended the Koyukuk to the head-waters. He came down the river in the spring of '99. This was a 1,600-mile trip.

February 2, 1893, A. H. Moore married Effie D. Hunter, of Port Townsend. They have three children, Willie, aged ten; Marion, eight; and Lucy, an infant.

NOME AND SEWARD PENINSULA, 1905

BENJAMIN P. MOORE

The entire territory of Alaska, with a seaboard greater than that of the whole United States, is comprised in a single customs district under the supervision of Collector Benjamin P. Moore, whose office is at Sitka, the capital town. Mr. Moore was born in New York in 1861, and spent his youth in that city at school. He is a son of the late J. S. Moore of New York, one of the best known tariff reformers in the United States, who was the author of the Mill's Tariff Bill, and a close friend of President Cleveland and Secretary

Carlisle.

In 1885 President Cleveland appointed Collector Moore as Indian agent in the then Washington territory, which place he filled for about two years, resigning in 1887 and associating himself with Mr. John W. Mackey and Senator John P. Jones and other eastern capitalists for the purpose of erecting smelting works, but after expending above $80,000, the enterprise proved unsuccessful. His appointment as collector for Alaska was not solicited, but Secretary Carlisle on May 12, 1893, offered him the appointment which was duly made on May 16, four days later he assuming the duties of the office on July 1st following.

Mr. Moore has always been active in the best interests of the territory. Visiting Washington in December, 1895, he appeared three times before the senate territorial committee, appealing for high license laws. He secured the passage of a bill appropriating $5,000 for the rebuilding of the government wharf at Sitka and was instrumental in securing the passage of the act whereby the secretary of the treasury is authorized to create such sub-ports of entry in Alaska as the increasing business may make necessary, and has done much else to improve the working of customs service in Alaska.

ALASKA MINING RECORD, January 1896

DR. H. S. MOORE

Dr. H. S. Moore first came to Nome in the fall of 1902. He returned to the states, where he spent the winter, coming back to Nome the following spring to become associated with Dr. Rininger. During the winter of 1903-'04, and while Dr. Rininger was outside, Dr. Moore had charge of the office and all the work connected with it.

He was graduated from the Indianapolis Medical College of the University of Indiana, in 1900, and entered the army as First Lieutenant Assistant Surgeon. He was with the 158th Indiana Regiment during the war with Spain. After the regiment was mustered out in

1899 he took the examination of the United States army for assistant surgeon, and was assigned to the barracks at St. Louis. From St. Louis he was transferred to the Presidio at San Francisco, and then sent to the Philippines, where he was promoted to Captain Assistant Surgeon, U. S. He was attached to the army service during a period of two years in the Philippines, and came to Alaska soon after his return from the islands.

During his stay in the Philippines, the country was ravaged by the plague. In some districts there was an appalling death list of native inhabitants. Dr. Moore volunteered his services, and was assigned to one of the worst districts of the island, and had charge of it until the abatement of the dread malady.

Dr. Moore is a native of Indiana, and was born October 26, 1874. Although a young man, he had a wide and varied experience in the practice of his profession.

He has traveled extensively, during which he devoted some time to the study of medicine in Milan, Italy.

NOME AND SEWARD PENINSULA, 1905

FRANCES KNAPP MORGAN

Frances Knapp was born October 5, 1869, in the college town of Middlebury, Vermont. Her father was in the printing business and later became editor of the MIDDLEBURY REGISTER. Before his gubernatorial appointment in Sitka, Alaska, he also became a lawyer. Her mother, Martha Severance Knapp was a painter with a strong interest in landscapes. She had two brother, George and Edwin, and a sister, Mary.

In 1890, upon graduation from Wellesley College, Frances "Fanny" Knapp joined her family in Sitka, Alaska, to act as secretary to her father, Judge Lyman E. Knapp, who had been appointed third territorial governor of Alaska. It was during her three years in Sitka that she observed the culture of the Tlingit Indians and collected tribal tales. In 1893, she moved with her family to Seattle where she wrote her book, THE THLINKETS OF SOUTHEASTERN ALASKA, containing the collection of Thingit tribal tales, but her notes and the manuscript were lost during the move to Seattle. In 1901, Frances Knapp married Everett R. Morgan. The couple lived, at various times, in Seattle, the Cascades, and Portland, Oregon. Everett Morgan died in 1946, one year after Morgan lost her eyesight at age 76. She wrote about her blindness in an article titled "Sight and Insight" concluding, "We, who are without physical sight, live, for the most part, in the realm of thought." It was this realization that led Frances Knapp Morgan to write her autobiography, OUT OF THE MIST.

In 1959, Frances Morgan recovered her lost notes and manuscript, and sent them to her cousin, Pauline Winchester Inman, for revision and publication. Rather than editing the tales as a companion volume, Inman collaborated with Frances Knapp Morgan to incorporate the published work, THE THLINKETS OF SOUTHEASTERN ALASKA, and the unpublished manuscript, TALES OF THE SITKA INDIANS, into one volume, a new enlarged version titled BLUEJAY FLY WITH ME. The manuscript was never published.

Frances Morgan's rekindled interest in Alaska led to her donation of her mother's paintings (Martha Severance Knapp) of Sitka and Wrangell, to the Alaska State Museum in Juneau in 1959, Alaska's year of statehood. Frances Morgan died on May 12, 1965 in Portland, Oregon.

ALASKA STATE HISTORICAL LIBRARY   (ms 127)

CLYDE L. MORRIS

Clyde L. Morris is the leading ditch contractor of Seward Peninsula. He came to Nome in the spring of 1900, and engaged in mining on the beach. He subsequently conducted mining operations on Osborne and Center Creeks, but failing to find a rich pay-streak he quit mining to engage in the transfer and freight business in Nome. From a modest beginning with two horses and a wagon, he has attained to the position of one of the largest contractors in Northwestern Alaska. This season, 1905, he has a contract for the construction of near 100 miles of ditches. To accomplish this volume of work he will take to Nome, on the first fleet of the Nome steamers, 108 head of horses and will employ not less than 500 men.

Since the beginning of ditch work in Seward Peninsula he has been prominently identified with that country as a contractor. He constructed the Hot Air Mining Company's ditch, a ditch for the Wild Goose Mining Company from Center Creek to the pumping plant, the Northland Mining Company's ditch from Balto Creek to Berg Creek on Snake River, a five-mile section of Flambeau-Hastings' Ditch, seven miles of ditch for the Midnight Sun Ditch Company in the Solomon region, and eight miles of ditch for the Solomon River Hydraulic Mining Co. He has now the largest equipment for ditch building in Northwestern Alaska, and will be the largest employer of men in the Nome country in 1905. His contracts for ditch construction this year amount to $300,000, and include contracts for the Seward Ditch and Cedric Ditch.

Mr. Morris is a native of Pomeroy, Washington. He was born September 2, 1876. When he was a small boy the family moved to Oregon and subsequently went to California. His early education was obtained in the public schools of San Francisco. In 1889 his family moved to Port Townsend, Washington, where his mother still resides. Mr. Morris attended the Port Townsend schools, worked a year at the printers' trade, was engaged in the dairy business and took a commercial course in the Acme Business College. In 1898 he went to Vancouver Island, British Columbia, and was employed as accountant by the Mount Sicker and British Columbia Development Company. Later he became local manager of the Lenora Quartz Mine, one of the company's properties, and held this position until the spring of 1900.

NOME AND SEWARD PENINSULA, 1905

OTTO S. MOSES

Otto S. Moses is a young man who has been

connected with the mercantile interests of Nome and has mined in the Blue Stone region.

He was born in Germany, November 18, 1872, and immigrated to New York when a small boy. He was educated in the New York public schools and in the City College. He received his musical education from private tutors. He went to Seattle in 1900, and in the spring of that year came to Nome.

NOME AND SEWARD PENINSULA, 1905

CORNELIUS D. MURANE

C. D. Murane was born in Freeborn County, Minnesota, February 6, 1867. He is a farmer's son and received his education in the high school of Austin, Minnesota, subsequently taking a course in a business college. He was graduated from the law department of the Northern Indiana Normal School in 1890, and opened a law office and began the practice of his profession in Valparaiso. He practiced also in Austin, Minnesota, and moved in 1892 to North Yakima, Washington. He practiced his profession in the State of Washington and during a part of this time was the attorney for a large mining corporation operating near White Sulphur Springs.

In February, 1898, he started for Dawson over the Stikeen route via Teslin Lake. He staid one year in Dawson and came to Nome in 1899, arriving in the month of October. He operated a rocker in the famous Nome beach diggings, and subsequently tried mining in the Nome country for a year, after which he resumed the practice of law. At the municipal election in April, 1904, he was elected to the office of municipal judge.

Mr. Murane was married in 1892. Mrs. Murane was formerly Miss Lydia E. Millard. He is the devoted father of three boys: Millard C., Edward Elmer and Ralph.

NOME AND SEWARD PENINSULA, 1905

GEORGE MURPHY

The political history of Alaska and the municipal history of Nome, would not be complete without mentioning George Murphy.

Alaska, like all frontier parts of the United States, had long been neglected by Congress and the matter of sending a delegate to Washington has been discussed. Mr. Murphy's successful handling of public affairs, and high personal integrity, made him a logical candidate for a representative. The Nome chamber of commerce by a unanimous vote elected Mr. Murphy, and instructed him to advocate such measures at Washington. Although a stranger in Washington, he secured one-half of all the revenues and licenses collected within municipalities in Alaska for school and municipal expenditures--a quarter of a million dollars has been retained in the territory for public needs.

His mission being successful, he was again induced the following year, this time by the city council, to return to Washington the next season, and attempt to secure the remaining half of all revenue and licenses, and while not securing immediate passage of this bill, it was framed and introduced under his direction, and passed at the next session of Congress.

Mr. Murphy has always been identified with the Democratic party; has never occupied a public office, but accepted the chairmanship of the Democratic Central Committee of Helena, Montana, in 1897, was a delegate from Nome to the National Democratic Convention at St. Louis in 1904, and was selected as chairman of the Alaska delegation.

Mr. Murphy was born in Carrolton, Illinois, July 22, 1862. He was reared on a farm and educated in the public schools of his native town. When twenty years of age he went west, and after a long and arduous trip, located in Montana, where he followed various business enterprises until the Klondike excitement in 1897. Soon after receiving news of the Klondike strike he started for the new gold fields via Skagway and Dyea Pass. Like the other pioneer prospectors who went to Dawson, he built a boat on Lake Lindeman. He arrived in Dawson October 3, , after a trip of fifty-eight days, and engaged in mining and merchandising until the following fall, when he went out for the winter, visiting his old home in Helena, Montana, intending to return the following spring. Upon arriving at Skagway in the spring of 1899, he learned that the ice in the lake had not broken, and he returned to Seattle to purchase merchandise to take to Dawson. When he arrived in Seattle the Nome excitement was at its height, and he changed his plans and secured passage on the steamer ROANOKE, bound for Nome and St. Michael He has since been identified with the commercial interests of Nome, and is the owner of both city and mining property in the town and district.

NOME AND SEWARD PENINSULA, 1905

A. J. NELSON

A.J. Nelson was born and raised on a farm in Minnesota. He departed for Seattle, Washington in December, 1896. While in this city visiting relatives, he heard of the Klondike placer strike, and on March 17, 1897, took passage on the steamer Alki for Juneau, from that point going to Dyea at the head of Lynn canal. There were three partners in Mr. Nelson's party, and among them they had 3,000 pounds of supplies. They packed this outfit on their backs over the Chilkoot Pass. When they arrived at the head of Thirtymile river, they whip-sawed lumber, built a boat and floated down to the head of Lake Labarge. To cross that large body of water, they hauled the boat and supplies on handsleds over the slush ice, to the head of the Yukon river. After camping there about a week, the ice began to break, and they followed the ice jams, reaching Dawson May 17th. Mr. Nelson spent eight years in the Dawson country, prospecting, working part of the time for day's wages, merchandising, mining on his own ground and freighting. He left for the new Fairbanks camp early in the summer of 1904, and while there was employed by Anderson Bros. & Nerland, as a bookkeeper, and later as bookkeeper and salesman for the Fairbanks

Lumber Company. For the last six years, Mr. Nelson has served as specialty salesman in Alaska, and writing insurance as a side line. At the present time, he is chiefly occupied as sales supervisor for the Willametter Building and Loan Association of Portland, Oregon. Mrs. Nelson was sister of the late Thomas Tonseth of Fairbanks and Mrs. J. A. Slipern, now in Los Angeles.

ALASKA WEEKLY, April 18, 1930

N. J. NICHOLSON

N.J. Nicholson is a construction pioneer. Since he went to Alaska in 1898, he has probably handled more construction of various kinds than any man in the Territory. It was early in May, 1898, that "Nick," as he is better known in Alaska, sailed out of the harbor of Seattle on the bark HAYDEN BROWN, bound for St. Michael. He landed at the mouth of the Yukon river on July 4th of that year after the ship had landed passengers on the Nome beach, and immediately went to work for the N.A.T.& T. Company. the following year he went to Nome where he worked at his trade as a carpenter and builder and then on to Fairbanks in 1904 and 1905. He afterwards returned to Nome, staying there until 1909. While in Fairbanks he was a member of the firm of Rutherford Raymond & Nicholson, which handled most of the construction work of that camp. Then Nick built oil stations for the Standard Oil Company at Petersburg and Ketchikan, and along in 1923 went with Bishop Peter Trimble Rowe to take charge of the construction work of the various churches, missions and hospitals that the bishop was building in Alaska. Since then Nick has built for the church buildings at Wrangell, Nenana, Tanana, Fairbanks, St. John-in-the-Wilderness, Stephen's Village, and other points. He has been in charge of the mission gas boat, THE PELICAN, and takes a portable sawmill with him on his trips, and wherever he lands near a stand of timber he is ready to start any kind of building that may be needed.

ALASKA WEEKLY, January 31, 1930

P. THOMAS NIXON

Mr. Nixon is a farmer's son, and was born near Maxville, Perry County, Ohio, November 10, 1876. His people are of Scotch ancestry, and have resided in America since Colonial days. He lived on the farm until he was eighteen years old when he resolved to seek his fortune in the West. He stopped in Dakota for awhile, afterward went to Vancouver, and the spring of 1899 found him at Skagway, Alaska. Later in the season he went to Dawson. He prospected in the Porcupine country, and in the spring of 1900 came down the Yukon in a row boat, following the ice. He stopped in St. Michael a couple of months, and did not arrive in Nome until October of that year.

In the winter of 1901 he and another man pulled a sled, loaded with 500 pounds of supplies, from Nome to the Kougarok District, most of the winter season being spent in prospecting in this region. But he didn't strike anything rich until the fall of 1902, when he and his partners found a fortune in an ancient channel on the left limit of Dry Creek.

Mr. Nixon is the owner of some producing properties on Banner Creek, a tributary of the Nome River.

NOME AND SEWARD PENINSULA, 1905

JOHN NOON

John Noon was born in Red Bluff, Ca. in August 10, 1859. He grew to manhood in the state of his birth, and followed mining for a livelihood, varying this occupation at times by running hotels. Twenty-five years ago, Mr. Noon went to Alaska going to Juneau. He remained in Southeastern Alaska for a few years, and then returned to his native state. When news of the great gold discovery in the Klondike was flashed throughout the world, Mr. Noon again headed for the Northland. The spring of 1897 found him in Dawson. He worked 37 above discovery on Bonanza and made some money, but the claim was not a bonanza. He joined the stampede to the new diggings at Nome in 1899, but returned to Dawson in the fall.

In 1900, he went to the Koyukuk country, returning to Nome in 1901. That same year found him and his old partner, Cal. Brosius, now a business man of Seward, building the first dock at Ellamar, where the Ellamar copper mine was being developed by J.D. Meenach, the mining man now of Seattle. Mr. Noon then went to Seward, construction work having started on the then Alaska Central railroad. From Seward, he went to Fairbanks, remaining there until 1905. Then the rich gold quartz mines of Nevada were struck and he was soon on the ground, going to Goldfield. But the lure of the North caused him to return, and in 1906, he ran a roadhouse on Thompson's Pass, on the Valdez-Fairbanks road. In 1908, Mr. Noon returned to Seward, again joining his old partner, Mr. Brosius in a manufacturing business.

Mr. Noon married Martha Kepfe in 1909. One child, John Henry was born March 22, 1911. While in Seward, he was a member of the Alaska legislative assembly, and served on the town council.

Mr. Noon died in Portland, Oregon, July 26, 1928. He leaves a wife and son.

ALASKA WEEKLY, July 27, 1923

JOHN A. OBRIEN

Captain John O'Brien was born in Cork, Ireland, January 29th, 1851.

He went to sea as a boy and served his apprenticeship on a deepwater fullrigged sailing ship. Sailing from China to San Francisco in 1888, with the first shipment of Chinese coolies ever transported to the united States. They rebelled and murdered several of the ship's officers, including the captain. O'Brien immediately took command of the situation, quelled the mutiny and brought the ALLIANCE to anchor in San Francisco Bay.

For Many years he conveyed Chinese labor to the united States and to Canada, to assist in the construction of trans-continental railroads. Several of these later became successful merchants in this country and were numbered among Captain O'Brien's closest friends.

In 1879, as master of the bark Alice Dickerman, Captain O'Brien took the first full cargo of Frazer River salmon to London, England. Five years later he figured in an exploit which established his prestige as a sailor. At that time the steamer UMATILLA was the largest passenger boat operating on the Pacific Coast and used both sail and steam as her motive power. During a snowstorm, this big ship went on the rocks outside Capt Flattery.

The captain, along with passengers and crew, abandoned the ship. But First Mate O'Brien and several crew members refused to abandon the ship. They managed to bring the steamer to Esquimalt, British Columbia, with the gunwales almost awash.

For five years Captain O'Brien was master of the steamship PREMIER operating between Puget Sound ports and Vancouver, B.C. He relinquished his command to take charge of the steamer CHAS. C. WETMORE, which he piloted from the Great Lakes around Cape Horn to San Francisco where this ship created considerable interest in marine circles as being the first whaleback steamer on the Pacific Coast.

The WETMORE proved to be a poor design and hard to steer. She was wrecked near Marshfield. The crew abandoned the ship, but Capt. O'Brien and a seaman named Holmes refused to leave their posts. They lashed themselves to the rigging and stayed with the ship, until they were rescued five days later.

Commanding the steamship ROSALIE, Captain O'Brien pioneered the gold rush to the Klondike.

During the month of June, 1874, Captain John A. O'Brien steered a ship into the harbor of Wrangell, Alaska. A gold strike had been reported in the Cassair and Capt. O'Brien had been commissioned to investigate the character and value of the new diggings. He explored the headwaters of the Yukon via Teslin Lake and upon returning to his ship and reporting his findings to his associates, resulted in the half century epoch of development of the great Northland.

Later he was transferred to the Seattle-Nome run and for many years commanded the steamer VICTORIA, which ship, battling its way through the ice field, was invariably the first to reach Nome. In command of the steamer YUCATAN on the Alaskan run over a quarter of a century ago, Captain O'Brien was seriously injured by an Italian laborer who ran amuck and stabbed the master mariner and two of the ship's mates.

Shortly after this episode the old skipper, saved the lives of five men and a woman who were blown out to sea in a small ship during a terrible off-shore storm. for five days they battled with the elements and were about to founder when rescued.

To Captain O'Brien the South Seas was a playground. He has visited every known group of islands in those waters, in the days of "wooden ships and iron men." Over a decade ago he commanded the steamer Buford on the world's first tour of the South Seas.

Among his passengers were many notables and millionaires. Jack London was a great friend of the old mariner's and his letters today assert the fact that Capt. O'Brien furnished him with several of the leading characters for his "Call of the Wild." Johnny O'Brien has been set out in Rex Beach's "Iron Trail." This Alaskan author enjoyed the close friendship of his sea-going friend and corresponded with him regularly.

On January 21, 1879, he married Emily Conroy, the daughter of Capt. John Conroy, who came to San Diego, Calif. in 1848, a captain of the first American troops landing there. The marriage took place in San Francisco at the old St. Mary's Cathedral. Four children blessed the union. Mrs. Kathleen Ackerman of Topeka, Kansas, and John A O'Brien, Jr. of Roseville, Calif., survive.

On the 21st of last January, Mr. and Mrs. O'Brien celebrated their golden wedding as Capt. Johnny expresses it "My first and only wife, just like whiskey, she gets better with age."

Captain John A. O'Brien died in Seattle, Washington, August 4, 1931.

ALASKA WEEKLY, Aug. 2, 1929, Aug. 7, 1931

HENRY OELBAUM

Henry Oelbaum was born near Hamburg, Germany, in 1860. At the age of fourteen he went to America and soon found his way to Chicago, where he conducted a decorating enterprise for twelve years.

In December, 1897, he left Chicago for the Klondike. He and his party of eight took passage in a small sailing vessel. The little boat was loaded with provisions, outfits, 200 dogs, twelve horses and 120 passengers. The weather was bad and she was sixteen days out from Vancouver to Skagway, landing January, 1898. Mr. Oelbaum met with the usual hardships encountered by early prospectors of that year who undertook the journey to Dawson over the Chilkoot. His party broke up before leaving Skagway, and he and his partner, P. Freitag, determined to make the journey alone.

The first day out from Skagway Mr. Freitag broke his leg, and that necessitated Mr. Oelbaum returning to Skagway, where he left his friend to receive medical aid. Mr. Oelbaum put to work and sledged the outfits over the pass to Bennett and then returned for his partner, who by this time was able to make the journey. Mr. Oelbaum had built a boat out of boards he had sawed, large enough to carry the outfits and party of three.

At Stewart River Mr. Oelbaum prospected for gold without success, and returned to Skagway overland. In the spring of 1899, he became influenced by Missionary Hultberg, who advised him to go to Nome. He arrived on the Roanoke, and pitched his tent on the tundra on the place where the city hall now stands.

Mr. Oelbaum did not work on the beach, but began looking over the country, and to him belongs the credit of gold discovery on Solomon River. He has opened up two valuable claims on

Solomon River, and has interests in Little Creek, Nome District.

NOME AND SEWARD PENINSULA, 1905

DOROTHY OGBURN O'KEEFE

Dorothy Ogburn went to Dawson, Y.T., with her parents, Mr. and Mrs. R.J. Ogburn, in 1904. For a year or more she lived on Last Chance Creek, then returned to Dawson City, where she attended school. In 1915, she married Larry O'Keefe. In 1918, she accompanied her husband to Nenana, where he assumed charge of the Northern Commercial Company store at that point. Mr. O'Keefe passed away in the spring of 1920, a victim of the "flu" epidemic. Two sons were born to Dorothy and her husband; Larry, Jr., born in Dawson, and Billy, born in Nenana. Dorothy came Outside in the fall of 1920 and went to Wichita, Kansas, where she lived two years. Upon her return to Seattle, she became manager of the Alaska Department of Frederick & Nelson's store, resigning recently to become Coast representative of a New York firm setting institutional supplies.

ALASKA WEEKLY, December 26, 1930

IRA D. ORTON

He was born in Princeton, Missouri, March 11, 1871. He was graduated by the Princeton High School and the State University of Iowa. From the State University he received the degrees of A. B. and LL. D. Mr. Orton's father is H. G. Orton, a well known attorney of Northern Missouri, and a descendant of an English colonist who came to America in 1640. Mr. H. G. Orton was a Union soldier in the Civil War, and was so severely wounded at the battle of Cross Lanes that he has been crippled ever since.

After Ira D. Orton received his law degree in 1892, he went to San Francisco, and was associated with the law firm of Reddy, Campbell & Metson. He came to Nome in 1900 and established an office. He is attorney for some of the largest corporations in the Nome country, a director of and attorney for the

Miners and Merchants Bank, the Electric Light and Power Company and the Moonlight Springs Water Company.

Mr. Orton was married in 1897; his wife was Claudia M. Ewing, daughter of a prominent lawyer of Iowa, and a member of an old family of the United States. The issue of this marriage is one child, a daughter, Helen, aged seven years. Mrs. Orton died in 1899. June 14, 1903, Mr. Orton contracted a second marriage with Miss Viola M. Codding, of Nome.

NOME AND SEWARD PENINSULA, 1905

JOHN Y. OSTRANDER

John Ostrander, one of the original townsite owners of Cordova, is a native son of Washington, having been born on a donation claim on the Cowlitz river at a place now know as Ostrander. It was during the early fifties when the great West was still mostly an unbroken wilderness that Dr. Ostrander, the father of the Cordova resident, came across the plains with a pack train from Missouri and settled in Washington. "Judge" Ostrander, as he is called most often by his Alaskan acquaintances, was educated in the public schools and studied law in Portland, Ore., under Judge Strong, the first chief justice of the territory of Washington.

In due course the young law student was admitted to the bar and first practiced in Dayton, Washington, in 1879. He was appointed register of the United States land office in Seattle, where he also practiced law, and later came to Juneau, having been appointed United States commissioner by President Cleveland. He served until the spring of 1898 and went into Dawson where he remained two years. He returned to Juneau and after a two years' residence moved on to Valdez, arriving there in 1902.

He came to Cordova in 1909 and built the Ostrander Block. Besides his real estate and property interests in Cordova proper, and his law practice, he is interested in copper mines on Fidalgo Bay. Mrs. Ostrander also makes her

home in Cordova and has had her share of pioneer experiences.
    ALASKA-YUKON MAGAZINE, December 1910

GEORGE W. OTTERSON

    George W. Otterson, internationally known mining engineer, president of the Otterson Engineering Company, inventor of the submarine telephone used by all divers throughout the world, was born in Atlanta, Georgia, February 22, 1864. He has been actively engaged in mining for the past thirty-five years in Canada and the United States, with Seattle as his headquarters throughout the years. He went to Dawson in 1897, going over the All-Canadian or Teslin trail. In Dawson, he was the superintendent of the installation of the telephone line from Dawson to The Forks. Later, he was associated with Captain Ellis in a lease on No. 3 below discovery on Bonanza. In 1900, he headed a party of three in the Omenica district of British Columbia, where he took out $9,000 on Manson Creek. He sold his interests and left that country, only to return in 1913 and locate ground on Slate Creek. Later, he sold this ground to the Kildare Mining Company. In 1926, he again went to the Omenica district and took an option on a large part of Manson Creek, and has devoted the last three winters in building a road and taking in a small dredge to his holdings. This season, he disposed of the plant, equipment, and lease. While not engaged in mining, Mr. Otterson has been doing big construction work. He went to Honolulu in 1894, and was employed in dredging the harbor there, which took over three years. It was here that he invented the submarine telephone. He was superintendent of the first regrade work in Seattle and later was a superintendent of construction on the Seattle-Lake Washington Waterway. He had charge of a channel on the upper portion of Snake river in Oregon. He is he inventor of the Otterson Automatic Jack for motor vehicles which is manufactured in Seattle by the Otterson

Engineering Corporation.
                ALASKA WEEKLY, October 18, 1929

CLAYTON H. PACKARD
   Clayton H. Packard was born in Wisconsin and came to Washington with his parents in 1870, where his father opened a trading post on White River, removing to Snohomish shortly after. As a young man, he attended the University of Washington, then situated in what is now the Metropolitan trading area in Seattle, and his first newspaper work was on the Seattle Post-Intelligencer. After a short time on the P-I he went to Snohomish and established the Snohomish Eye. From that time on his life was a series of newspaper and mining adventures.
   In 1897 he went to Alaska with the Ingraham party and spent a year in the Kotzebue Sopund country; came Outside for a short time and returned to Nome in 1900 with his son, Irving, spending the next two years on a law on Hunter Creek. Subsequently he was associated with various newspapers in the Northwest states, and in Alaska, including the Seward Gateway, and from 1915 to 1919 the ANCHORAGE TIMES. Always seeking the end of the rainbow, his newspaper work was plentifully interspersed with prospecting and mining in Alaska, British Columbia and Washington.
   Many years ago as a result of a strenuous prospecting trip in the Cascades he suffered a stroke, which paralyzed one side of his body, and from which he never entirely recovered.
   Clayton Packard died in Colorado Springs, March 2, 1932. Two sons, Irving A. Packard and Frank H. Packard, both of Bainbridge Island, Washington, and a sister, Mrs. Nell Witherell of Bridgeport, N.J., survive him.
                ALASKA WEEKLY, May 6, 1932

ROBERT J. PARK
   R. J. Park is one of the pioneers of Nome. He is a conspicuous figure in its history, and a well known and successful citizen of the community. He is a native of Ontario, Canada,

and will be forty-four years old June 22, 1906. He accompanied his folks to North Dakota in 1871. In 1885 he began a line of work, traveling as a salesman for safes, cash registers and bicycles, which he followed for fifteen years.

The Klondike strike gave him the gold fever, and he went to Dawson in 1898. Since that time the northern country has been his home, and the place where are located his business interests.

While descending the Yukon late in the season of 1898 he was "frozen in," and compelled to go into winter quarters on Dall River. His wife was with him and a participant in this experience. Sending her to the states via Dawson after the severe part of the winter had passed, he left Rampart in March, 1899, with two dogs and a sled, without tent or stove, and started alone on a trip down the Yukon to Nome. An account of this trip is an interesting story of itself. He was thirty days on the trail, camping whenever it was possible with wood choppers or natives. There were three nights, however, when he was compelled to make a camp in the snow and sleep before the camp fire.

Arriving in Nome early in April he was what appeared to him to be the most desolate looking country he ever beheld. Near Nome he had fallen in with two men who had a tent, and the party had been augmented by another stampeder who had a stove. The Nome beach where the town now stands, was covered with seven feet of snow. There was no evidence of a town or camp at that time. The prospectors were compelled to dig a big hole in the snow to find ground upon which to pitch their tent. The tent was erected where the Eldorado Saloon now stands.

He arranged with R. T. Lyng, manager of the Alaska Commercial Company, for the purchase of a large tent and a stock of liquors and cigars. The tent was a striped one, and is shown in an engraving in this book, which was the first photograph ever made of Nome.

Seventy days after buying this lot he sold a one-quarter interest in it for $22,000. As the result of his business during this summer, and his speculations in mining and city property, he left Nome in the fall with $70,000 in cash, and he owned property valued at $100,000.

In the early summer of 1905 Mr. Park disposed of his interests in Nome, and returned to the states. He married Miss Louisa Couteron, of San Francisco, December 5, 1895.

NOME AND SEWARD PENINSULA, 1905

JOHN P. PEARSON

J. P. Pearson has shown his faith in the future of quartz mining in Seward Peninsula by his investments in quartz property near Nome and in the Solomon River region during the past two years. He came to Nome in 1903, and has been active in the industrial field since his arrival. Besides being a large stockholder and director in two quartz mining companies, he owns some placer ground, is associated with a ditch enterprise, and has a road-house and mercantile business on Solomon River.

Mr. Pearson is a native of Sweden, and was born September 1, 1856. He is the son of a farmer, and was educated in the schools of Tirup and Alfredstorp, receiving a special course in agriculture, which qualified him for the work in which he was subsequently engaged in his native land. After leaving school he was employed as the superintendent of a three-thousand-acre farm, one of the largest in Sweden, at Sunnerborg, State of Smoland. He also had charge of a flour mill on the estate. He filled this position during a period of five years, when he decided to go to America. In 1882 he arrived in the State of Minnesota, and engaged in the creamery business. Until 1890 he was extensively interested in this industry, and in addition thereto owned a large milk business in St. Paul, being one of the organizers and vice-president and superintendent of the Minnesota Milk Company.

In 1890 he sold out and went to the State of Washington, where he lost money in real estate investments. Undiscouraged, he went into dairy and stock farming. For a period of four years from 1891 he had the management of stock farms and dairies in Oregon, and for five years subsequently was in the dairy business in California. During this latter period he was prominently identified with the dairy industry.

In 1900 he became a member of the firm of Sutherland & Pearson, grocers, in Oakland, California, and disposed of his interest in 1903 to go to Nome.

NOME AND SEWARD PENINSULA, 1905

GEORGE W. PENNINGTON

Pennington was born in Fredricktown, Md., October 12, 1856, one of nine sons. As a youth he became a traveling representative of a Boston Mercantile company in the western states.

Called by the lure of gold, he headed for Dawson in 1897.

After several unsuccessful attempts at mining he went into the mercantile business with North American Trading & Transportation Co. and to the mutual profit of the company and himself he brought his wide mercantile experience into practice.

His mercantile career, merged into his years in the lumber business in which he was associated with one of the leading lumber dealers in the Territory.

For many years beginning in 1904 he lived in Fairbanks, later moved to Nenana and remained there until 1919, when he came to the United States to visit his children. He never went back.

In Alaska he took a prominent part in the development of the Territory. He served two terms as Senator in the Territorial Legislature. He was instrumental in building the Alaska Railway and in service of the government contributed largely to shaping the educational system of the rapidly growing country. He was president of the Alaska Petroleum Co., which he formed in 1926. He was also secretary-treasurer of the Dixon-Creek and

McIlroy oil companies in Texas for many years.

An incident during his career in Alaska as told by his friends revealed part of his fine character. While in the employ of a trading company in Forty Mile, he learned that a motherless child was in danger of dying, if it remained with only the father to care for it in a remote section of the frozen northland.

He hitched up his dogteam and made a dangerous trip across the frozen wastes in two days and nights to the remote shack. he packed the girl child which was only a few days old into the sled and made the return journey safely. After the child grew to womanhood, he met her in the United States.

There is behind the Pennignton line a colorful history. In pre-revolutionary days, a Captain Pennington established himself in New Jersey after he had killed an admiral of the British navy in a duel. An early descendant of Captain Pennington served as governor of New Jersey.

He married Mollie Rittenhouse in Butte, Montana in 1898.

George W. Pennington died November 4, 1933 in Amarillo, Texas. A son, George W. Pennington, Jr., a Wilmington, Del., trader and two daughters survive him. The daughters are Mrs. Nellie Clark, Hollywood, Cal., and Mrs. Anna Trott, Wilmington, Del.

ALASKA WEEKLY, November 17, 1933

WILLIAM T. PERKINS (Col.)

Col. Wm. T. Perkins lived in the Northland from 1898 to 1909. He is known throughout Alaska, having been one of the moving forces in the commercial, as well as in the mining development of the territory. He was a delegate for the republican national convention of 1904 and 1908.

William Perkins was the Alaska manager of the old Northwestern Steamship Company(now merged with the Alaska Steamship Company), and with the late John Rosene opened up Northeastern Siberia to trade and organized the Northwestern Fisheries. He surveyed the proposed Alaska Midland railroad from Haines, via Lake Kluane to Dawson and Fairbanks, was associated with the Powell Bros. in the building and operation of the first dredge at Nome, the forerunner of the great dredging plants now in operation; was associated with the late J. M. Davidson in obtaining the properties sold to the Fairbanks Exploration Company.

Col. Perkins, for the past twenty years, has been a resident and an active factor in the upbuilding of Seattle, with offices at present in the Central building. He is president of the Northern Securities Company and treasurer of the Puget Sound Mortgage Securities, Incorporated, and an active trading member of the Seattle Stock Exchange and the Seattle Curb and Mining Exchange. He is personally sponsoring the development of thirteen crown-granted claims on Bear River, known as the Vancouver Mines, Limited, in the Portland Canal district.

He was appointed by Gov. Lister as a member of the Board of Regents of the University of Washington and was chairman of the committee that brought Dr. Henry Suzzallo to Seattle as president of the institution. He is a graduate of the University of Michigan and an attorney and member of the Washington Bar.
ALASKA WEEKLY, June 15, 1928

NELS PETERSON
Nels Peterson was born on the Island of Szaland, Denmark, October 23, 1850. His father tilled a small farm on the island, and the boy obtained his education in the public schools of his native land. Mr. Peterson has been a bread-winner ever since he was eleven years old. In 1872 he left the old country and went to the United States. He spent two years in the iron mines of Lake Superior, and another two years in the city of Chicago. From Chicago he went to the northern parts of Michigan and Minnesota, and during a period of nine years was a railroad contractor engaged in construction work. His last railroad work, in

1885, was on the Canadian Pacific.

Quitting railroad work he engaged in mining in British Columbia, and two years later went to Seattle. He resided in Seattle from 1887 to 1894, and during this time he was engaged in the grocery and transfer business, and the work of contracting to clear land for city improvements. In June, 1894, he went to Southern Oregon and for three years prospected and mined in this state. Returning to Seattle in 1897, he outfitted for Alaska, and on March 25 sailed on the City of Mexico for Dyea.

He arrived in Dawson, May 20. His entire assets upon his arrival in the Yukon mining camp were ninety-five cents. Working a month for wages at $15.00 a day, he obtained a "grub-stake" and started prospecting. He located 5 Below on the left limit of Bonanza Creek, and was the first man to find pay in the benches of this stream. He borrowed three sluice-boxes from "Tex" Ricard, and in three weeks cleaned up $1,100. The famous Gold Hill of the Klondike gold fields lay between his claim and Skookum Creek. Careful observation by Mr. Peterson of the character of gold in Bonanza and Eldorado Creeks and in Skookum Creek, convinced him that an ancient channel or deposit of concentrated placers existed in Gold Hill. So when Nathan Kresge, his partner on the trail to Dawson, came to his camp, Mr. Peterson induced him to locate a bench claim on the right limit of Big Skookum where he thought the old channel might be discovered. On the claim located by Mr. Kresge, in which Mr. Peterson was to have a half interest, the first stroke of the pick removed the moss covering of a gravel deposit and turned over a $10.40 nugget. Taking a pan of the gravel to water he washed it and secured $8.00. With rockers made of tomato boxes, in eight days he and his partner cleaned up $6,375. Two days after they made the strike there were a thousand people on Gold Hill locating claims.

In the spring of 1899 he cleaned up all of his mining interests and bought the river steamers Bonanza King and Eldorado, paying for them $50,000. But he found the transportation business different from mining. He came into active competition with the Canadian Development Company, and in the fall of 1900 he landed in Seattle broke.

In the spring of 1901 he sailed on the Centennial for Nome and arrived in this camp in worse financial condition than he was in when he arrived in Dawson. He didn't have a cent. But his wife who had remained in Dawson the previous winter reached Nome a few days after his arrival, and she had $800, which she had managed to save out of the wreck of his Klonkike accumulations. Mr. Peterson went to Teller and prospected in the Agiapuk region, but meeting with no success he returned to Nome.

In November 1904, he went into a partnership with John Johnson, who had a lease on the Portland Bench. They drifted on bedrock at total distance of 160 feet, and finally they struck the pay. It proved to be the richest gravel deposit ever found in any of the northern gold fields, possibly the richest ever found in the world. A pan of gravel taken from bedrock yielded $1,200, and Mr. Peterson says that a pan could have been picked that would have yielded $3,000, possibly $5,000. In sixty days the claim yielded gold valued at $413,000.

Mr. Peterson was married in Dawson, July 4, 1899. They have one child, Nels Joseph Peterson, born April 12, 1900.

NOME AND SEWARD PENINSULA, 1905

VIRGINIA CLARK PODMORE

Mrs. Virginia Clark Podmore was born in Virginia, January 20, 1895. Her father is a Presbyterian minister who had various pastorates and finally accepted a charge in Alaska, where he resided with his family for a period of eighteen years, many in Wrangell. Here Virginia Podmore received her earliest school training. She graduated from the Academy at Tacoma, Wash., and later received a diploma from the Whitworth School of Oratory. Her A.B. degree she received from the

University of Washington at Seattle. She pursued the study of music all through her regular college course and later specialized in music at the New England Conservatory at Boston. It was while she was at the University of Washington that she met J.A. Podmore, her future husband. He is also a graduate of that institution. During the World War she taught school on Kodiak Island in Alaska. After the war she took post graduate work at the Emerson School of Oratory at Boston. During that year her parents, the Rev. and Mrs. J.S. Clark moved to Florida, taking up their residence near Sanford where they still live. Virginia came at the end of the school year to be with her parents. It was there that she was united in marriage with Mr. J.A. Podmore, her father performing the wedding ceremony, September 10, 1920.

After their marriage Mr. and Mrs. Podmore came to Winter Park where they began teaching in Rollins College. Mr. Podmore in the Department of Mathematics and Mrs. Podmore in the Department of English and Oratory, where her patience, tact and skill have endeared her to a host of Rollins graduates and former students. Many students have been heard to say that no woman connected with Rollins College ever left so deep an impression on the college and community as did Mrs. Podmore.

Virginia Clark Podmore died in Orlando, Florida, August 7, 1926. She was a member of the Woman's Club, of the Camp Fire Girls' organization and the Eastern Star, Pioneer Chapter No. 99. At the college she was active in the work of two sororities, the Phi Beta and the Sigma Phi.

ALASKA WEEKLY, September 24, 1926

ANTONIO POLET

Antonio Polet is a native of Calabria, Italy, and was born April 29, 1881, and went to America with his parents in 1892, locating in Seattle. When he was fifteen years old he began his business career, his first venture being the purchase of a cigar store with money

that he had earned and saved following the trade of a boot-black. By close application to business and economy he added to his little store of wealth. Realizing the need of a better commercial education he disposed of his business and took a course in Wilson's Modern Business College. After graduating he came to Nome in 1900 with a stock of groceries, and in partnership with Frank Aquino established the Snake River Grocery. In the fall of 1900 Mr. Polet bought his partner's interest and is now the sole proprietor of the business.
NOME AND SEWARD PENINSULA, 1905

ERNEST M. POLLEY

Mr. Polley was born on June 9, 1887 in South Boston, Mass. He was educated at Winchester High School in that state and later took a correspondence course in architecture from the International Correspondence School.

He came to Alaska as a youth in the early 1900s and was employed as a carpenter for the Alaska-Juneau mine for 14 years prior to 1918. In the summer of that year, Mr. Polley volunteered his services to the army and was sent to Camp Humphries, Virginia, and was assigned to the U.S. Engineers Training Regiment. He was discharge in February 1919, and returned to Juneau, shortly thereafter moving with his family to Sitka.

At Sitka, he assisted in the Formation of the American Legion Post and was one of its first commanders. He was elected to the Territorial Legislature for the 1923 session on the Republican ticket, and returned to Juneau in that post. He served as a Representative from the First Division.

On May 15, 1923 Mr. Polley was appointed Tax Collection Clerk for the Territory and served in that capacity for 12 years.

Mr. Polley was particularly active in American Legion affairs. He was instrumental in arranging a five-year program of activity in child welfare work for the American Legion of Alaska at the Legion's Territorial Convention in Petersburg in 1931, when he was chairman of the Child Welfare Committee for the Legion in Alaska. He also held the position of Advisory Member of the National Child Welfare Committee. Mr. Polley appeared before a number of sessions of the Territorial Legislature, endeavoring to secure better laws for incorrigible and indigent orphan children.

In 1938 he was elected Commander of the Alaska American Legion Department at the Ketchikan Convention. In 1940 he represented Alaska at the National Convention of the American Legion.

In 1935 Mr. Polley became associated with the Forest Service as Storekeeper.

Mr. Polley was a member of the Territorial Board of the Alaska Tuberculosis Assoc. and also was the representative of the American Legion on the Juneau Health Council. He also was very active in Juneau Civilian Defense and headed the Evacuation Division of that organization.

Ernest Polley died in Juneau, February 26, 1942. He is survived by Mrs. Polley, and one son, Dr. Clayton Polley, dentist at Skagway, now at Chilkoot Barracks.

DAILY ALASKA EMPIRE, February 27, 1942

FREEMAN B. PORTER

F. B. Porter was in Seattle in the early part of 1898 when he decided to join the Kotzebut Sound expedition, and arranged for transportation on the schooner M. Merrill. He wrote his fiancee, Miss Stella H. Scofield, of New York, and she came to Seattle where they were married May 27, 1898.

Mr. and Mrs. Porter spent the winter of 1898-'99 in the Kotzebue Sound country. They built a cabin on the upper waters of the Inmachuk, not far from the hot springs. They were the first white people who ever wintered in this part of the Arctic slope.

When the news of the Nome strike reached the Kotzebue Sound, Mr. Porter and his wife abandoned their cabin and took passage on the steamship Townsend for Nome. During his sojourn on the Arctic slope he found prospects on the Inmachuk River and decided to return to that area, locating one of the best mines in the country.

Mr. Porter is a native of Freeport, Maine, and was born May 3, 1869. Through his mother he is a descendant of Col. Ethan Allen. He received a public school and academic education, and at the age of sixteen went to Boston where he obtained a business course under a private tutor. He began the serious work of life as a stenographer, and was at one time stenographer for John Alexander, first vice-president of the Equitable Life Assurance Company. He filled the position of private secretary for Congressman Logan H. Roots. He has also filled positions in the offices of Kimball & Bryant, of New York, and the Mingo Smelting Company of Salt Lake. While employed by the latter company he acquired a knowledge of ores and an inclination for mining. At a later date he was connected with the Smith Premier Typewriter Company, and was in the employ of that company when he joined the Kotzebue Sound stampeders.

When he came from Kotzebue Sound in the spring of 1899 he resided in Nome continuously until 1902. He then returned to Portland, Oregon, and took up his old line of work as manager of the typewriter company, but still retained his mining interests on the Inmachuk and Kugruk Rivers and Candle Creek. Mr. Porter leased the Polar Bear Group on Inmachuk River and in the fall of 1904.

NOME AND SEWARD PENINSULA, 1905

WALTER W. POWERS

Walter W. Powers was born in Lake City, Minnesota, in 1864. He was an early-day Seattle pioneer, and was in the real estate business in this city when the Klondike strike was made. He joined in the stampede, reaching Dawson May 20, 1898. He made one trip outside in 1903, taking passage on the S.S. Islander, which was wrecked en route south. Mr. Powers swam ashore and escaped, but $28,000 in gold dust, which he was taking outside, went down with the ship. On his return North, he went to Fairbanks, then a new camp just coming in. He established himself in business there and remained for over two years, when he came outside again, locating in Seattle.

Here he organized the Seattle Park Company, which controlled the Luna Park amusement resort in West Seattle. He had real estate interests in this city, and desiring to devote more time to this industry he sold out a half interest in Luna Park May 1, 1927, and went into partnership with his old friend, Herbert S. Turner, with offices in the Securities building.

In 1897 Mr. Powers married Miss Mate M. Miller in Durand, Wisconsin. Walter Powers died April 1, 1930, in Seattle, Washington. He as a member of the Seattle Real Estate Board and the Order of Railway Conductors.

ALASKA WEEKLY, April 4, 1930

J. J. PRICE

J. J. Price, perhaps better known to the sourdoughs as Jack Price, is one of the best known mining men in all Alaska, and is almost equally well known in the yukon territory. He joined the stampede from the outside to the Klondike in 1898, reaching Dawson in the early part of that year. He mined on Skookum Gulch for a couple of years, and then in 1900 joined the stampede to the Nome gold fields. When the Fairbanks camp came in, Mr. Price was early on the ground and acquired property on the famous Cleary Creek, perhaps one of the richest creeks of the district. He was also early on the ground when the Iditarod camp came in and in company with Ellsworth Ives, another well-known Northern mining man, secured very valuable holding on Glen Gulch, a pup of Otter Creek. Mr. Price then came outside and purchased a large, improved farm in Idaho, where he lived for several years. But life on a farm was a little too slow for a he-man type like jack Price. He had been a successful mining operator and this fascinating game still had an attraction for him, as he was in fine physical

condition and still in the prime of life. With
associates, he acquired the Dan Creek Mining
Company's extensive placer holdings on Dan
Creek, in the Copper River country, from Howard
Birch, a brother of Stephen Birch, and formed
the Nicolai Mining Company. Associated with
him in this mining project as L. A. Levensaler,
the widely known mining engineer, and the heirs
of the estate of Charles E. Peabody. This is a
hydraulic operation and Mr. Price is the
general manager in charge. The opening of rich
pay on the benches of Dan Creek this season
insures a long life for this property and
altogether a profitable mining venture.
          ALASKA WEEKLY, November 2, 1928

CHARLES C. PYNE
     Charles C. Pyne was born near Brockville,
Ont., and in 1889 removed to the State of
Washington with his family. Here he followed
lumbering for a few years and then went to
Dawson by the way of St. Michael. He
prospected and mined on Bonanza and gold run
for about a year, when he left there and went
to the Koyukuk District. On this trip Mr. Pyne
used his dog-team, it taking him forty days to
make the trip over the ice, a distance of six
hundred miles. Here he prospected and mined
until the fall of 1900, when he went to Seattle
by the way of Dawson and Skagway, remaining
there until January, 1901, when he went to
Valdez. He was one of a party of eight, known
as the Casey bunch, that sledded their outfit
to the head of the Delta with horses and dogs
and landed at Casey's cache in May, 1901. He
then went down the Delta in a poling boat and
landed in the Tanana Valley in August. With
him was his partner, W.R. Smith, and these two
men built the first trading-post in the Tanana
for the firm of Hendricks & Belt. They then
went up the Chena river in October and located
what is known as Pyne Creek, and here they
prospected for two years. They returned in the
fall of 1903 and located claims on Pedro,
Goldstream and Cleary Creeks. they prospected
and mined on those creeks until the spring of

1905, when Mr. Pyne moved to the now famous Ester Creek.

Mr. Pyne owns several claims but does not work the ground himself since the fall of 1907, preferring to let his claims out on lays. Three sets of lay men are at present actively engaged in opening up and developing the bench claims opposite No. 1 above discovery, and opposite No. 1 below.

The claim on the right limit of No. 4 below has not been worked, but will be developed in the near future. There is rich pay all around it, and no doubt No. 4 bench contains the same pay.

ALASKA-YUKON MAGAZINE, January 1909

ELI QUIGLEY

Dr. Eli Quigley was born in Iowa in 1849 and was a graduate of the Kukuw Medical Institute of that state. He followed his profession several years in Grand City, Mon., afterward coming to the Pacific coast and thence to Alaska in 1893.

Dr. Eli Quigley, aged 48[?] years, died at his home in Douglas City Friday morning of paraplegia caused from injury to the spine. He leaves a family of four children, two boys and two girls, who reside in Seattle. He was buried yesterday afternoon in the new cemetery near Juneau.

ALASKA MINING RECORD, May 13, 1895

GEORGE RAABE

Captain Raabe went North from Puget Sound in 1898. He put in one year as steamboat pilot on the Stikine river, and in 1899 began his career as a pilot on the Yukon and with the close of the season, just ended, has a total of thirty full seasons to his credit as pilot between Dawson and Whitehorse. Allowing an average of sixteen round trips between the two points, he covered 14,720 miles of upper Yukon each year. At this rate, his grand total of mileage on the river in the thirty years is 441,600 miles.

Before going North, Captain Raabe was

a steamboat man on the Columbia and Willamette rivers, sailing out of Portland, Oregon. It was there he started as a young man and worked up to pilot, where he became one of the most skilled pilots of inland waters.

Born of hardy stock in old Norway, George Raabe came to America with his parents, and when but fourteen years of age sailed round Cape Horn to the Columbia river with them, and ever since has been a staunch Oregonian. His wife crossed the plains by prairie schooner from Iowa when a little girl with her parents in 1852. Despite his years Captain Raabe is alert, keen of sense in every respect. As the dean of the Yukon river fleet he retires with the highest esteem of his fellow navigators and confreres and the many with whom he has been in contact.

ALASKA WEEKLY, October 26, 1930

HARRY J. RAYMOND

Mr. Raymond was born in New York State in 1871 and resided there into young manhood. He was a graduate pharmacist but did not follow that profession after coming west.

He came to San Francisco in 1895. There he met and became associated with Mr. McBride. It was through the latter that he came to Sum Dum in 1897 as storekeeper for the Sum Dum Mining Company. In 1898 he returned to San Francisco and was married, bringing his wife back to Sum Dum. He came to Juneau in 1901, making this his home while he represented Alaska for the larger wholesale hardware firm on the Pacific coast. In 1912 he organized the H.J. Raymond Company which was operated here until 1917. Later he was connected with the Alaskan Hotel.

In 1923 he went to Bell Island Hot Spring near Ketchikan and opened a health resort. Selling out there in 1925, he returned here and went to Baranof where he opened a general merchandise business and hot springs.

In his residence there, Mr. Raymond took an active part in civic as well as business affairs. He wa a member of the City Council a number of times He was also active in the Elks Lodge for many years.

Mr. Raymond passed away in Juneau, Wednesday, December 26th from effects of blood poisoning, originating from a slight injury received some two weeks ago. He was 57 years of age, and is survived by a widow.

DAILY ALASKA EMPIRE, December 26, 1928

GEORGE HERBERT HUNTINGTON REDDING (Dr.)

In the spring of 1850 B. B. Redding arrived in San Francisco. He was one of a company of young men that brought a schooner and a cargo of lumber around the Horn to California. When they got into port they found the market well stocked with lumber. Redding was the son of the American consul at Yarmouth, Nova Scotia, at which place he was born.

B. B. Redding was successful in mining ventures and business enterprises, followed journalism for the time, was in the legislature when the capital was in Benecia, filled the position of the first secretary of state. He was also the first president of the fish commission of California.

Half a century after the arrival of B. B. Redding in San Francisco, his son, Dr. G. H. H. Redding, came to Nome, and brought a cargo of lumber, and found the market in a condition similar to the market his father found fifty years before in California.

While this venture was not the financial success anticipated at the beginning, Dr. Redding remained in Nome for two seasons, and wound up the affairs of the business with profit. Their company, the Riverside Lumber Yard, furnished most of the lumber for planking the streets of Nome. In 1903 he and A. H. Dunham purchased the Geiger toll bridge, which has since been acquired by the city. He is interested in mining property in the peninsula, and is vice president of the Alaska Placer Mining Company, with holdings on Flambeau River. This is the first Nome company organized under the laws of Alaska.

Dr. Redding was born in Sacramento, Cal.,

Dec. 16, 1860. He is descended from the early Massachusetts Colonists, who came to America in 1634 during the regime of Governor Winthrop. He traces his lineage through his mother's family to Israel Putnam. Dr. Redding was educated in the schools of Sacramento, the California Military Academy of Oakland and the Urban Academy of San Francisco. He received his degree in medicine from the Cooper Medical College, and was graduated from Bellevue Medical College, New York. He spent three years walking the hospitals of Europe, during which time he visited nearly all the notable cities of the Continent and of England. Returning to California in 1889 he practiced medicine for eight years in San Francisco. He was the first house surgeon of the San Francisco Polyclinic. He was police surgeon of San Francisco in 1894, and was also the surgeon of the Midwinter Fair. He relinquished his practice to engage in mining on the Mother Lode in California. After selling the famous Tarantula Mine he went to Karluk, Kodiak Island, in 1898, and relieved his cousin, J. A. Richardson, superintendent of the fish hatchery of the Alaska Packers Association. He was in Karluk a year, in charge of this extensive industry. Dr. Redding has made five trips to Alaska, three to Nome, one to Karluk and one to Sitka.

    He has two brothers, Albert Putnam, secretary Pacific Surety Co., and J. D. Redding, the latter one of the leading members of the bar of California and New York.

                  NOME AND SEWARD PENINSULA, 1905

ALBERT W. REED

    Dr. Reed was a native of Bakersfield, Vt. He came to Pocatello in 1890, and followed his profession in dentistry until the outbreak of the Spanish-American war in 1898, when he entered the army as chief musician of the First Regimental Band, Eighth Army Corps. Serving approximately two years in the Philippines, he was mustered out in San Francisco and returned to this city.

From 1900 until 1911 he practiced dentistry in Skagway, Alaska, after which he again took up his residence in Pocatello. He was a former member of the Idaho State Dental Society, and past president of the Southeastern Idaho Dental Society. He was a member of the United Spanish War veterans.

Dr. Albert Reed died in Pocatello, Idaho, September 26, 1930. He is survived by a wife, Helen C. Cosgrove Reed, and a daughter, Mary Lea, of Pocatello.

    ALASKA WEEKLY, October 17, 1930

THOMAS MELBURNE REED

Thomas Reed's father came West from Kentucky in the early days of California's golden career and located in Placer County, California, where Judge Reed was born January 27, 1857. The Reeds came north a few years after that to Olympia, then the chief city in Washington Territory. Thomas M. Reed, Sr. became Territorial Auditor and served in that capacity until Statehood, except for the period of Democratic control during the first Cleveland administration. He was the last Territorial auditor and became the first state auditor. For many years he was secretary of the Grand Lodge of Masons for Washington Territory and State.

Thomas M. Reed, the second, followed closely in his father's footsteps. He was prominent almost from the beginning, partly on account of the prominence of the Reed family but more on account of his own merit and ability. He graduated from the public schools at Olympia and went to Princeton where he was given an A.B. degree in 1878 after four years attendance. He was admitted to the washington bar in 1881 at Olympia and practiced there until 1889 when he was appointed Register of the U.S. Land Office at Seattle by President Harrison. In the meantime he served in the last Washington Territorial Legislature in 1887 and the first State Legislature in 1889. In 1893 he was appointed to membership on the State Land Commission by Gov. John H. McGraw.

In 1895 Gov. McGraw appointed him superior court judge for Thurston County to fill a vacancy. He was defeated for re-election two years later. Shortly thereafter Judge Reed moved to Nome where he served as United States Commissioner or practiced law until 1921 when he was appointed U.S. District Judge of the First Division. He served in the sessions of 1919 and 1921.

Judge Reed died April 30, 1928 in Juneau(?). He is survived by a wife, a son and a daughter by a former marriage, and a brother, Mark E. Reed of Shelton Wash. who is a state representative.

ALASKA WEEKLY, May(4, 11,) 25, 1928

W. B. REINHARDT

W. B. Reinhardt was born in Lincoln County, North Carolina; he graduated from the North Carolina State College, and came to Seattle to work in the drawing room of Moran Bros. Shipyards on the battleship Nebraska. After a few months, he went to Dawson, Y.T., where he was associated with the Dawson Electric Light and Power Company for almost twenty years, and where he met and married Miss Lilly Buckles. Mr. Reinhardt left Dawson in 1922, and settled in Seattle. Later he became affiliated with the Franklin-Wicks Company as a salesman. In 1929, with Mr. O.F. Kastner, another Yukoner and owner and publisher of the Dawson Daily News, he bought out Mr. Wicks interests, and now runs the business under the name of the Kaster-Reinhardt Franklin Company. Mr. Reinhardt is the president and manager.

ALASKA WEEKLY, November 15, 1919

FRANK H. RICHARDS

Frank H. Richards was appointed United States Marshal of the Second Judicial Division of Alaska June 4, 1901, and he held the position until the fall of 1904. He was born in McHenry County, Illinois, March 21, 1858. He lived on a farm until he was twenty-four years old. He immigrated to the Puget Sound country in 1883, and was with Eugene Canfield when he made the first survey of the railroad between British Columbia and Seattle. Later he studied law at the Columbia Law School and was admitted to the bar, but never engaged in the practice of the profession. He was appointed Harbor Commissioner of the State of Washington July 1, 1890, and resigned the office in January, 1893. He was elected state senator from Whatcom County, and served in the biennial session of '91 and '93. He was chairman of the Fisheries Committee and the first legislator in the interest of the fish industry in Washington.

The panic in 1893 swept away his accumulations and a few years later he went to Alaska. After prospecting in Southeastern Alaska he went to the Forty-Mile country in 1899, and arrived in Nome in 1900. October 8, 1903, he married Miss Bessie Wilke, of Chicago. When he was a school boy her father was his teacher.

NOME AND SEWARD PENINSULA, 1905

GEORGE A. RICHARDS

George A. Richards, the new Department Commander of the American Legion in Alaska, has been the commander of Ketchikan Post, the largest post in the territory, since last November. The post has activities, such as three very successful plays; a special edition of the Ketchikan Alaska Chronicle which attained a circulation of 5,000, and other affairs, has succeeded in raising over one thousand dollars for its building fund.

Commander Richards was born in Lawrence, Kansas, moving to a cattle ranch in Montana with his family when a small boy; then in 1911 to California, where he graduated from the Long Beach Polytechnic High. During school years he was a star man on the track and football teams and was interested in dramatic and other school activities.

The commander has seen service on the Mexican border, volunteering in August, 1915 in the 7th California National Guard, which was later the 160th Infantry of the 40th division, and being sent to Nogales, Arizona.

Prior to the declaration of war he was assigned to Rockwell Field on North Island for guard duty until the building of Camp Kearney, where he was commissioned 2nd Lieutenant June 1, 1917, and later transferred to Camp Pike, Arkansas, where he assisted in organizing one of the first replacement camps in the country. Five days before his outfit was to go overseas he was transferred to be instructor at the Infantry Central Officers' Training School where he received his promotion to a 1st Lieutenancy and was discharged at the close of the war in December, 1918.

He came to Ketchikan in April, 1919 to become manager of the store department of the New England Fish Company and is still serving in that capacity. He was married in September, 1919 to Bernice Lambert of Long Beach, California. One son was born to this union.
PATHFINDER, May 1922

WILDE P. RICHARDSON (GENERAL)

General richardson was on duty in Alaska from 1898 to 1917, at which time he joined the service in the World War, being sent to Russia. It was here that he was awarded the Distinguished Service Medal and was elevated to the rank of brigadier.

When he first went to Alaska, General richardson was in charge of troops on the Yukon river and St. Michaels. In 1905 the Alaska road commission was created and General richardson was placed at the head of this road and trail building organization. In this position, he remained until 1917, when he was recalled in regular army duty. During his long tenure as president of the Alaska road Commission, General richardson had charge of the construction of some 4000 miles of roads and trails. His most notable achievement was the Richardson Highway.

General Richardson, age 67, died May 20, 1929, in Washington, D.C. He will be buried in West Point, the military Academy from which he graduated.   ALASKA WEEKLY, May 24, 1929

WILLIAM V. RINEHART, JR.

William V. Rinehart, Jr., is the son of W. V. Rinehart, Sr., of Seattle. The subject of this sketch was born July 31, 1867, in Jefferson, Oregon. He was educated in Washington University and at Ann Arbor College, receiving the law degree from the latter institution in 1889. He took a post graduate course the following year and the Master's Degree was conferred upon him. When a student in the University of Washington he stood at the head of his rhetoric class, and at the graduation of his class was awarded a gold medal for oratory.

During his residence in Washington, Mr. Rinehart was prominently identified with the National Guard, and was adjutant of the First Regiment. He received a medal for being the best drilled man in the regiment. He was Lieutenant of Co. G in the Spanish-American war.

After his graduation from Ann Arbor, Mr. Rinehart entered the law offices of Lewis, Gilmore & Stratton, of Seattle, and subsequently worked a year in the office of Judge Thos. Burke. Mayor Phelps appointed him to fill an unexpired term as municipal judge.

Mr. Rinehart came to None in 1900, and has been identified with the country ever since. In 1890 he married Miss Martha A. Waltz, of Ann Arbor.

NOME AND SEWARD PENINSULA, 1905

EDMUND MARBURG RININGER (Dr.)

Dr. Edmund Marburg Rininger was born in Schellsburg, Pa., March 7, 1870, of Pennsylvania Dutch parents. His father served in the Civil War as a non-commissioned officer, USA. His father was a cabinet maker who moved to Kansas and engaged in farming, and two years later, in 1876, removed in a prairie schooner to Ohio. Most of the boyhood days of Dr. Rininger were spent on a farm near Tiro, Ohio, where he obtained a common school education. When a mere youth he taught school during winters, and with the money thus earned attended the summer terms of the O. N. U. at Ada, Ohio. After three years of this kind of work he attained his majority. During this period he was ambitious to go to West Point, but politics instead of merit determined the selection.

He then began the study of medicine in the office of Dr. Hatfield, of Crestline, Ohio. He then entered the Ohio Medical College, which he attended for a year. He then went to the Marion Sims Medical College of St. Louis. By arising at 7 in the morning and working until 2 A. M. he was able to finish a three years course in two years, receiving a graduation next to the highest honor in a class of eighty-two students. After graduating, the position of assistant to the chair of Bacteriology and Physiological Chemistry was tendered him. He got the opportunity to take a doctor's practice in New Washington, a neighboring town. By 1896 he had paid off his school debts and accumulated a little money, and he started west with the intention of locating in some live mining camp. He traveled until 1897, and at one time thought of locating in Salt Lake. He passed the examination of the State Medical Board of Utah, and opened an office, but went to California a few months later.

Attracted by the Klondike boom he started for Dawson, but too late to get in that season, 1897. He stopped in Douglass, and here conceived the idea of opening an hospital at Sheep Camp on the Dyea Trail. He put up a drug store, erected an hospital that contained twelve beds, and hired two trained nurses. Dr. Rininger's hospital accommodations were inadequate. Only a small percent of the ailing could be received at the hospital, but the doctor never failed to respond to a call if it were possible to attend. Day and night, from February 1 to June 1, he was busy, much of the time on horseback, between Lake Lindeman and Dyea, a distance of twenty-five miles. Mrs. Rininger was with him, assisting him in his work.

When the army of gold hunters had passed

over the trail, Dr. and Mrs. Rininger went to Lake Lindeman, built a boat and followed the procession to Dawson. As the Canadian laws would not permit him to practice his profession he turned his attention to mining. During this winter he operated on Gold Bottom, Quartz and Hunker Creeks, but as he did not find mining profitable he decided to go to Nome.

He arrived in Nome September 20, 1899, bringing with him a supply of drugs obtained in Dawson and St. Michael, and opened the Pioneer Drug Store, the first in the town. He began the practice of medicine, and the demands for his services have kept him busy ever since. At the close of navigation in 1900 he was appointed by Nome citizens as one of three delegates to Washington to place before Congress the need of better laws for Alaska.

Dr. Rininger went from Washington to New York, and took a post graduate course. In the early part of the season of 1902 he established an hospital in Nome, and turned it over to the Sisters of Charity later in the season when they arrived in Nome. He went to the states in 1903, and spent the winter in New York, doing laboratory and clinical work. Returning the following spring, he resumed his practice. In the fall of 1904 Dr. Rininger left Nome, and located in Seattle.

July 11, 1893, Dr. Rininger and Miss Nellie Powers were married at Tiro, Ohio. They have one child, Dorothy Helen, born February 2, 1900.

NOME AND SEWARD PENINSULA, 1905

EDWARD MARBURG RININGER

Dr. E.M. Rininger, a pioneer of the Klondike and Nome gold fields, is now one of the leading physicians of the City of Seattle, having splendidly equipped offices in the Alaska building. Dr. Rininger was born in Ohio in 1870 and received the education which fitted him for his profession in the Ohio Medical College and the Marion Sims Medical College at St. Louis. He went West and located in Utah in 1897, but remained there only a short time, as he was attracted to the far North by the great stampede to the Klondike. He arrived at the head of navigation in Lynn Canal too late to cross the summit. In the fall of 1897 he located temporarily in Douglas, Alaska. Foreseeing the great rush over the Dyea trail in the spring of 1898, he conceived the idea of establishing a hospital at Sheep Camp. By the time the rush started he had fitted up a drug store, and a hospital with twelve beds, and had hired two trained nurses. Probably this season was the most strenuous in all of Dr. Rininger's busy life. There was an epidemic of cerebro spinal meningitis and typhoid pneumonia and many accidents on the trail.

The doctor always responded to calls and spent much of his time on horseback between Lake Lindemann and Dyea, a distance of twenty-five miles.

When the last gold seekers passed over the trail he moved to Dawson. In the latter part of the summer of 1899 he joined the Dawson stampeders to Nome. He immediately established a drug store and began the practice of his profession, and for five years was a citizen of Seward Peninsula. In 1900 he was selected at a meeting of Nome citizens as one of the three delegates to go to Washington and lay before Congress the need of better laws for Alaska. He established a hospital in Nome and at a later date turned it over to the Sisters of Charity.

During all Dr. Rininger's busy career and strenuous life in the Northland he was accompanied by Mrs. Rininger.

ALASKA-YUKON MAGAZINE, February 1908

SOL. RIPINSKY

Col. Sol. Ripinsky, a resident of Southeastern Alaska for the past twenty-three years, owner and founder of the townsite of Haines Mission. He is an artist, sculptor and linguist. He was United States commissioner to Alaska under Judge Johnson. He was a colonel on Gov. Thayer's staff in Oregon over twenty-five years ago, and all told, his has been a life of varied phases. Mr. Ripinsky was born April 15, 1859, in Rypin, Poland, near Strassburg, Western Prussia. He received a good European education and studied at some of the best military schools in Europe. Here he acquired a thorough knowledge of daughting and considerable skill in sketching, drawing and painting.

Mr. Ripinsky graduated with the rank of second lieutenant of cavalry and being too young to enter the service, visited many of the principal cities of Europe.

Coming to the United States he made a partial tour of the Eastern and Southern States and located at Shreveport, La., where he engaged in merchandise.

He moved to Sacramento, California and he opened a studio where he painted several fine oil paintings. After a short residence in California he located at Salem, Oregon, in 1878, and became identified with the State Militia, rising rapidly to the rank of colonel. In 1878 he received from the Oregon State Fair Association and Mechanics fair, at Portland, Oregon, and first prize for the emblematic Masonic chart. Under the administration of Governor W.W. Thayer, Mr. Ripinsky was honored with an appointment on His Excellency's staff as aide-de-camp, with rank of lieutenant colonel. He is a High Free Mason and a Sir Past Chancellor Commander K. of P. He is also a member of the Arctic Brotherhood.

Colonel Ripinsky came to Alaska in 1884, with the famous Arctic explorer the late Lieutenant Frederick Swatka. Under Attorney-General Haskett he was appointed clerk and in 1885 commissioned to establish a United State Government school in Western Alaska. Transferred from Unalaska to Chilkat, he became principal of the school at that place, and served one term. From 1887 to 1890 he was connected with the Pyramid Harbor salmon cannery, and during the latter year opened a general merchandise store on his own account at Chilkat, Alaska.

In view of his services to the Government,

one of the Chilkat mountains has been named for him, Mount Ripinsky is 3,680 feet high.
ALASKA MONTHLY, May 1906

W. FLEET ROBERTSON

W. Fleet Robertson had a distinguished professional career. He was born in Montreal in 1858 and educated at Montreal High School and Galt Collegiate Institute. From 1876 to 1880 he was a student of McGill University, graduating with a degree of B.A. Sc. After leaving McGill he was assistant engineer to Henry M. Howe, then rated as the world's greatest authority on iron and steel. He was also engaged in construction of the copper smelting works of the Orford Copper Co. at Eustic, Quebec, and was associated with Mr. Howe in the development of the first large copper blast furnace. In 1882 he was engaged as superintendent of the Chemical Copper Company's smelting and refining plant at Phoenixville, Pennsylvania.

During the following years, he was assistant superintendent of the Orford Copper Company at New York Harbor and at Constable Hook, N.J., where considerable research work was done.

In 1885 he resigned his position with the Orford company to join the militia and served in the Northwest Rebellion. The following year he was appointed engineer for the coal mines and railway of the Cumberland Coke & Coal Company at Springfield, N.S. In 1887 and 1888 he filled the position of superintendent and consulting engineer at Copper Smelting Works at Gia Solell, Coronada in Spain, where he was in charge of the construction and operation of the copper smelting plant, which had four thousand employees.

In the latter part of 1888 he was employed in designing, construction and operating the copper refining works of the Tamarack Osceola Copper Company of Dollar Bay, Mich. In 1889 he was chief engineer and metallurgist in charge of the Boston and Montana Smelting and Refining Company's plant at Great Falls, Montana. From

1899 to 1892 he was assistant superintendent of the Orford Nickel Company's smelter and refinery at Constable Hook. In 1892 he was superintendent of the copper plant of the Buffalo Chemical Company at Buffalo, N.Y. resigning in the fall of that year to open offices as consulting mining and metallurgical engineer in New York city. He continued in this practice for five years, being engaged in examining and reporting on properties and metallurgical works all over the U.S. and Canada.

In 1892, W. Fleet Robertson was appointed as Provincial Mineralogist for British Columbia, a position he held until his retirement in 1925. He died at Everett, Washington, June 12, 1929.

ALASKA WEEKLY, July 5, 1929

JOHN RONAN

John Ronan was born on a farm in Leavenworth, Kansas on June 28, 1871. He attended the public schools in his home state until the age of twenty, when he left home to seek for himself a fortune in the hills and plains of Nebraska, Iowa, and Dakotas, Montana and Washington. For several years he worked and prospected among the western hills. In 1896 he worked in logging camps in Washington State. In the spring of 1898, he started for the Klondike. His money gave out at Lake Bennett, and he went to work on the White Pass Railroad. From there went to Atlin, B.C., where he was engaged in mining for about a year. During the winter of 1899, he drove team for the White Pass Railroad from Lake Bennett to Whitehorse. In the spring of 1900 Mr. Ronan went direct from Atlin to the Faith Creek country, in Alaska, where he remained until the following winter, and then went to Dawson, staying there a short time, thence to Circle, where he prospected and mined, and finally, went to Fairbanks in the spring of 1903, and has been a resident there ever since.

Mr. Ronan, together with Matt Matheson, purchased a third interest in the mining claim known as No.5 above, left limit, a three-quarter interest in No. 1 above, left limit, and the entire claim No. 11 below, all located on Cleary Creek. Here the partners operated their ground for a period of three years. In 1904 they sold out their interests in No. 5. The partners operated No. 1 above for a short time, after which they sold out to other parties, but their claim on No. 11 below they operated for three years, employing as high as fifty men at a time. From this ground was taken out over $275,000 by Mr. Ronan.

Mr. Ronan has always been interested in politics, and in the fall of 1907 ran as delegate to Congress, but was unsuccessful.

Mr. Ronan has interests on Cleary, Chatham, Fairbanks, and Engineer Creeks.

ALASKA-YUKON MAGAZINE, July 1908

MOSE ROSENCRANZ

Mose Rosencranz came to Nome June 27, 1899. He was a passenger on the schooner Erma and was among the first arrivals from the states to the new mining camp. His entire capital consisted of the sum of one dollar and thirty-five cents. He secured some of the first lumber shipped to Nome and began the construction of the first frame building of the town. Possessing a money-making instinct he accumulated near $12,000 during the summer season of 1899. He was engaged in real estate, the handling of mining properties and a general brokerage and commission business.

As illustrative of the conditions in Nome during this season, he tells of an incident when he was offered fifty dollars to carry a letter from town to Anvil Creek, a distance of not more than four miles, and he declined the offer as an opportunity presented itself for a more profitable employment of his time.

He was born in San Francisco, June 3, 1865. He has a business record in San Francisco where he accumulated considerable money while engaged in the business of loaning money on real estate. Meeting with business reverses he was induced to go to Alaska. A

brother of Mr. Rosencranz is a physician of San Francisco, and he has a sister who is also a physician. At present Mr. Rosencranz is associated with Simson Brothers, on of the largest mercantile institutions of Seward Peninsula. In the list of his mining properties is a one-half interest in Poor Man's Bench adjoining the Maudeline and "Caribou Bill's" claim, a very valuable bench between Anvil and Dexter Creeks. He is also the owner of considerable town property.
NOME AND SEWARD PENINSULA, 1905

PETER TRIMBLE ROWE (Bishop)
Peter Rowe was born November 20, 1856 at Meadowville, Canada, and graduated from Trinity College, Toronto where he received his master of arts degree; received his doctor of divinity degrees from Hobart College and Toronto University and was ordained to the Episcopal priesthood in 1880.

The bishop was married twice. His first wife was Dora H. Carry, who died in 1914. They had two sons. In 1915 Bishop Rowe married Miss Rose Fullerton of Winnipeg. Three sons were born to them.

He became the first missionary bishop of Alaska in 1895 and for years after that traversed all the navigable streams by rowboat or canoe and "mushed" thousands of miles across the frozen wastes and was the first white man to visit many Eskimo villages.

Bishop rowe made his first airplane flight in August, 1926, being piloted from Nome to Tigara by Noel Wien.

In later years the Bishop of the Arctic trail did most of his traveling by plane, but often turned to dog sleds to reach otherwise inaccessible spots to carry on his gospel and medical work

At 82, on a brief vacation in New York, he looked back to his 43 years in the North, recalled gold rush friendships with Jack London, Rex Beach, and Tex Rickard, and remembered preaching several sermons in Rickard's gambling place in Nome.

There were only three churches in his territory when he started, but by 1939 there were 37 and three hospitals.

The oldest Bishop in the service of the Episcopal Church in the world, Bishop Rowe spent his summers in his Far North diocese of 39 mission stations; generally made his winter headquarters in Seattle; and spent whatever spare time he had for rest and relaxation at his Victoria residence.

Bishop Rowe died June 1, 1942 at his home in Gordon Head, British Columbia. He is survived by his sons, Jack and Richard Rowe of Victoria, and his wife, Rose. Also surviving are two other sons, Lieut. Paul Rowe, now serving a Canadian Expeditionary Force in England, and Leo R. Rowe, Seattle.

ALASKA WEEKLY, June 5, 1942

JOHN RUSTGARD

John Rustgard is a lawyer and miner of Seward Peninsula who has the distinction of having served one term as mayor of the City of Nome. He is a Norwegian by birth and an American by choice. In his youth he worked in saw mills, lumber yards and as a carpenter, and with his own earnings paid his way through high school and college. He was graduated from the law school of the University of Minnesota in 1890. For two years prior to his graduation and admission to the bar he was a teacher in one of the high schools of Minneapolis, Minnesota.

In 1899 he went west, and came to Nome in the early summer of 1900. Since his residence in Nome he has been stampeding, prospecting, mining and practicing law and speculating in mines and merchandise. At the Nome municipal election in April, 1902, he was elected to the common council by the largest vote cast for any of the candidates, and was elected by that body as president and ex-officio mayor.

NOME AND SEWARD PENINSULA, 1905

KATE RYAN

Kate Ryan was born in Johnsville, New Brunswick, Canada, in 1868. In 1898, accompanied by Minnie Lamereux, she mushed over the Stikine route to the Klondike...It was a long and tedious trail and the journey, through an unbroken country was completed in two months. Later, at Whitehorse she entered the service of the Royal Canadian Mounted Police where she was assigned to special detail to prevent the smuggling of gold out of Yukon territory without payment of royalty to the government. She was the only woman member of the Royal Canadian Mounted Police.

Known throughout the upper Yukon in the early Klondike days as "Big Sister," or Sergeant Kate, Kate Ryan never hesitated to mush over boggy tundra or frozen waste to bring comfort to the sick and needy.

Sergeant Ryan died in Vancouver, B.C., February 20, 1932.

ALASKA WEEKLY, February 26, 1932

RICHARD STANLEY RYAN

Dick Ryan was born in Limerick about 1861. He received his education at the Royal University of Dublin and on leaving college joined the Irish National League. Dick Ryan worked for the cause with the result that in 1885-86 a large number of Nationalist members were returned to Parliament and their pressure on the British government led to Gladstone's plan by which Ireland was to receive a parliament of her own. Dick Ryan made an extended trip from Ireland to the united States in the interests of the National League and was instrumental in raising a large fund to further the cause.
Returning to Ireland Dick continued his work for the National League.

In 1900 Dick Ryan chartered the steamer Garonne and loaded with passengers and freight set out for Nome. He became active in politics in the Northland and was elected as delegate to the national republican convention in 1908. He left for the states shortly after.

Ryan considered that one of the greatest honors conferred upon him in the northland was his election to the office of mayor of Nome.

Richard S. Ryan died at his home in Berkely Springs, West Virginia, November 28, 1931. He is survived by his wife, Margaret.
ALASKA WEEKLY, December 11, 1931

CHARLES ELLIOTT RYBERG   (Rev.)

The Rev. C. E. Ryberg is the pastor of the Congregational Church at Nome. He is a native of Chicago, Illinois, and was educated at Carleton College, Northfield, Minn., and was graduated with the degree of A. B. in 1898. He began preaching when he was a student at college. Before coming to Alaska he was pastor of one of the oldest churches in Minnesota, at Cannon Falls.

A chum of his boyhood days, who had struck it rich at Nome, wrote him and urged him to come to Alaska. He accordingly left his work in Minnesota and started for Nome. Arriving here in the summer of 1900, he secured a situation as foreman on No. 9 Anvil Creek. After he had worked long enough to secure a "grub-stake" and horse, he went to the Kougarok District on a prospecting trip. During this trip he located a claim on Garfield Creek. He went to the states that fall, and came back the following spring with a big outfit to work the Garfield claim. But the prospects he had obtained were deceptive and what had appeared to be a very rich claim proved to be valueless.

Rev. Ryberg returned to Nome late in the season discouraged and hungry. He was endeavoring to arrange to return to the states when Missionary Karlson wrote him from Unalakleet asking him to come to the mission and help with the work. He went to Unalakleet and lent his services to the missionary work.

Returning to Nome in the spring of 1902, he staid and thus became pastor of the Congregational Church. During his ministerial career in Nome he has been the agent for the establishment of the Quartz Creek Mission for natives. This work was begun under his supervision in the fall of 1903, and at the close of last season 100 Eskimo or more had been gathered at this mission.

NOME AND SEWARD PENINSULA, 1905

JOHN L. SANDSTROM

John L. Sandstrom was born in Alton, Norway, August 12, 1866, and received his education in the public schools of Norway. He went to America with his parents in 1885, and resided for a year in Chicago. In 1886 he went to Los Angeles, and a year later to Portland, Oregon. During the early nineties he resided in Silver City, Idaho, and for a period of five years was engaged in quartz mining. In 1899 he prospected in the Buffalo Hump country, and came to Nome in 1900.

For three years he was mine foreman for Magnus Kjelsberg, operating property in the Nome District. Mr. Sandstrom is the owner of No. 2 bench on the left fork of Dexter Creek. He is one of the owners in the Louisa and Golden benches adjoining this property.

In 1893 he and Miss Amanda Peterson of Boise City, Idaho, were married. They have two children, Esther and Harala. His home is in Portland, Oregon.

NOME AND SEWARD PENINSULA, 1905

LADOWICH LATHAM SAWYER

L. L. Sawyer is one of the best known citizens of Nome. During the past two years he has filled a position on the school board, being elected thereto by a large majority, and selected by the board to perform the duties of secretary of that body. He is a Connecticut Yankee and the son of Jeremiah Nathaniel Sawyer and Emeline Kelly. His father's ancestry is English and his mother's Irish. He was born October 27, 1832, in Mystic, Connecticut. He is the third son of a family of seven children, five boys and two girls. His ancestors were among the Pilgrim Fathers. They were seamen and his father was a captain and owner of vessels. His elder brother was a lieutenant in the United States Navy during the Rebellion, and subsequently was United States Consul at Trinidad, W. I. Jeremiah N., the second son, was a sea captain and one of the owners at Galveston, Texas, of the Charles Mallory Line of Steamers between New York and Galveston. He was agent of the company.

In the period of Mr. Sawyer's boyhood there were not the opportunities for acquiring an education that exist today. Mr. Sawyer's alma mater was a cross-road's country school in Mystic, Connecticut. At the age of sixteen he was left an orphan and thrown upon his own resources. Following the hereditary instinct he went to sea as a sailor. In 1849 he shipped before the mast and went around the Horn to San Francisco, California, and resided in this state a number of years. He and Julia E. Price were married in California in 1857. The issue was a son and a daughter, both deceased. Mrs. Sawyer, who has been his inseparable companion for near half a century, is with him in Nome.

In 1855 he and his brother, Jeremiah, filled a vessel in San Francisco to go to Bering Sea on an expedition to trade for fur and ivory. The vessel was crushed in the ice after having been loaded in less than a month with a cargo obtained from the natives and valued at $80,000. The vessel and cargo were lost. Mr. Sawyer engaged in mining in California, and went to Frazer River, British Columbia, during the excitement over that camp in 1858. In 1860 he followed the stampeders to Caribou, carrying a pack on his back from Fort Hope to Caribou, a distance of several hundred miles.

In 1870 he left the Pacific Coast and returned to Connecticut, engaging in manufacturing in Meriden. He organized the Meriden Curtain Fixture Company, to manufacture a shade spring window roller which he had patented. This company is now the largest manufacturer in this line in the world. He made a fortune out of this enterprise, and lost it through the mental aberrations of his partner who became insane.

After severing his connection with the company and being reduced to poverty, he turned his attention again to the business of mining;

forming companies and putting up stamps and amalgamating mills in North Carolina, Colorado and elsewhere. After accumulating another fortune the demonetization of silver left him "broke" again in 1897. In 1898, when near three score, he returned to the Pacific Coast undiscouraged by adversity, and firm in the belief and the hope of acquiring another competence. He started the business of a mining broker in Seattle, and in 1900 came to Nome where he has since resided. Mr. Sawyer is largely interested in the tin mines of Cape Mountain. There is a good prospect that their development will bring him the object of his search in Alaska.

NOME AND SEWARD PENINSULA, 1905

W. J. SCANLAN

Wm. J. Scanlan was born in Charlestown, Mass., May 20, 1874. He received his education in the public schools of his native state and the Allen Institute of Boston. He has filled the positions of private secretary to several multi-millionaires in the East, and also acted in the capacity of secretary to a number of corporations.

In 1901 he went to Nome as the secretary of several mining companies operating in Seward Peninsula. Prior to going to Nome he was a broker in the city of New York, engaged in the bond and mortgage business. He has traveled extensively in America and abroad.

Mr. Scanlan and Miss Katharine M. Hagan were married in New York, February 1, 1905.

NOME AND SEWARD PENINSULA, 1905

ALBERT SCHNEIDER

A. Schneider is the French Vice-Consul in Nome. He is also largely interested in mining and ditch construction, being president and general manager of the Northwestern Ditch Company.

A. Schneider was born in Paris, March 3, 1864. He received his education in the Chaptal College of Paris, and subsequently engaged in

the commission exportation business. He left this business to go to Dawson in 1899, and came to Nome the following year. In 1901 he was appointed Vice-Consul for France at Nome, and has filled this position satisfactorily to his country and to the French residents of Northwestern Alaska. Besides his mining and ditch enterprises, Mr. Schneider is a director in the Miners and Merchants Bank of Nome. He and Mlle. Marguerite Bourgeois were married in Paris in 1890. Two daughters, Simone and Helene, are the issue of this marriage.
                    NOME AND SEWARD PENINSULA, 1905

GEORGE D. SCHOFIELD

He was born in Portland, Michigan, August 23, 1864, and received his education in the Northwest University, and Normal School at Dixon, Illinois. He was admitted to the bar at the age of twenty-one in the State of Washington.

Mr. Schofield comes from a family of lawyers. His grandfather was a lawyer in the state of New York, and his father was district attorney of one of the four districts of Nebraska from 1876 to 1880. In 1883 he went to the State of Washington.

In 1883 a party of six, of which he was a member, started from Butte to Juneau, but Mr. Schofield stopped in Montesano and entered his father's law office. He later began the practice of law in Nebraska City, Nebraska. In 1898 he was elected senator from the Sixteenth District of the State of Washington.

He came to Alaska in the spring of 1900 but returned to Washington in the fall. He came back the following summer and has resided in Nome ever since. In the spring of 1904 he was appointed by the Nome City Council to the office of city attorney.

His wife was formerly Miss Sarah E. Amidon, of San Francisco. They have two children, George D. and Mary Gwendolin, aged eight and five years respectively.
                    NOME AND SEWARD PENINSULA, 1905

ANTON C. SCHOW

Anton C. Schow is the owner of large mining interests in Seward Peninsula. He is better known as Frank Schow. In his younger days he went to sea as a sailor, and when the crew was drawn up in line and the mate asking each one his name, several natives of Portugal gave their names as Anton. When the mate asked Mr. Schow his name, he promptly replied, Frank, and by the name of Frank he has since been known.

Mr. Schow is a native of New York, and was born August 25, 1860. He was educated in the public schools, and went to sea when he was fourteen years old. He followed the sea for seven years. After 1876 his home was in California. He was assistant foreman for Goodall, Perkins & Company, of San Francisco, at their Broadway wharf, prior to the discovery of gold in the Klondike. Upon receipt of the news of the Dawson strike in 1897 he started for that region. He and thirty-nine other men paid $500 each for the schooner South Coast, in which they embarked for St. Michael. At St. Michael he realized that the plans of the company would not enable him to get to Dawson that season, so he shipped as a mate on one of the river steamers. ON the way up he purchased five tons of outfits for $300, and when he arrived in Dawson with them he was offered $8,500 for the supplies they contained.

He engaged in mining in the Klondike country and during his residence there owned twelve mining claims. He came down the river during the summer of 1899, arriving in Nome June 1. Shortly after his arrival the beach diggings were struck, and Mr. Schow claims the distinction of having weighed the first product of the beach, which consisted of dust valued at fifty-two dollars.

In 1899 he got a bench claim off Discovery Claim on Anvil Creek. This claim adjoins the property where the big nugget was found. Mr. Schow sold this claim in 1903 for $32,000 cash. He is now interested in 6,000 acres of mining land in various parts of Seward Peninsula, and

is an owner in some valuable water rights. In
the fall of 1899 Mr. Schow went to the states
and took a trip to Europe.
             NOME AND SEWARD PENINSULA, 1905

MATTHIAS SCHULER
     Matt Schuler is one of the successful
miners of the Nome country. He is a pioneer
Alaskan, having spent ten years in the northern
country. He was born in Siskiyou County,
California, November 19, 1870. He was educated
in the public schools of California and in
Atkinson's Business College in Sacramento.
After working at farming a short time he went
to Alaska in 1890 via Chilkoot Pass and down
the Yukon. He camped and ate dinner on the
banks of the Yukon where Dawson now stands,
before the discovery of gold in the Klondike
country. His objective point in Alaska was
Circle City. Mr. Schuler engaged in the
business of teaming in Circle, and was the
owner of the first wagon on the Yukon. After
the strike at Dawson he made big money out of
the teaming and freighting business. In those
days the price received for a day's work with a
team was $100. He went from Circle to Dawson
in June and remained there until the spring of
1900, when he came to Nome, where he has
interest in claims on Summit Bench and Arctic
Creek.
             NOME AND SEWARD PENINSULA, 1905

HAL B. SELBY
     Born 1868 in Jerseyville, Illinois, Mr.
Selby entered the newspaper business as a young
man and remained active in it until shortly
before his death. Before coming to Alaska he
published newspapers in many parts of the
United States and spent some years engaged in
his chosen field in Florida. Mrs. Selby and
he were married in Florida and came to Alaska
together in 1915, when they settled in Valdez,
then a thriving mining community.
     For several years Mr. Selby published both
a daily and weekly newspaper in Valdez, calling
the former the PROSPECTOR and the latter the

VALDEZ MINER. He was publisher of the VALDEZ MINER at the time of his death. From 1915 until 1921 he remained in Valdez and then moved to Seward, where he published the SEWARD GATEWAY until 1926 when he went south for his health.

After spending several years in an effort to regain his health, Mr. Selby returned to Alaska and spent some time in Juneau as publisher of STROLLER'S WEEKLY here. He returned to Valdez in 1934.

Hal B. Selby died in Valdez, Alaska March 10, 1942. He is survived by his widow, and a daughter, Mrs. Ruth Pedersen, who resides in Valdez; a sister, Mrs. Maude Angel, of Pasadena; a son, Harry B. Selby, of Seattle; a son, F.J. Selby who lives in Juneau, and six grandchildren.

DAILY ALASKA EMPIRE, March 12, 1942

GEORGE SEXTON

George Sexton, proprietor of the Coleman House, Seward, is a native of Indiana. He went to Alaska in 1898, settling at Skagway, where he engaged in the hotel business. In 1900 he was selected to take charge of the census work in the Prince William Sound and Copper River country. He located at Seward in 1903, where he has since been engaged in the hotel business. For several years he was deputy United States marshal.

ALASKA-YUKON MAGAZINE, July 1911

LOUIS P. SHACKLEFORD

Louis Shackleford was a pioneer of Alaska, going to Juneau during the rush to the Klondike. A lawyer by profession, he was long a member of the legal firm of Shackleford & Lyons, with headquarters in Juneau. This long and successful partnership was only severed when Judge Thomas P. Lyons was appointed district judge in the First division by President Taft.

Mr. Shackleford, a brilliant attorney, found time, despite the large practice of the firm, to devote some of his time to politics, and for many years he served as Republican National Committeeman for Alaska. This [position made him well known throughout the Territory.

When Mr. Shackleford quit Alaska a number of years ago, he went to California, making his home in Los Angeles. He came north some two years ago and made his home in Seattle until the death of a brother, a lawyer of Tacoma, whose practice he assumed.

Louis P. Shackleford died in Tacoma, Washington, July 27, 1929. He was 52 years old. He is survived by a wife, son, and daughter.

ALASKA WEEKLY, August 2, 1929

L. F. SHAW

Born at Chico, California, his boyhood was spent in Port Townsend where he did his first newspaper work. At the first call of the northern stampede he left the Sound city for Alaska, stopping at Valdez where he edited the VALDEZ PROSPECTOR. From then on his adventurous spirit led him from one camp to another. During 1904-5 he was in charge of the NOME NUGGET for the late Governor Strong. About that time the Northeastern Trading Company obtained some concessions in Siberia and called for prospectors and he spent the next eight months in Siberia. Returning he went to Seward where for the succeeding six years he edited the SEWARD GATEWAY, leaving Seward to go on the ANCHORAGE TIMES where he remained for the next three years.

L. F. Shaw, for the past eight years news editor of THE ALASKA WEEKLY, died at the Providence Hospital, Seattle, on the morning of March 14. He had been ill but five days. Death was due to complications resulting from intestinal flu. He is survived by his widow, Margaret E. Shaw, to whom he was married in 1912 at Walla Walla.

ALASKA WEEKLY, March 20, 1931

JAMES SHEAKLEY

The late James Sheakley, fourth Governor

of Alaska, was born at Sheakleyville, Pennsylvania April 26, 1829, and died at Greenville, Pennsylvania, December 17, 1919.

In early life he lost his father, and lived with his widowed mother and brothers and sisters on their farm until young manhood. He attended the common schools and became a teacher.

In 1851, when 22 years of age, he joined the rush of gold seekers to California, going via the Isthmus of Panama. As a gold miner he was successful, and returned to Pennsylvania two years later with a moderate competence. He purchased the old Sheakley farm homestead, which had passed to other hands, and in 1855 he married Miss Lyndia Long. They made their home in the Sheakley homestead, residing there for several years. Three children were the fruits of this marriage, two daughters who died as they were growing into young womanhood, and a son, Frederick E. Sheakley, now a resident of Sitka, Alaska.

Several years after his marriage, Governor Sheakley sold the old homestead and moved to Greenville, Pa., where he engaged in the dry goods business for several years. About this time petroleum was becoming known, and was struck in western Pennsylvania, and among the names of the great pioneers of the petroleum industry that of James Sheakley frequently appears. In these early days of this great industry it is recorded that he was known among his associates as "Pap" Sheakley, and was president of a club composed of oil men known as "Ali Baba and the Forty Thieves." Although a Democrat of the old school type, he was sent to the Forty-Fourth Congress from the oil district of Pennsylvania, a Republican stronghold.

He was always deeply interested in education and the improvement of the public schools. He, with others, was instrumental in locating a college at Greenville, Pennsylvania, and in building for that time, the finest school building in the State.

Mr. Sheakley was appointed by President

Cleveland as Superintendent of Schools in Alaska and United States Commissioner, with headquarters at Wrangell. He held this position for about two years, and while living at Wrangell was admitted to the practice of law.

He was one of the two delegates from Alaska to the Democratic National Convention which nominated Cleveland as candidate for the Presidency for the second time, and in 1893 President Cleveland appointed Mr. Sheakley Governor of Alaska, in which capacity he served for four years. His son, Frederick E. Sheakley, was Secretary to the Governor.

At the expiration of his term of Governor of Alaska, Mr. Sheakley went o San Francisco, and represented the Chamber of Commerce, Board of Trade and the Alaska Trade Commission. Then, he returned to Greenville, Pa. where he held several political offices. James Sheakley and his wife both died in 1918.

PATHFINDER, Feb., 1921

MARIE N. SILVERMAN

Marie Silverman came to Alaska in 1908. She was married that year in Ketchikan to the late Solomon Silverman, who was employed by the ANCHORAGE TIMES prior to his death nearly 30 years ago. Mrs. Silverman then joined the staff of the TIMES and was revered as the newspaper's oldest employee.

From Ketchikan, the Silvermans had moved to Prince of Wales Island, then to Seward, where he was employed by the Brown and Hawkins store. Then, in 1912, they moved to the then bustling town of Knik where Silverman was with the same firm.

With the decline of Knik, the Silvermans moved to Anchorage where for many years their home was on the present site of the J.C. Penney Co. store.

"I saw Anchorage before the trees were cut in the townsite," Mrs. Silverman, who lived in Anchorage before the town began in 1915, and recalled over the years.

Mrs. Silverman was a charter member of the

Anchorage Chapter 3 of the Order of Eastern Star formed back in 1918. She served as the lodge's worthy matron in 1929. She was also a charter member of the Order of Amaranth Alaska Court No. 1 and active in the Pioneers Auxiliary and the Sons of Norway lodge.

Queen regent of the 1930 Fur Rendezvous, Mrs. Silverman also had received other honors. Job's Daughters honored her in 1958 by naming her "honorary mother" and that same year Pythian Sisters initiated her as "temple mother."

Mrs. Silverman was loved and respected by many who looked upon her as "mother." Her work with the USO during the war years here led to long friendships with many servicemen with whom she corresponded up until the time of her death.

Mrs. Silverman was born May 9, 1878 in Norway, and died in Anchorage, Alaska in April 7, 1967.

ANCHORAGE DAILY TIMES, April 28, 1967

CHARLES SIMENSTAD

Charles Simenstad, mining engineer went to Valdez, Alaska, in 1898. He mined in the Slate Creek district and was part owner and operator of the Jack Pot placer claim. He later discovered and sold copper properties on Prince William Sound, after which he spent four years as a special student of the College of Mines, University of Washington. He was a member of the first city council of Valdez and was a stockholder of the Cliff mine near that town. He opened an office as consulting mining engineer in Seattle in 1918, and has since been engaged in mining consulting work in the Pacific Northwest, British Columbia, and Alaska. In addition to metal work, he designed and put in operation many successful coal washing and coal handling plants, including the plants at the Evan Jones coal mine and the Healy river coal mine. He directed the deeper development of the Nikolai copper mine near Kennecott, and at present is managing engineer for the Copper Creek Copper Mines of Alaska, carrying on extensive development work on Copper Creek, Kotsina river valley. He is a member of the Arctic Club and the American Institute of Mining and Metallurgical Engineers. Mr. Simenstad spends from eight to nine months a year in mining work in Alaska and is entering his thirty-first consecutive year of work in that territory.

ALASKA WEEKLY, april 13, 1928

ROBERT NIEL SIMPSON

R. N. Simpson is connected with the commercial interests of Nome, being associated with one of the largest mercantile and transportation companies of Seward Peninsula. He had the foresight to see the benefits to be derived from a street railway in Nome and secured from the Nome Council a franchise for a street railway. This is the first franchise of this character ever granted in Alaska.

R. N. Simpson was born in Oakland, California, March 17, 1867. His father, Thomas B. Simpson, was a well known mining man of that state, being largely interested in the Blue Gravel Mine at Smartsville and the Excelsior Ditch at the same place. During then years of R. N. Simpson's business career he was in the canning business and interested in several Alaska salmon canneries. Five years prior to his coming to Nome he was in the insurance business. On his arrival in Nome the prevalence of litigation and the aspect of conditions as a result of this litigation caused him to change his plans, and instead of engaging in mining he took a position as cashier of the Northwestern Commercial Company, and has been connected with the company ever since.

Mr. Simpson married Jessie B. Grayson, of Hillsboro, New Mexico, August 7, 1888. Mrs. Simpson is with her husband in Nome.

NOME AND SEWARD PENINSULA, 1905

ABRAHAM SIMSON

The Simson Brothers own one of the largest mercantile businesses on Seward Peninsula, conducting stores in Nome and Council. Abe Simson is one of the pioneer merchants of Nome and was the first members of the firm to arrive in this camp. He came down the river from Dawson and landed in Nome September 6, 1899. He did not bring a stock of goods with him, as the object of the trip was to investigate the new camp and see what opportunities it might offer for the establishment of a business. But after arriving he thought it best to stay, and began business in a small way by buying and selling goods and handling merchandise on commission.

Abe Simson is a native of Haverstraw, New York, and was born November 15, 1869. He is the second son of a family of eight, six boys and two girls. His father was a merchant. When he was four years old the family moved to Germany and the subject of this sketch did not return to the United States until he was sixteen years old. His education was obtained in Germany. He started in business at the age of seventeen and began by taking retail orders. When he was nineteen years old he opened a store in Croton, New York, and subsequently with his eldest brother, S. Simson, established another store in Suffern, New York. It was the largest mercantile institution in this town. In 1898 he sold out his interest in New York and with his brother Ben started for Dawson, via Chilkoot Pass. They pulled their freight over the trail and built the boat in which they descended the Yukon. After several months devoted to prospecting in the Klondike region, they got weary digging for gold and determined to engage in business with which they were familiar. They began by buying and selling outfits. They returned to the states that winter and in the spring of 1899 came back to Dawson with a stock of goods and opened a small store. The reports from Nome induced Abe to make a trip to the new camp. In the spring of 1900 Ben Simson arrived in Nome with a stock of goods. This was the first stock of goods received in Nome this season. The firm did an extensive business, but on account of the fire

risk they retired from the field at the end of the season of 1903. But Ben got the fever to go to Nome again, and in the spring of 1904 he returned and bought out the N. A. T. & T. Co.
NOME AND SEWARD PENINSULA, 1905

BEN SIMSON

Ben Simson was born in Middletown, New York, February 20, 1974, and began business in mercantile lines in Suffern, New York, when he was seventeen years old. In 1898 he and his brother Abe started for Dawson. They had a narrow escape from the great snow-slide at Sheep Camp, and subsequently lost most of their outfit in a tent fire.

Not meeting with success at mining in the Klondike gold fields, he turned his attention to merchandising. He went outside in the fall of 1898 to buy goods, and got back to Skagway in January with a three thousand-dollar stock, which he took to Dawson. He got a letter from his brother Abe, who had gone to Nome, telling him to go to the states and buy a stock of goods, and get it to Nome at the earliest possible date. In the spring of 1900 he arrived in Nome with a stock of merchandise. The firm of Simson Bros. made money in Nome, and is now one of the largest mercantile institutions in Northwestern Alaska.
NOME AND SEWARD PENINSULA, 1905

SKOOKUM JIM

Skookum Jim, the well known Indian who was with George Carmack at the time the great discovery of the Klondike camp was made on August 17, 1896, and who passed away at his home at Carcross on July 20, 1916, was the most widely known Indian of the North and no doubt was the richest native ever in the Yukon. It is estimated that at one time he had close to $100,000 in virgin gold. This he proceeded to spend. The late Bishop Bompas and Percy Reid, former mining recorder here at Carcross, took particular interest in Jim and assisted him in such a way as to make the money last him practically until his death.

Soon after Skookum made his strike on Bonanza he journeyed with his wife and George Carmack to Seattle, and there they enjoyed the ways of the cheechaco for several months.

Returning North, Skookum was around Dawson for a time, and finally moved to Carcross. He was a native of the Tagish Lake district.

Skookum naturally preferred to spend the last of his days in his native district, and there settled down at Carcross. His mining ground was sold to others and he spent much of his last several years prospecting for new placer camps. A great deal of his money went in that way. His last stampede was made last winter to the head of the Liard, beyond Atlin. He traveled many weeks through the bitterest weather, reaching 60 or more below zero, with no companions but the dogs which drew his sleigh. Soon after returning to Carcross he was taken ill, and never recovered. For a time he was at Tenakee Hot Springs, Alaska; then in the government hospital at Whitehorse, and finally back at Carcross. His full name, given him, it is believed, on suggestion of Bishop Bompas, was James Mason.--DAWSON NEWS.
ALL-ALASKA REVIEW, August 1916

DR. JOHN M. SLOAN

Dr. John M. Sloan is a native of Huron County, Ontario, Canada, and began this life with the first day of the new year, 1868. His ancestors were Scotch, and after graduating from the Clinton Collegiate Institute and the Manitoba University he went to Scotland to perfect his education for the profession he had selected, and was graduated from the Edinborough and the Glasgow Colleges of Physicians and Surgeons. From the Edinborough College he received the degree of L. R. C. P. and S., and from the Glasgow College, L. F. P. S. After graduating he went to London, and spent a few months in the Moorfield and London Hospitals.

When he returned to America he located in Chicago, where he began the practice of medicine. This was in 1894, and during that year he received the appointment of Professor of Surgery in the Harvard Medical College. Later he was Instructor of Surgery in the Post Graduate Medical College of Chicago, and held both of these positions when he started for Nome in the Spring of 1900.

After arriving in Nome he went to the Port Clarence and York Districts, and was one of the first in on the Bluestone strike. After three years of hard work, Dr. Sloan returned to Nome and opened an office in the Golden Gate Hotel. His brother, Dr. W. Sloan, is the operating manager of their mining interests, which are extensive, comprising gold mines in the Bluestone and Gold Run country and tin properties in the vicinity of Ear Mountain and elsewhere in the York District.

NOME AND SEWARD PENINSULA, 1905

WILLIAM SLOAN

When the first news reached "the outside" of the discovery of gold in the yukon, William Sloan, with three friends, embarked for the far north. After prospecting in the vicinity of the Stewart River for the greater part of the season without success, his party came on Eldorado Creek, where the future minister of mines staked No. 15, and his friends adjoining claims. It was No. 15 that first reached bedrock and proved the fabulous richness of the creek.

It was the "strike" on this property that led to the great Klondike rush. In 1898 Mr. Sloan returned to British Columbia a rich man.

Following his return from the north the young miner evinced an interest in politics. He first essayed to enter the House of Commons as a candidate for Vancouver district, but was defeated in the general election of 1900. Four years later he received the nomination for Comox-Atlin and was elected by acclamation. In the following election, 1908, he was once more acclaimed as member for the district.

In 1916 he was appointed minister of mines, a portfolio which he held under the Brewster, Oliver and MacLean administrations.

Premier Brewster also added to his responsibilities the commissionership of fisheries.

In 1924 William Sloan was appointed provincial secretary.

Called by his political opponents "the master-mind of the government," and the "political general" of the cabinet, he was nevertheless the most popular man in the government.

Mr. Sloan was twice married. His first wife was Flora McGregor Glaholm, whom he married at Nanalmo in 1891. By this marriage there was one son, Gordon McGregor, a practicing barrister of Vancouver. Several years after the death of his wife Mr. Sloan married, in 1916, Catherine McDougall. There is one son, William McDougall, by this union.

William Sloan died in Victoria, British Columbia, March 2, 1928.

ALASKA WEEKLY, March 9, 1928

EDMUND SMITH

Judge Smith was admitted to the bar in what was then Dakota Territory in 1878. He was elected prosecuting attorney for Custer County in 1888, the youngest prosecuting attorney in the then territory. He was elected to the state senate in South Dakota in 1898, and was a candidate on the democratic ticket for judge of the supreme court in 1900. During his residence in the Black Hills, he had gained a reputation as a mining lawyer. In 1903, Judge Smith went to Valdez, Alaska, to assist in the trial of a great mining case(what is now the great Kennocott copper mine, being involved in this action), and taking a fancy to the town decided to locate there. Here he formed a law partnership with Fred M. Brown, who some years later was appointed federal judge in the Third division, and this partnership lasted for many years.

He moved from Valdez to Seattle in 1912, and established law offices in the American Bank building, with his law partner Julian O. Matthews.

Judge Smith died February 20, 1930. He was born in Adams County, Iowa, and was 69 years of age. He was a member of the Valdez Lodge, F. & A.M., and the King county, State and American Bar Association.

He is survived by his wife, a daughter, Mrs. Floy Webber, and a son, Donald J. Smith, who is with the Associated Oil Company in Seattle.

ALASKA WEEKLY, February 21, 1930

FRANK S. SMITH

Frank S. Smith went to Dawson via the Chilkoot Pass in 1898. His brother, Ed. S. Smith, and P. W. Koelsch accompanied him. They arrived in Dawson June 22.

In the Klondike country he acquired an interest in a beach claim on Hunker Creek and mined it for two years. Having an opportunity to sell it for a fair price he disposed of his interest and came to Nome in 1900. His first venture here was on Hungry Creek, in the Cripple River region. After mining the property and taking out of it a considerable quantity of gold, he acquired other property in the vicinity, constructed a road-house and made his Alaska home on Oregon Creek; he studied the country, prospected in creeks and benches, and continued to acquire property. He staked and acquired water rights, and in June, 1904, began the construction of ditches which will supply water for hydraulic mining in the region of the upper waters of Cripple River. He has mined on Trilby Creek, Oregon Creek and Nugget Gulch. He established the Oregon Creek Road-house, and is engaged in the transportation business, owning teams that make round-trips every two days between Nome and Oregon Creek.

Mr. Smith owns Trilby Creek, a tributary of Hungry. His property on this stream consists of Nos. 1, 2 and 3 creek claims, and the Sullivan, Saturday, McCibbia, Smith and Accidental bench claims. On Hungry Creek he owns No. 2 and 500 feet of the Le Clair fraction. Among other promising claims that he owns are No. 3 above the mouth of Oregon, and the Eureka bench opposite 6 below. He has secured long-term leases on other properties and staked water rights on several streams.

F. S. Smith is a native of Utah, and of English and Scotch blood, by virtue of his father's and mother's lineage, respectively. He was born in Tooeley City, April 24, 1870. He is next to the eldest son in a family of four boys and one girl. His father owned and operated a farm and a saw mill in Utah. In 1880 the family moved to Idaho, and resided in Albion, Challis, Wood River and Boise City, the latter place being their present home. Mr. Smith's father followed stock raising and ranching in Idaho, and the subject of this sketch received the benefit of a public school education in the schools of Idaho.

NOME AND SEWARD PENINSULA, 1905

HENRY SMITH

Henry Smith was born on a ranch in Lavoca County, Texas, December 28, 1856. His early life was spent on the ranches of the "Lone Star State." When fifteen years old he rode the range and did the work of a man. He subsequently learned the trade of a blacksmith and carriage maker. In 1888 he went to Tacoma, Wash., and engaged in the real estate business; and also conducted a blacksmith shop in the same city. His home has been in Tacoma ever since he went to the Northwest.

In 1898 Mr. Smith went to Skagway and established a blacksmith shop at Canyon City on the trail in Dawson, and in the fall of that year went into Dawson with a stock of goods, which he sold and then engaged in mining. His first mining ventures were in 1886 in the Slocan country, British Columbia. In the Klondike country he mined on El Dorado, Dominion and Canyon Creeks, meeting with varying success.

When he left home in 1898 he planned to be gone two months, but did not return until after the lapse of five years. In 1901 he and Jeff McDermott came down the Yukon together to Nome. During this season he began mining operations on Dry Creek, opening Claim No. 5. He had an option on this property, but failure to secure a title compelled him to abandon. In 1902 he mined on Oregon Creek. During the winter of 1901-02 he prospected on El Dorado Creek near Bluff. In 1904 he conducted extensive operations on Dry Creek on Nos. 6, 7 and 8 below. At one time fifty-seven men were employed by him on these claims. The result of this work was very satisfactory. Mr. Smith is interested in the McDermott Ditch, a valuable water right and ditch property in the Solomon River region.

NOME AND SEWARD PENINSULA, 1905

LYNN SMITH

Lynn Smith was born in Indiana on March 4, 1872. Early in 1898, he arrived at Rampart, where he and Volney Richmond, now president and general manager of the Northern Commercial Co. built a log cabin. They spent considerable time on the various creeks and gulches in that region.

In 1901 Lynn went over to Glenn Gulch, where he worked on the property of the Eagle Mining Co. for two years. When the Fairbanks boom started he decided to go there in 1903 and looked over the Eagle Mining Co.'s holdings on Ester Creek. The year 1906 found Lynn at the strike on Cooney Creek near Hot Springs, where he spent two years prospecting and mining in company with Capt. A.D. Williams, with whom he was associated for many years. He returned to Fairbanks for a time, but went back to Hot springs where he mined on American and Woodchopper creeks until the strike at Ruby about 1911.

With the discovery of gold in the Ruby district, the town of Ruby sprang up and Mr. Smith soon had a jewelry store in operation there in addition to trading in furs. Lynn operated this store from 1912 to 1920, after which he was appointed deputy U.S. Marshal at Flat in the Iditarod district, a position he filled for two years. From 1925 until 1926 he acted as agent for the Northern Commercial Co.

at Ruby and it was while holding this position that he was appointed U.S. Marshal.

Mr. Lynn Smith passed away of a heart attack at Providence Hospital, Seattle, March __, 1933. Besides his sister, Mrs. Mary S. Heller of Newcastle, Indiana, he is survived by a niece, Miss Mary Louise Heller, his assistant at Fairbanks; three brothers, Clarence and Arthur of Newcastle and Harry of Fort Wayne, Indiana, and a nephew, Herbert Heller.

ALASKA WEEKLY, March 17, 1933

NORDAHL BRUNE SOLNER

N. B. Solner has been identified with the banking interests of Nome since the early spring of 1900. He is the manager of the Bank of Cape Nome. He came to Nome in June, 1900, and supervised the construction of the bank building.

Mr. Solner is a native of Janesville, Wisconsin, and was born January 10, 1864. In 1880 he entered the First National Bank of Moorehead, Minnesota, and in 1884 was cashier of the Tobacco Exchange Bank of Edgerton, Wisconsin. In 1886 he went to California on account of ill health. Two years later he visited Seattle, where he obtained employment as teller of the First National Bank of that city.

Subsequent to the establishment of the Bank of Cape Nome he was elected vice-president of that institution. In 1903, he helped to organize the Union Savings and Trust Co., of Seattle, and was selected as cashier of that institution.

Mr. Solner fills both positions - that of manager of the Bank of Cape Nome, and cashier of the Union Savings and Trust Co., of Seattle. He visits Nome during the summer season, and exercise a general supervision over the Nome bank.

NOME AND SEWARD PENINSULA, 1905

PHILIP STARR

Philip Starr was one of the oldest of Alaskan pioneers and during a residence of nearly a quarter of a century in the territory had become known in nearly every resident of the southeastern section and all who knew him were his friends. He was one of the number who joined the rush to the Frazer river mines in 1858, thence in to the Caribou country and in 1874 to the Cassiar district. Until 1881 he mined in Cassiar spending the winters in Wrangel, coming during that year to Juneau where he has since resided, becoming associated with the late Stillman Lewis, their relations continuing until the death of the latter in April, 1891. His first mining in this district was on Montana creek, where during the season of his arrival he prospected with Lewis, Billy Nixon and Joe Falkner. During his residence here Mr. Starr acquired a comfortable competence in mining and city property Two sisters survive him, and are made the beneficiaries of his will. One of these, a Mrs. O'Brien, has her residence at Port Henry, N.Y., the address of the other is unknown.

Philip Starr was born in Tipperary county, Ireland in July 1842, and died in Juneau on December 29, 1896.

ALASKA MINING RECORD, December 30, 1896

HARRY G. STEEL

Harry G. Steel, editor and manager of the Nome News, is a native of Pennsylvania, where he spent his boyhood days and received his newspaper training. He is the youngest son of Col. J. Irvin Steel, treasurer of the National Editorial Association, and one of the oldest living newspaper owners in the Keystone State, having been actively engaged in the profession of near half a century. The father and five sons own in all fourteen newspapers.

H. G. Steel was city editor of the Ashland Evening Telegram, Mauch Chunk Daily Times and Pottsville Daily Republican prior to 1893, when he purchased the Shamokin Daily Herald. All of these papers are published in Pennsylvania. In 1899 Mr. Steel took a seventy-five ton plant to Dawson and started the Daily News, the first daily newspaper in the Klondike. That fall he

sent a plant to Nome and there established the
News, the first newspaper in that camp. He
went to Nome in the spring of 1900, and assumed
the active management of the News and has since
been at the head of that paper. When the
wireless system was completed between St.
Michael and Safety, Mr. Steel had the
distinction of receiving the first commercial
message over the line, and the News received
and printed the first wireless press messages
received in the North.
NOME AND SEWARD PENINSULA, 1905

JOHN L. STEELE
John L. Steele went to Alaska in 1899
and was the first mayor of Valdez. He was
involved with early legislation for Alaska. He
helped write the homestead bill; helped secure
appropriations for the Alaska cable; appeared
before the U.S. lighthouse board on three
occasions in an effort to get lighthouses in
Alaska; assisted in getting appropriations for
the Alaska Road Commission and for the U.S.
Coast and Geodetic surveys, and prevented the
passage of the bill giving Alaska a commission
form of government. He made the first
commercial gasoline in Alaska. Mr. Steele
moved to Los Angeles in 1924. He is a member
of the Alaska committee of the Los Angeles
Chamber of Commerce.
Mr. Steele has done special work for
the Los Angeles county flood control, and is
president of the Interstate Conservancy
Association for California, Arizona, Nevada and
Utah, working on the improvement of the
Colorado River and securing a permanent supply
of water for Southern California.
ALASKA WEEKLY, January 31, 1930

JAMES GORDON STEESE
General Steese made his first trip to
Alaska in 1913 for the purpose of inspecting
the proposed rail route, prior to the beginning
of construction. After that short visit he was
assigned to duty with General Goethals in the
Panama Canal zone returning to the North, in

the spring of 1920 as president of the Alaska Road commission. It was under his direction that much of the important work which has given the Alaska Road commission such an enviable reputation as a highly efficient organization was done. The Richardson Highway was transformed from a wagon road to an automobile highway, the Chistochena, Nebesna and Sushanna projects all important links in the International highway, were started under his supervision as were the Ruby extension and the Mt. McKinley highway. Seventy airfields were constructed, the Wrangell Narrows were dredged, the Nome jetty built, the Alaska Railroad was completed--in fact the transportation arterials of the entire territory are indelibly stamped with the mark of his administration ability and engineering skill.

During his northern trip General Steese was fittingly accorded the first honorary degree to be conferred by the Alaska College and School of Mines. In presenting him with the honorary degree of Doctor of Science, President Bunnell enumerated the various outstanding services which he had rendered to his country and to the engineering science as well as a list of the numerous decorations and honorary fellowships bestowed upon him by governments, societies and educational institutions. He has six times been decorated by governments and these signal honors include the Greek Croix de Guerre and a medal for bravery from Montenegro. He is a Fellow of the Royal Geographical Society and of the American Association of Adv. Science, Member Am. Society C.E., Am. Institute Mining and Metallurgical Engineers, Academy of Political Science and of many others.

General Steese has had a life full of activity. In 1926 he represented the United States at the International Navigation Congress in Cairo, Egypt, and in 1931 he again represented his country at the 15th Congress at Venice, Italy. That same year he was a delegate from the United States to the Congress of Geography held in Paris. After leaving

Alaska in 1927 he went to South America in charge of the exploration and development work of the Gulf Oil Company in Colombia, Venezuela and Panama.

ALASKA WEEKLY, July 1, 1932

CHARLES L. STEINHAUSER

Charles L. Steinhauser is a pioneer Alaskan. In 1887 he went to Point Barrow, most northwestern extremity of the territory. During the month of January, 1888, he mushed over the old Russian American Telegraph line to Unalakleet, on the Bering sea coast, and from there went to Fort Yukon and later to the Fortymile. He worked for the famous Jack McQuesten, a pioneer trader of the Yukon country, for a period of nine years. Later on, when the Klondike camp came in, Steinhauser went there, but made a failure in mining in the Dawson country. From Dawson he went to the Cook Inlet, Alaska, country, and mined with success in the Sunrise camp there. When the Nome district was discovered, he went there and worked for the Alaska Commercial Company. In 1902, in company with two partners, he went to Nelson Island, Bering sea, and started a trading post. Two years later, he sold out his interest, and started a trading post at Unalakleet. He ran this post for seven years, sold out and bought a trading post at Nulato. He ran this post for a period of ten years, and made good. He sold the Nulato post to O.P. Russell and came outside. He and his wife reside in Seattle, where Mr. Steinhauser is the president and treasurer of Sam Shucklin Company, Inc., wholesale dealers in men and boys clothing, furnishing goods, and ladies and misses and girls wearing apparel.

ALASKA WEEKLY, September 6, 1929

A. GERTRUDE STERNE

Graduated from the Church Training and Deaconess House in Philadelphia with the Class of 1916, Miss Sterne offered herself for Alaska, was appointed and arrived on the field that same year. Her first duty was at Anvik where she served as the teacher in the mission school. It was during this period of her service that she was set apart as a Deaconess by Bishop Rowe. After five years of service at Anvik, Deaconess Sterne went out on her first furlough.

Returning to the field the next year, she was sent to the Mission of our Saviour at Tanana, where she spent the rest of her Alaskan service. During some of those years she served under other member of the staff. Later she was placed in full charge of the mission and of all work at Tanana.

She retired December 31, 1935 and left for the States. A few years later she retired to Tanana for ten years. She left Tanana in 1948 and retired to Quincy, Illinois.
ALASKA CHURCHMAN, 1936

SYLVANUS HARLOW STEVENS

S. H. Stevens, editor and publisher of the Nome Gold Digger, is one of the most widely known citizens of Seward Peninsula, having held the position of councilman of Nome ever since the organization of the town. He was born in Humboldt, Kansas, June 1, 1873, but his boyhood days were spent in Chicago, where he received a public school education. His father was one of the oldest members of the Chicago Board of Trade, and at the time of his death was flax inspector for that institution. Mr. Stevens began his newspaper career on the Chicago News, and during the World's Fair, was reporter for the Graphic. At the close of the fair, he accepted a position with the Field Columbian Museum in the Art Building of the World's Fair, which was set aside for it.

He first came to Alaska in 1897, arriving in Skagway. In 1898 he started over the trail to Dawson, but stayed only a short time in the Klondike country, as his destination was Eagle. He spent two years mining in Eagle. He organized a longshoreman's union in Eagle, on account of an attempt to cut wages, and this was probably the first organization for the protection of labor in Alaska. He arrived in

Nome in the fall of 1899, but returned to the states that winter. In the spring of 1900 he went back to Nome. From Nome he started out with a pack on his back to find a job, and succeeded in securing work as a miner on Hastings Creek. In September of that season he returned to Nome and obtained employment on the Gold Digger. The editor of this paper, Mr. Coe, was in ill-health and in the hospital. His first work on the Gold Digger was in both capacities of editor and printer. He worked at the case without copy. Mr. Coe's health compelled him to return to the states that fall, and Mr. Stevens remained with the paper with which he has been connected ever since. He is now the owner of this journal.

At the time of the incorporation of the city of Nome he was elected to the council, and was appointed to the position of chairman of the law and ordinance committee, and was also a member of the finance committee. Lively interest has been taken every subsequent municipal election on account of the attempt by Mr. Stevens' opponents to defeat him. He is the only one of the councilmen who has been re-elected at every succeeding election.

He and Miss Alma Day were married October 22, 1903. Mr. Stevens is an aggressive man, and on account of the policy of his paper commands the general support of the laboring classes of the community.

NOME AND SEWARD PENINSULA, 1905

ALEXANDER CAMPBELL STEWART

Alexander Stewart came to Nome in the spring of 1900, and to quote his own language, "landed on the beach with $7 and a sprained ankle." He was one of the early arrivals in the camp. his first employment was cooking in a restaurant. The wages he received were $1.50 an hour. After earning some money, he put a pack on his back and started for the creeks. He secured some property this season, and started to go outside for the winter. At Dutch Harbor he found employment as a cook in the United States Marine Hospital. He filled this position until the hospital closed, three months and a half later.

In the spring of 1901, he returned to Nome with his brother, J.W. Stewart. They prospected during the summer season, and having the promise of a grub-stake, made preparations to remain in the country the ensuing winter. but the last boat sailed, and the promised grub-stake had not arrived. Mr. Stewart's entire available assets consisted of forty-two dollars in dust and a tent on his Cooper Gulch Claim. He lived in this tent during that winter. On February 1, 1902, he was sent to the Arctic slope. It was one of the severest and worst trips that he ever had in this country. During this trip he was in a bad blizzard, and for forty-four hours his dog team of eight dogs was buried under the snow.

He arrived in Candle City. He got a job working for Baker & Long on Candle Creek at ten dollars the day and after working twenty-nine shifts he started in mid-summer to return to Nome with a park horse across the peninsula.

After he returned to Nome the balance of the season was occupied in doing assessment work on the property he had previously acquired. He also did some prospecting on Snake River, and there and then resolved to concentrate his efforts and confine his work to this Creek. Between this date and the spring of 1903, he acquired water rights and secured surveys for the ditch which he now has partially constructed. In 1903 he went back to Green Bay, Wisconsin, and organized the Golden Dawn Mining Company. A ditch thirteen miles from Bangor Creek to Sunset Creek will be finished this year, 1905, and the work of mining by the latest improved methods will begin.

Mr. Stewart was born January 23, 1874 at Kingston, Ontario. He is of Scotch parentage and spent his boyhood days in Kingston, Ontario where, when he was ten years old, he distributed the Kingston daily papers to country subscribers. At the age of sixteen years he was a sailor on the lakes. When he was nineteen years old he went to North Michigan and became a prospector in the iron region. He worked in the woods as a lumberman. When twenty-three years old he was in Montana prospecting and mining. While he was a sailor on the lakes he learned the art of cooking and baking, and he frequently has followed his avocation as a cook to obtain funds which to go prospecting.

NOME AND SEWARD PENINSULA, 1905

FRANK P. STEWART

In the early days, Frank Stewart crossed the plains from his parents' home in Indiana, where he was born in 1852, and settled in Candelaria, Nev.

He built the first house there and located the Mt. Diablo mine, of which he was foreman for many years. While in Nevada, he married Camilla McFee.

In 1896 he came to Seattle to live, and in 1898 he joined a party headed for the Klondike. Later, he went with a party to find the headwaters of the Nass River, and after reaching it, headed for the coast, coming out in which is now the Portland Canal camp. He was the founder of the town of Stewart, British Columbia, and located the first mining claim in the Portland district, called the "Mountain Boy."

Frank P. Stewart died in his home in Renton, Wash., Friday, October 3, 1930. He is survived by his widow, Camilla Stewart, who is now with her son, F.F. Stewart of Renton; eight children, fifteen grandchildren, and four great grandchildren. His sons are F.F. Stewart of Renton; E.B. Stewart of Carson City, Nev.; M.I. Stewart of New York City; T.L. Stewart of Hoover, Wash.; C.E. Stewart of Allen, Nev.; and M.B. Stewart of Newcastle, Wash. His daughters are Mrs. W.M. Penrose of Wabuska, Nev.; and Mrs. Grace Kaiser of Seattle.

ALASKA WEEKLY, October 10, 1930

EDWIN RAWSON STIVERS

E.R. Stivers was born in Knoxville, Tenn.,

in 1865. Graduated from the University of Michigan, he enlisted shortly afterward in Company C, 14th Minnesota Infantry, and served during the Spanish American War. He was mustered out as a Sergeant Major.

Though a graduate pharmacist, Mr. Stivers never followed his profession. He came to Alaska about 1900 with the U.S. Customs service and remained here until he retired in 1935 on account of reaching the age limit. He was stationed in Nome, Hyder, St. Michael, Skagway, Juneau and Seward. He was a member of the Arctic Brotherhood.

Since leaving the Territory, he has made his home in Ocean Beach, California.

Edwin Rawson Stivers died October 1, in Los Angeles. Surviving are his wife, Mrs. Irene O. Stivers; a daughter, Virginia Stivers Bartlett; his son, Edwin R. Stivers and his brother, Col. Daniel Gay Stivers, U.S.A., retired, of Butte, Montana.

NOME AND SEWARD PENINSULA, 1905

WALTER STORY

Captain Walter Story, a pioneer in the salmon canning industry in Alaska built the first plant in the vicinity of where the present town of Cordova now stands.

Captain Story early became identified with the Alaska Packers' Association and remained with that big canning concern until his retirement from active work in 1911. It was in 1887 that Captain Story built a cannery on Wingham Island, near Controller bay. Later the plant was moved to Kokenhenic island, and still later it occupied the site now covered by the railroad yards of the Copper River & Northwestern railroad at Cordova.

The railroad town looked good to Captain Story, who resigned from the Alaska Packers' Association and threw in his lot with Cordova. James MacCormac was brought to Alaska by Captain Story and he and the Captain opened a mercantile establishment in Cordova. Later, they sold the store and erected a hotel building which was called the Alaskan hotel.

Captain Story's experiences around Eyak lake where he operated a cannery would make an interesting story. The natives from up and down the Copper river and from what is now called Katalla made annual pilgrimages to the Eyak cannery to trade their furs for supplies. Captain Story was probably the first white man to see the real deposits there. He burned coal at the cannery over thirty-five years ago.

Walter Story died in Alameda, California, in February of 1925. He is survived by his wife, Mrs. Grace Story, and by two married daughters, all living in California.
    ALASKA WEEKLY, February 13, 1925
    DAILY ALASKA EMPIRE, November 1, 1939

W. H. STOUT

Judge Stout was well known throughout Southeastern Alaska. He went to Skagway in 1898 and in 1899 located at Haines where he has since resided. He was United States Commissioner there for many years, and for nearly twenty years has been practicing law. He is survived by a daughter, Mrs. Fred E. Handy, at Haines, a daughter in Portland, and a daughter and son in San Francisco. A son residing in Portland died a year or so ago.

Judge W. H. Stout died in Haines, Alaska, April 9, 1926. Judge Stout was about 84 years of age at the time of his death.
    ALASKA WEEKLY, April 23, 1926

STRANDBERG, DAVID AND CHARLES

The Strandbergs went to the United States from Sweden, when very young and settled in Elk County, Penn., where their father was engaged in the timber business. The elder brother(David?) went to the Klondike with the rush of 1898, remaining there until 1905. During his stay in the Klondike he prospected and mined.

The younger brother went to the Klondike in 1901 and followed the same pursuit. In September, 1905, the Strandbergs went to the Tanana Valley and settled on Ester Creek. The partnership of the Strandberg Brother was formed, and they worked several claims in that area.

In the fall of 1907 the firm of Strandberg Bros. & Johnson was formed.

ALASKA-YUKON MAGAZINE, January 1909

GUY M. STREET

Captain Guy M. Street first went to Alaska in 1896, running coastwise. In 1898, he was on the Excelsior on the Yukon River and in 1900 transferred to the government steamer Jefferson Davis. In the years following, he was on the Hamilton, Cudihee and T.C. Powers, of the N.A.T.& T. Line, and then went over to the N.C. Company, running the Schwatka. Captain Street knew all of the camps of the North from St. Michael to Fort Yukon, and after a while, tiring of the river, stopped ashore for a couple of years and opened a store at Sullivan Creek, in the Hot Springs district. In 1912, he took over a White Pass Route job and for a time was on the Robert Kerr, of the Pacific Cold Storage Company. With the breaking out of the war, Captain Street came outside and for a time was in the Transport Service running troops and supplies to Europe. The war over, he returned to the Pacific Coast and for a time was on the Oriental run, but one day he saw one of the new Franklin cars and decided to trade his ship for a Sedan and go ashore and try his hand at selling the same. Since then, Captain Street has been driving and selling Franklins in the Seattle agency.

ALASKA WEEKLY, May 16, 1930

JOHN H. SULLIVAN

John H. Sullivan, 78 years of age, Navy veteran of the Civil War, went to Alaska just after this country purchased the territory from Russia. Mr. Sullivan also had a long and colorful career as an Indian fighter and was enroute with reenforcements for General Custer when that officer and all his men were killed in the battle of the Little Big Horn.

If not the oldest Alaska pioneer, Mr. Sullivan was among the oldest, for in 1869 he went North with Battery I, 21st Artillery, and was barracked at Wrangell. Here Alaska's first weekly newspaper began life, with Mr. Sullivan as its editor. It was issued from a hand press in the barracks.

Mr. Sullivan, born in Cork, Ireland, came to the United States at the age of 4. Upon his father's death in the Civil War, he enlisted in the Navy at the age of 16 and served for the duration of the war. He then enlisted in the Army and served for sixteen years, much of the time with the rank of first sergeant. He participated in the major Indian campaigns of the West, including the Snake-Piute, Bannock, Nez Perce and Sheep wars.

Mr. Sullivan's career also included distinction as an early professional baseball player with the Southern League and as an Army sharpshooter. He had resided in Seattle and Alaska the last forty-three years. John H. Sullivan died in February 1926.

ALASKA WEEKLY, February 19, 1926

MARK L. SULLIVAN

Mr. Sullivan was a native of Main, born 1868. Early in life accompanied his parents to Michigan and received his education at the University of Michigan at Ann Arbor. After graduation from the law department of this university he removed to San Francisco. He was associated with William H. Metson.

Mr. Sullivan relocated to the Northern territory. He remained at Nome until the discovery of the great Tanana gold fields, when in 1903 he cast his loft in the new district. At Fairbanks he formed a law partnership with John L. McGinn under the firm name of McGinn & Sullivan. This firm was connected with much of the mining litigation that marked the early history of the Tanana Valley. The firm was dissolved last year, when Mr. Sullivan"s commercial and mining interests took him to the Iditarod district, where he, in addition to practicing law, was interested in business and mining with his brother-in-law, Charles Suter.

Mr. Sullivan died at Fairbanks, Alaska,

March 23, 1911.
ALASKA-YUKON MAGAZINE, May 1911

MICHAEL J. SULLIVAN

Michael J. Sullivan is a miner from Dawson who has been identified with Northwestern Alaska since the spring of 1900, and is now a prominent mine operator of the Gold Run and Solomon River regions of Seward Peninsula.

He was born on a farm in Iowa, February 9, 1867, and received his education in the public schools of his native state. From the time he was nineteen years old, and for a period of ten years, he was connected with the train service of railroads in the United States and Mexico. He began his railroad career on the Union Pacific and concluded this line of work in Mexico.

In 1897 his was one of the first outfits to go over White Pass. His trip across the lakes and down the Yukon was a memorable experience. While he was in Dawson he mined on Hunker Creek, and he came down the river to Nome in the spring of 1900. This camp has been the seat of his mining operations ever since that date. Mr. Sullivan is connected with several important mining enterprises, and is the owner of some valuable and promising properties.

NOME AND SEWARD PENINSULA, 1905

LOUIS W. SUTER

L. W. Suter, the jeweler, is one of the prominent and reputable business men of Nome. He came to this country in the spring of 1900. He owns and conducts the leading jewelry store of Nome, and probably carries the largest and best selected stock of jewelry of any merchant in Alaska.

Mr. Suter was born in Rouse's Point, New York, Dec. 23, 1869, but the family moved to Swanton, Vt., when he was an infant. His trade came to him by inheritance, as he is the son of a jeweler. The early part of his life was spent in Swanton, where he was educated and began life in mercantile pursuits, being placed in charge of a store when he was seventeen years old. He went to Seattle in 1891 and was employed by the McDougall & Southwick Company, and at a later period was on the road as a traveling salesman in jewelry lines.

Mr. Suter is a member of the Masons, the Arctic Brotherhood and the Eagles. He was president of the Anvil Masonic Club one year. Since he resided in Nome Mr. Suter has taken one journey to the states, in 1903. It was during this trip he arranged for carrying the large stock which gives his store the eminence among jewelry stores of Alaska.

NOME AND SEWARD PENINSULA, 1905

INGVARD BERNER SVERDRUP

Among the first men to arrive in Nome in the spring of 1899, was I. B. Sverdrup, of Valdez, formerly of San Francisco. Since this early date he has been identified with the Nome country, but has spent most of the winters in San Francisco. He is extensively interested in mining in the vicinity of Nome, owning among other valuable properties, No. 6 Dexter Creek, which he has successfully operated. He was in Nome during the winter of 1902-1903, and took active part in the promotion of out-door sports, being one of the organizers of the ski club. He was prominent in the construction and management of the skating rink. Having lived during the days of his boyhood and early manhood in Northern Europe he was familiar with the winter out-door sports in high latitudes, and believed that their introduction in Nome would be beneficial to the miners who were patiently waiting for the long winter to pass. This was the inception of the most popular winter sport of Nome. Men, women and children have learned the art of skiing, and include it in exercise for pastime, or utilize their knowledge of the use of the ski in traveling over the country.

Mr. Sverdrup was born in the northern part of Norway December 24, 1864, and educated at Trondhjen. His father was a merchant, and the family, which emigrated from Schleswig to

Norway in 1620, is prominent in the political, educational and scientific affairs of Norwegian history. Prof. George Sverdrup helped to frame the Constitution of 1814, and Captain Otto Sverdrup, a cousin of the subject of this sketch, was commander of the Fram in Nansen's first polar expedition. He accompanied Nansen twice in Arctic voyages, and in 1900 was at the head of an expedition which entered the Arctic region through Baffin's Bay, and is accredited with having accomplished the most valuable scientific work of any of the explorers in the Frozen Sea.

Mr. Sverdrup came to America in 1888, and located in San Francisco, where he conducted a grocery business for ten years.

NOME AND SEWARD PENINSULA, 1905

ELLA LEOTIA SMITH SWANTON

Ella Leotia Smith was born in the Middle West and was married in the '80s to Frank W. Swanton of Minneapolis, Minn. She was a graduate of the Emerson School of Oratory in Boston, Mass. and gave Shakespearean readings on Chautauqua circuits and abroad. With her husband she visited Great Britain and the continent and at one time presented a Shakespearean program for the late King Edward.

As the wife of Mr. Swanton, who was the first postmaster at Nome, Mrs. Swanton entertained in her home many national and interesting figures. Both Amudsen and Peary, Arctic explorers, were personal friends of the family.

Mrs. Swanton was a famous cook, and frequently remarked, "There was three things I know--Shakespeare, cats, and cooking." During her residence in Portland, where she had lived since 1906, Mrs. Swanton devoted herself to the work of the humane society, to her gardening and entertaining, and housed at her residence a fine private collection of Alaskan curios. Mr. Swanton who died about 14 years ago, was in the flouring mill business in Portland, managing the Columbia Milling company.

Ella Leotia Smith Swanton died near

Portland, Oregon, May 30, 1933. She is survived by a brother, Charles Smith, Sioux City, Iowa; and a sister, Mrs. Alice C. Nash, Minneapolis, Minn.

ALASKA WEEKLY, June 9, 1933

FRANK W. SWANTON

During the fall of 1897 and spring of 1898, Frank W. Swanton, with others, organized a company known as the Minnesota-Alaska Development Co. of Minneapolis, Minn. This company built, at Tacoma, Wash., two river steamers, the Minneapolis and the Nugget, for the purpose of exploring Alaska and incidentally of securing some of the gold of this new Eldorado. He arrived in St. Michael about August 1, 1898, with the intention of going up the Yukon to Dawson, but reports received of the immense riches of the Koyukuk, and its tributaries, they changed their plans and proceeded to ascend the Koyukuk. On September 13, at a point above Bergman, a town some 600 miles up the Koyukuk, the steamer landed on a bar and there it remained, all efforts to get it off proving futile. He prospected all that winter, going up the Koyukuk as far as its head, but found nothing that seemed like pay, and when the ice broke in the spring, came down to Nulato. At that point the big strike at Nome was first heard of, and he consequently determined to go there, and arrived at Nome August 15, 1899. He went to work on the beach with a rocker, located some town lots and some mining claims. He was municipal clerk of the first government ever formed in Nome, and when the Nome Mining District was formed in compliance with federal statute, he became deputy mining recorder and later postmaster of Nome, which position he still holds.

Mr. Swanton was born in Clommell, Iceland, December 29, 1863, and educated in a private school and Queens College. He went to the United States in 1883 and was employed by the Pillsbury, Washburn Flour Mills Co. of Minneapolis. At a later date he was in

business for himself in the steam specialty line, representing a number of large manufacturers of steam supplies.
    NOME AND SEWARD PENINSULA, 1905

ALFRED P. SWINEFORD

    Alfred Swineford was born in Ashland, Ohio, September 14, 1836. He received a common school education and became a printer's apprentice at fifteen years of age. After working at his trade in the office of the "Ashland Press" he joined the staff of the "Ohio Statesman" at Columbus, O.; later came to Wisconsin in 1853, and read law for three years while working at his trade. Late in 1856 he moved to Minnesota and was there admitted to the bar in April, 1857. He established the "Freeborn County Standard" at Albert Lea, Minnesota, and was later associated with the "La Crosse Democrat" in 1859. During 1860 this enterprising young journalist published "The Milwaukee Daily Empire" until after the election of that year. From Milwaukee he moved to Fond du Lac, Wisconsin, and there published the "Democratic Press" daily and weekly. This field of endeavor claimed his best efforts until early in the winter of 1867, when he moved to Marquette, Michigan, and there founded the "Mining Journal," which he conducted as editor and proprietor until appointed governor of Alaska by Hon. Grover Cleveland, in 1885.

    In 1889 Governor Swineford resigned and again resumed the profession of journalism in Wisconsin. During President Cleveland's second term Governor Swineford was appointed surveyor general of the district land offices of the United States. While in office he made a number of journeys to Alaska. He again made Alaska his home and established THE MINING JOURNAL at Ketchikan.
    ALASKA'S MAGAZINE, January 1906
    ALASKAN, November 1886

TILLIE PAUL TAMAREE

    Although Mrs. Tamaree was born in Victoria, B.C., practically all her life had been spent in Alaska. She was among the first pupils in Mrs. Amanda McFarland's school, which began in Wrangell in 1877. She married Mr. Louis Paul and both were commissioned missionaries by the Board and sent to the village of Klukwan. Later Mr. Paul was drowned, leaving Mrs. Tamaree with three sons, William, Louis, and Samuel. Sheldon Jackson then assigned her to the Sitka Training School, where she was on the staff until 1904. Mrs. Tamaree also labored at Petersburg and Kake. In 1905 she married Mr. Tamaree and had made her home in Wrangell since.

Mrs. Tamaree was one of the few workers to be honored with a 50-year pin for missionary service by the Board of National Missions, and was the first woman elder of the Presbyterian Church in the United States after the General Assembly authorized their election.

Mrs. William Tamaree, age 90, a Presbyterian missionary died at her home in Wrangell August 20.

VERSTOVIAN, September 1952

JULIA VALENTINE TANNER

Julia Valentine was born at Dowagiac, Michigan, December 15, 1853. In 1868 she crossed the plains with her mother and brother, Emery Valentine. The family located at Central City, Colorado, where she was married April 25, 1871, to Josias H. Tanner. To this union was born three children, Mrs. Maud Schutzman and Mrs. Jessie Grieves, both living at Tacoma, and Fred E. Tanner, resident of Skagway. Mrs. Schutzman and her husband, Charles Schutzman, lived at Skagway in the earlier days of the history of that town.

Mr. and Mrs. Tanner moved from Colorado to Tacoma in 1892 and went to Juneau in 1895, Mr. Tanner becoming manager of the People's wharf for Emery Valentine. Mr. Tanner later was in a grocery store that was owned by Mr. Valentine. He was one of the first to locate in Skagway early in 1897, and Mrs. Tanner joined him there shortly afterward. They have resided there, where Mr. Tanner was engaged in the hardware business, except when Mr. Tanner was United States marshal for more than five years, when they resided in Juneau. Mrs. Tanner also visited Juneau during the two sessions of the territorial legislature when Mr. Tanner was a member of the territorial senate.

Julia Valentine Tanner died in Tacoma, Washington February 27, 1927. In addition to her husband, daughter and son, and brother, Mrs. Tanner is survived by two sisters, one residing in Colorado and the other in Iowa.

ALASKA WEEKLY, March 11, 1927

LEWIS B. TANNER

L. B. Tanner came to Nome in the spring of 1900 and started a lumber yard. By 1902 the business had grown to considerable proportions. This fact, together with Mr. Tanner's plans to reduce the price of lumber by buying timber and operating a sawmill, and shipping direct from his own plant, induced him to seek a man for a partner.

This man was found in W. A. Clark, and the firm of Tanner & Clark took charge of the business. Mr. Tanner went out to Washington at the close of the season of 1902, and bought timber land equipped with a sawmill plant in King County, and in two years the firm has cut and shipped to Nome near 12,000,000 feet of lumber. Much of this material has been shipped in chartered schooners. The yard in Nome at the close of navigation of the past two seasons has contained between 5,000,000 and 6,000,000 feet of lumber. A complete planing mill is a part of the equipment of this yard.

Mr. Tanner is a native of Canada. He was born in Brantford, Ontario, January 17, 1866, and was educated in the public schools of the province. He learned the trade of a builder and contractor, which he followed, with the exception of a few years devoted to mining in the Rossland and Trail Creek country, B. C., and the Klondike region, until he came to Nome. He emigrated from Canada in 1890, going to Seattle and subsequently to Portland, Ore. In 1898 he went to Dawson, but returned to Seattle

the following year. He came to Nome in the spring of 1900 on the steamer Alpha, and began the successful business career narrated in the foregoing. September 4, 1900, L. B. Tanner and Miss M. N. Pickard were married in Tacoma.
NOME AND SEWARD PENINSULA, 1905

CHARLES MURPHY TAYLOR

Charlie Taylor was born at Elmira, New York, June 7, 1866. When he was seventeen, he moved to California and from there he migrated to Leadville, Co., where he was an assayer in his uncle's smelter for several years.

In 1895 he joined the rush to Cook Inlet, Alaska. He then returned to the States and entered the employ of the Seattle Hardware Company. He then went to Ketchikan in 1906 to enter the employ of J. H. Heckman.

It was in the same year that Mr. Taylor and Lula B. Gorst were married in Port Orchard, Washington. They then went to Ketchikan and have made their home there ever since.

Three years later, Mr. Taylor entered the employ of the Alaska Steamship Company, and in 1911 he became agent for that organization.

This position he held until 1921 when he assumed charge of their building department holdings until his death in August of 1928.
NOME AND SEWARD PENINSULA, 1905

CHARLES W. THORNTON

Charles W. Thornton is one of the pioneers of Northwestern Alaska, having been a member of the Kotzebue Sound expedition in 1898. Mr. Thornton is a son of Wesley Coates Thornton, who was a grandson of William Thornton, of the Revolutionary Army. Mr. Thornton's mother was Rachel Livingston, whose grandfather was also a soldier in the Army of the Revolution.

The subject of this sketch was born in Le Seuer, Minnesota, March 25, 1869. He lived on a farm in Hennepin County in that state until he was thirteen years old. The death of his father, his mother having died six years prior, caused the family of three boys and one girl to decide to leave the old home and take up their residence with various friends and relatives, where they could continue their schooling. The little property left by the father was not available for the purpose of supporting the children while they were in school, so they were thrown upon their own resources. Charles, having determined to become a lawyer, was enabled through hard work, strict economy, and diligent study to obtain a college education.

Early in the spring of 1898 and while he was a resident of Seattle and reading law, he was attracted by the excitement over the Alaska gold fields, and joined the stampeders to Kotzebue Sound. During the winter of his residence in Northern Alaska he was on the trail for forty days, and during thirty days of this time the sun never showed itself above the horizon, and the average record of the thermometer was 62° below zero.

Not finding any gold mines in the Kotzebue Sound country he went to Nome in the summer of 1899. His first work in the Nome camp was mining on the beach. In 1890 he engaged in the general merchandise business, and was the head of the firm of Thornton & Keith. The big storm of September 12-13 of this year wrecked their building and caused them such financial injury that they discontinued business. Mr. Thornton again took up the study of law, and was admitted to the bar in the District Court of Nome in August, 1902.

Subsequent to this date he was associated with the Archer, Ewing Company, prominent merchants of Nome, and during 1903-'04 was the manager of their store in Solomon. He also practiced law in Solomon. During his Alaskan career he has acquired some valuable mining property. He spent the winter of 1904-'05 in the states, and will return to Nome this season for the purpose of disposing of his interests there with the intention of locating in Chicago for the practice of law.

ALASKA WEEKLY, August 17, 1928

CONRAD M. THULAND

Conrad M. Thuland is the son of a

Norwegian school teacher, and was born in Bergen, Norway, May 7, 1868. During his boyhood he resided in Christiana for a period of eight years, and attended the Latin school in that city. In 1884 he emigrated with the family to Decorah, Iowa, where he attended Luther College. He was graduated from this institution 1885, with the degree of A. B. He took a post-graduate course the following year at the University of Minnesota, and in 1887 began his career as a journalist by establishing a Norwegian newspaper in La Crosse, Wis. He was subsequently connected with the publication of several papers, both English and Norwegian. He moved to Seattle in 1889 (before the fire) and established the Washington Tidende, which was afterward merged into the Washington Post. His knowledge of the law requisite for admission to the bar was obtained in the office of Wiley & Bostwick, of Seattle.

He opened an office in Seattle in 1895, and was enjoying a lucrative practice when the Nome strike was made. In the spring of 1900 he came to Nome to defend the interests of some of his clients, acquired some valuable mining property while here, and after returning to Seattle in 1903, has come back to Nome to stay indefinitely. This season he is building a cottage on First Avenue, where he and Mrs. Thuland will reside.

Mr. Thuland has been successful in a number of suits involving valuable mining property. During the winters of 1901-'02 and 1902-'03, Mr. Thuland was acting vice-consul in Nome for Norway and Sweden. He was married in Seattle Dec. 28, 1897.

NOME AND SEWARD PENINSULA, 1905

J. C. TOLMAN

J.C.(Dad) Tolman first went to Alaska in June, 1889, sailing from San Francisco on the steam schooner Bertha. He landed at Oonalaska(Unalaska) and followed the coast north to Kodiak. Enroute, at Karluk, he participated in a baseball game on the Fourth of July. He arrived at Kodiak on July 6, where he was stationed as deputy collector of customs until 1891, when he was transferred to Wrangell, where he remained until the summer of 1895. In 1896, he went as purser on the steamer Dora, operated by the A. C. company, on the run between Juneau and Dutch Harbor. At the close of the season, in December, he started for Circle City, crossing the Chilkoot Pass and making a boat at Linderman. At the breakup, he went down the river and landed at Dawson June 9, 1897. He had intended going to Circle, as he had interests there, so continued on down the river, but returned to Dawson on the first boat. Here he mined on Bonanza, with Captain Watson, during the season and went outside in the late fall. In January, 1898, he started in over the White Pass, with a big outfit; built a scow and boat and reached Dawson June 11. He bought and worked ground on Sulphur, Dominion and Lovett Hill, none of which paid. He took the first boat from Seattle to Nome in 1900, and secured an interest in No. 1 Daniels creek, which later proved to be one of the richest claims on the Seward peninsula, but was "gyped" out of his equity. In 1902, he was in on the first stampede to Candle creek and remained there until 1904. In March, 1905, Tolman took the newly-appointed U.S. Marshall Powell in over the trail via Valdez and Fairbanks, and served as deputy marshal and later was named chief deputy marshal at Nome. While in Candle, Mr. Tolman organized Igloo No. 2, Pioneers of Alaska, and is a life member of that organization. His sons, Crit and Chester are both members. He left Nome in the fall of 1908, but was back in Alaska the next year, as deputy marshal at Seward under U.S. Marshal H. P. Sullivan. Later he served as senior game warden at Seward under Gov. Walter E. Clark. His two sons served in the World War. His permanent home is at Point Loma (San Diego), California.

ALASKA WEEKLY, October 26, 1928

A. H. TRAPHAGEN

Delmer H. Traphagen was born in Michigan October 14, 1874. He graduated from the Michigan State College in 1898; taught school for two years until the lure of gold brought him to Seattle, where he took a boat for Nome.

He was superintendent of schools in Nome in 1902, and then returned to Seattle to teach in the Central and Broadway high schools and to become principal of the public night schools. Later he organized the Summit and Interbay schools, and served as principal of each, at the same time studying law at night.

In 1904 he went back to Nome and engaged in mining until 1907, when he returned to Seattle and entered the construction field. He built the Hanford irrigation project and the first unit of the Tieton project, and was also the builder of the Inglewood Country Club and Broadmoor.

Mr. Traphagen found time to devote to civic affairs. Among other matters, he was a member of the city zoning commission and director of the National Bank of Commerce.

He is survived by his wife Mrs. Pearl Traphagen of Seattle, and two sisters who live in the East.

ALASKA WEEKLY, June 6, 1930

DEEMAR H. TRAPHAGEN

He was born near Fenton, Michigan, October 14, 1876 and grew up on a farm. After graduating from the high school he took the examination for teachers which he successfully passes. He succeeded in obtaining a country school, and after teaching one year attended the University of Michigan, paying for the tuition with the money he had earned. By teaching and selling school supplies he earned the money with which he obtained a university education and fitted himself for the profession of teaching. He was principal in the Owaso public schools in his native state in 1900, when he resigned to go to Nome.

Arriving in Nome he undertook the work of mining on the beach. He made some money operating on the beach, and later in the season went to Teller. In 1901 he was interested in the mines of the Kougarok District. But these ventures not being so successful as he anticipated, he returned to Seattle in the fall of 1901 with the intention of taking a post graduate course. In Seattle he organized the night school and taught mathematics in the high school during the winter. In the spring he resigned and returned to Nome, where he spent the summer season, returning to Seattle in the fall of 1902. During the winter of 1902-'03 he was principal of the Interbay School, and was re-engaged to teach this school the succeeding term when he secured the principalship of the Nome School.

NOME AND SEWARD PENINSULA, 1905

CLARENCE M. TUCKER

Clarence Tucker was born May 17, 1863, in Tippecanoe County, Indiana, where his father engaged in farming and where he grew to manhood, receiving a common and high school education. At the age of 22 years, he came to Washington, first locating at Port Townsend, from where he went to Whitby Island. The summer of 1885 was spent on a farm near Dugulla Bay and in the autumn he moved to Irondale, Jefferson County, where he was employed for some time by a flouring mill company.

In the fall of 1886 he went to San Juan County, locating at Argyle, where he engaged in farming and was instrumental in organizing the Argyle Milling Co. Soon afterwards he bought out his partner's interest in the enterprise. For several years he continued its operation and while thus engaged his interest in public life commenced, first as postmaster at Argyle and as justice of the peace of that precinct. Later he was elected and served eight years as county treasurer. With the exception of the time he spent in 1898 and 1899 in the Yukon, his residence is San Juan County was continuous.

Soon after the arrival of the gold ship Portland in Seattle, Mr. tucker and a man named

Hill embarked for Skagway and succeeded in transporting their outfit to a point near the Skagway Summit. Hill remained with the cache and Tucker returned to the States, but went back to Skagway early in February of 1898. They moved their outfit to Bennett, built a boat and arrived in Dawson about the middle of June. During the summer or late fall they were joined by a party of old acquaintances, consisting of John "Doc" Kelly, Fred Knight and Tom and Al Paxson, and spent the winter of '98-99 prospecting on Fortymile, building a large cabin on O'Brien Creek.

The party separated in the early spring and Mr. Tucker spent some time prospecting on Nugget, Eula and Napoleon Gulches. late in the fall Mr. Tucker returned to his home in Friday Harbor.

He was married December 23, 1900 to Miss Marie Jensen.

Throughout his long residence in San Juan County, Mr. Tucker took an active part in political and business affairs which brought him a large acquaintance. He was probably best known through his affiliation with the San Juan County Bank, which he entered in December 1906, and in which institution he was soon made vice-president. It was through ill-health that he was compelled to resign from active duties at the bank, January 1, after twenty-six years of service.

Mr. Tucker died at his home in Friday Harbor, October 5, 1933. He is survived by two sisters, Mrs. Albert Lerable of Seattle and Mrs. Matthias Stone of LaFayett, Ind., and one brother, Charles G. Tucker of Bellingham.

ALASKA WEEKLY, October 27, 1933

JOHN RANDOLPH TUCKER

Judge Tucker was born in August, 1854, a member of one of the most distinguished families of Virginia, where he spent his boyhood and young manhood. He received his early education in Washington and Lee University, and later studied law at the University of Virginia. He was elected judge

of the circuit court for his judicial district
in 1898; and in 1908, he was elected to the
state senate where he served with outstanding
ability until his appointment in 1913, as
federal judge of the Second division of Alaska
by President Wilson.

Mrs. Tucker is the daughter of the late
General Wade Hampton of South Carolina.
0   Judge Tucker died in Bedford, Virginia,
D0ecember 18, 1926.

ALASKA WEEKLY, February 11, 1927

PHILLBERT TURNELL (REV.)

Rev. Phillbert Turnell, S.J., beloved
pioneer priest of Alaska, passed away in his
89th year in Sacred Heart Hospital, Spokane,
last Saturday.

Father Turnell was born in Venice, Italy
in 1850. He was a member of a family of royal
lineage, and bore the title of Count up to the
time he entered the Jesuit Order at the age of
22. Father Turnell had made some priestly
studies before joining the Society of Jesus at
Monaco, Italy in 1873. He was ordained in
Lerris, France in 1878.

Father Turnell arrived in San Francisco in
1878 and taught for three years each at Santa
Clara University and San Francisco University.

In 1881, eight years before Washington
Territory was admitted to statehood, he was
attached to Saint Francis Regis Mission,
Colville, Washington, as the district mission
worker. From that mission he frequently rode
horseback to the Spokane Indians on Peone
Prairie, a distance of 94 miles. Often there
were detours for sick calls over the hills and
back to the valley trail. From 1883 to 1886
Father Turnell was at De Smet Mission with the
Coeur d' Alene Indians, and taught English to
the Indian youth. In Montana he labored among
the Blackfeet Indians, the Cheyennes, the
Flatheads, and the Crows from 1887 to 1898.

In 1898 Father Turnell went to Skagway
which at that time embraced a vast mission area
reaching to Sitka on the South and to Valdez
and Seward from his Skagway headquarters until

1905 when he was transferred to Valdez and Seward. In 1908 he returned to Skagway and remained there for ten years. For a time Father Turnell was pastor in Douglas and later in Anchorage and afterwards assistant pastor in Fairbanks and Ketchikan.

Father Turnell had the long record for 34 years of service in Alaska. For the past five years he has been at Mount Saint Michael's, Spokane. He died in Spokane, Washington on October 29, 1938.

ALASKA CATHOLIC, November 5, 1938

H. S. TURNER

H.S. Turner was born at Nashville, New York, and spent his early boyhood days on a farm in Sauk County, Wisconsin. He left for the West when he was about twenty years old stopping in Helena, Montana for some little time and coming to Seattle just after the fire in 1899. Mr. Turner says that the first work that he did in Seattle was shingling a house.

Getting the gold fever when the gold boat, Portland, came into Seattle in 1897, he left on August 5 on the old steamer, Islander, for Skagway, being one of the first to go over the famous Skagway Trail. Mr. Turner arrived in Dawson just eight days before the freezeup. Mr. turner stayed in Dawson and at different times owned sixty-seven different mining claims, none of which proved to be of much value.

Mr. Turner left for Nome on one of the first boats down the river in the spring of 1900, coming back to Dawson that fall with Eddie Whittemore, a well-known Alaskan. Upon coming back to Dawson they started in to develop two claims on Lower Hunter and at that time had the only claims in the district where they had two steam hoists on their property.

They left for Seattle in 1900, at which time Mr. Turner went into the Real Estate business and was quite prominent in platting Capitol Hill, H.S. Turner's University Tract, and H.S. Turner's Interlaken District and several other districts which now constitute

the best residential districts of the city.
      Mr. Turner is better known among his fellow realtors as "Regrade" Turner and was prominent in the development of the old regrade and is now giving practically his whole attention to the property in the new regrade district.

ALASKA WEEKLY, November 16, 1928

ALBERT L. VALENTINE

Albert L. Valentine came to Nome in 1900 as manager of Nome Trading Company. Mr. Valentine was elected to the Nome council at the municipal election held in April, 1902, and was unanimously selected by that body as mayor of Nome.

Mr. Valentine was born in Fontanelle, Adair County, Iowa, June 18, 1868. He went to California with his parents in 1875. The death of his mother a few weeks after their arrival, was the cause of the boy going to Seattle to reside with his uncle. Mr. Valentine's education was obtained in the Seattle public schools. At the age of sixteen he began to earn his own livelihood. In 1886 he was employed by the Puget Sound and Gray's Harbor Railroad Company as a member of the surveying party. This employment probably determined much of his future career. From 1887 to 1890 he was in the Seattle city engineer's office. Later he was associated with the Northern Pacific Railroad Company, in connection with the Seattle terminals. From 1892 to 1897 he was assistant engineer and chief clerk of the O. I. Co., now the Pacific Coast Co. In 1897 Mr. Valentine was employed by the Northern Pacific Coal Company, but went back to the O. I. Co. in the fall as manager of the store at Franklin. Here he remained until 1899. In the following year he came to Nome, where he resided three years. He is still interested in mining and ditch property in the Nome country.

At the state and county election in 1904 Mr. Valentine was elected to the office of surveyor of King County, Washington, a position which his training and wide experience eminently qualifies him to fill. February 14, 1894, Mr. Valentine married Miss Martha Sidebotham. The issue of this union is one child, Albert L. Valentine, Jr., born October 13, 1896.

NOME AND SEWARD PENINSULA, 1905

EMERY VALENTINE

Born in Dowagiac, Michigan in 1858, Mr. Valentine lived almost all the years of his life in pioneer countries. His ancestry dated back on his mother's side to William Bradford, who came to America on the first trip of the Mayflower in 1620, and served as governor of the Plymouth colony for many years, and his father was Joseph Valentine, whose ancestors came from Hamstead, England, in 1630.

As a boy to ten years he crossed the plains from Michigan to Colorado, riding a small pony all the way with an old overcoat for a saddle and rope for stirrups.

He grew to manhood in Colorado, early engaging in metal mining, which pursuit he followed until an accident deprived him of a leg. He then apprenticed himself to a jeweler and learned the goldsmith's trade. Leaving Colorado in 1884, he went to Montana, and following two years residence there he went to Alaska, arriving in Juneau in May, 1886, and since that time has made that territory his home.

Almost from the very outset of his residence in Juneau, and until a few years ago, Mr. Valentine took a personal interest in civic and political affairs as well as business enterprises. He opened a jewelry store in Juneau immediately after arriving, and continued it through all the intervening years.

He was organized of the present Juneau Volunteer Fire Department, and its first chief. He had been an honorary member of that organization for many years. He is credited with being the father of the Juneau public library, and his activities in the building of private and municipal wharves have been of material benefit to the community in both transportation and trade.

Since Juneau was incorporated in 1900, Mr. Valentine had served as its mayor for six terms, between 1908 and 1918, and member of the city council in 1902.

In national and territorial politics he was a Republican, but in 1912 cast his fortunes with the Bull Moose movement. He was one of the leaders in the insurgent movement in Alaska and presided over the Territorial convention that sent delegates to Chicago when Roosevelt was nominated.

Emery Valentine died in Juneau, September 10, 1930.

ALASKA WEEKLY, September 19, 1930

H. R. VANDER LEEST

Mr. Vander Leest, known to many Alaskans only as "Van" was born in Grand Rapids, Mich. on May 22, 1882. He first came to Alaska in 1908. At that time he entered the employ of the Butler Mauro Drug Co. as a pharmacist at their Nome store. In 1914 he opened a branch store for the company in Juneau on South Franklin Street. In 1932 he completed purchase of the company from the owners and continued to operate the Butler Mauro Drug co. until 1952 at which time he sold out his interest and retired.

During his more than fifty years of residence in Alaska, "Van" was prominent in civic, state and fraternal activities. He was a life member of the Elks and the Pioneers. He served on both local and state Chamber of Commerce board of directors. He was a member of the board for the Pioneer's Home for a period of 15 years, the latter part as president. He was president of the Territorial Board of Pharmacy for many years. In 1955 he was elected as the Juneau representative to the Alaska Constitutional Convention.

Mr. Vander Leest died in Sitka, November 1964. He is survived by his wife, Lexie Vander Leest of Juneau, two brothers William and Garrit Hulstra of Grand Rapids, Michigan; a sister Emma Howard of Long Beach, California, two daughters, Mrs. G.C. Ricke of Woodland Hills, California and Mrs. Felix J. Toner of Juneau; eight grandchildren and two great-grandsons as well as several nieces and nephews.

ALASKA EMPIRE, November 6, 1964

CORNELIUS L. VAWTER

Cornelius Vawter came to Alaska in 1898.

Prior to 1898, Mr. Vawter was a successful silver mine operator in Montana. Then came the slump in silver and the subsequent closing of many of the mines throughout the western states. In the year 1898 Mr. Vawter was appointed a deputy and was stationed at St. Michael. At this time there was but one judicial division in Alaska. The headquarters of the court was at Sitka. In 1898 Mr. Vawter took a number of criminals from St. Michael to Sitka, among whom was Homer Bird, who was convicted of murder after two sensational trails and was hanged at Sitka. He was the first man legally executed in the territory.

In 1900 the Second Judicial division, with headquarters at Nome, was established, and Mr. Vawter was appointed United States marshal for the new division. Mr. Vawter was marshal all through the stirring days of the regime of the notorious Judge Noyes. He was the officer who took the infamous Alexander McKenzie to San Francisco under arrest upon charges of contempt of court of the Circuit Court of Appeals. Mr. Vawter was an important witness against the Noyes and McKenzie crowd, made famous by Rex Beach's story THE SPOILERS.

Subsequently Mr. Vawter returned as deputy marshal stationed at Unga, and when H.K. Love was made marshal of the Fourth division, Mr. Vawter accompanied Marshal Love to Fairbanks and has since served as deputy in the Fourth division at Iditarod, and for the past several years at Fort Gibbon.

Mr. Vawter served 23 years as an official of the Department of Justice. He is leaving Alaska and will take up residence in San Diego, California. STROLLER'S WEEKLY, Feb. 18, 1922

IOANN VENIAMINOF

Born in Siberia at the beginning of this century, Ioann Veniaminof was trained to the priesthood, and immediately after ordination the Archbishop of Irkutsk sent him, in company with two other missionaries, to the Russian Colonies on the American coast. Veniaminof's first and principal station was Oonalashka Island, where he arrived in 1823, and labored for many years with remarkable success among the Aleuts. In 1824, on the first of August(o.s.), the first solemn liturgic service was held on the island, and the anniversary of that event is observed to the present day. In the following year Veniaminof opened a school, and on the 29th of June, 1826 the first church was dedicated.

The zealous apostle made voyages to the Pribylof and other more distant isles, and in 1829 and 1832 he visited the populous villages at Nushegak on Norton Sound, making many converts. He translated portions of the New Testament, a brief catechism and sacred history into the Aleut language, and had them printed as early as 1831. Baron Wrangell, during his administration of the colonies, recognized the great merits of Veniaminof and had him transferred to a wider field of usefulness at Sitka in the 1834. Here he labored among the Kolosh, whose language he acquired as readily and thoroughly as that of the Aleuts. He officiated at the first church service ever held on the Stickeen river and made many converts. In 1840 he was made a Bishop by the Holy Synod, and proceeded to Siberia to be consecrated, and on that occasion he adopted the name of Innocentius or Innokentiy, which he bore to his death. On the 26th of September, 1841, he returned to Sitka, established a seminary, and superintended the translation of religious works into the Kolosh and Kadiak language and had them printed. The Bishop's see was subsequently transferred to Kamtchatka, from there to Yakutsk, and then to Blagovestchensk in the Amoor country; but Innocentius continued to devote his special

attention to the welfare of the American members of his diocese. His unceasing efforts met with deserved recognition, and finally the son of a poor Siberian couple was elevated to the highest position in the Church of Russia by being appointed Metropolite of Moscow, a dignity he held until his recent death.
ALASKA APPEAL, April 22, 1879

WILLIAM A. VINAL
William A. Vinal is the Nome representative of the Alaska-Boston Construction and Mining Company, a Massachusetts corporation operating in Seward Peninsula. Last season, 1904, Mr. Vinal acquired extensive interests for this company in the Solomon River region.

Mr. Vinal was born in Orono, Maine, March 14, 1860, and was educated in the University of Maine, and followed the profession of surveyor and engineer for nine years. During a period of eleven years of his life he was engaged in the lumber business in his native state. He came to Nome in 1900 and engaged in mining on Hungry Creek. He was successful in this venture, and subsequently mined on Kasson Creek in the Solomon country. He has also operated on Anvil Creek.

Mr. Vinal is a member of an old and prominent family of Massachusetts who trace their lineage back to English and Scotch ancestors. He is married. Mrs. Vinal was formerly Miss Hattie Sutherland, a relative of Miss Sutherland, one of the teachers in the Nome public school.
NOME AND SEWARD PENINSULA, 1905

JUDGE WALKER
Judge Walker, the district attorney for the Third Division of alaska, was born at Akron, Ohio. He was educated in Yale.

Several years after graduation Judge Walker became a member of the faculty of the college at Jacksonville, Ill. Later he took a law course and practiced in Chicago.

In 1906 President Roosevelt appointed

Judge Walker district attorney of the Southern District of Indian Territory, in charge of two federal judges and including eight court towns, and having the heaviest criminal district of the territorial courts.

Judge Walker holds his appointment as district attorney for the Third Division of Alaska, appointed by President Taft.

He has a wife and two sons, the latter aged 16 and 18 respectively. The younger is at Valdez, and the older son and mother will join the judge in a short time and make their home in Alaska.

ALASKA-YUKON MAGAZINE, December 1910

ADDIE CRAWFORD WARREN

Mrs. Warren was born in Oregon City, Oregon, February 24, 1854, first child of a union of two of the earliest pioneer families of the Northwest. Her parents crossed the plains, then a six months' journey by wagon train in 1847; her father, Ronald C. Crawford, to join his elder brother, Medorem, who had crossed in 1842 with the first party to bring families prepared to settle, and her mother, Elizabeth Jane Moore, with her father, James M. Moore, to join his father. The latter, Robert Moore, is famous as a member of the celebrated "Peoria Party" which left Illinois in 1838 and as a leader of the effort to make Oregon the property of the United States, he and Medorem Crawford participated in the forming of the provision government at Champoeg, Oregon, the first effort of American citizens to establish law and order west of the Missouri River. Following their marriage in 1852, Mr. and Mrs. Crawford spent their seventy-one years of married life and reared their seven children entirely within the limits of Oregon territory, mostly in what is now the state of Washington. Their eldest daughter, Addie, was educated in the schools of Oregon City and married in early womanhood Moses E. Warren, with whom she pioneered in Centralia, Washington, their home, until 1898 when they joined the gold rush to Alaska. They spent five years mining on

Victoria Gulch a tributary of Bonanza Creek, and on Gold run.

Since 1903 Mrs. Warren has made her home in Seattle. When her father relinquished his brokerage business at the age of 89, Mrs. Warren took it over and conducted it until two months before her death, June 13, 1929.

Mrs. Warren is survived by three children, Marian Warren Kelly, Helen Warren Brace, and Dr. Crawford Warren, Seattle dentist; and a brother Ronald M. Crawford; and a sister, Mrs. Laurence Booth.

ALASKA WEEKLY, June 21, 1929

P. H. WATTS

P. H. Watts was born in Chillicothe, Ohio, in 1876, and was graduated from Miami University with the degree of B. A. in 1897. He went to Seattle that fall, and was a member of the expedition that went to Kotzebue Sound in 1898. He passed the winter of 1898-'99 in a cabin on Kobuk River, and came to Nome the following spring, arriving July 25. Until 1902 he was engaged most of the time in the business of mining. He relinquished this kind of work to accept to clerkship in the Bank of Cape Nome, and subsequently was appointed assistant postmaster of Nome, a position which he still holds.

Mr. Watts is a charter member of Camp Nome No. 9, Arctic Brotherhood, and in October, 1904, was elected to the office of Arctic Chief. He has been prominently identified with the work of the Brotherhood since the organization of the Camp, serving one term as Keeper of Nuggets, five terms as Recorder and one term as Vice-Arctic Chief. He was a delegate from the Nome, Council and St. Michael Camps to the Third Annual Grand Camp meeting at Skagway, August 1903. Mr. Watts is interested in a number of claims in Cape Nome Mining District, and is the local agent of the Cripple River Hydraulic Mining Company, of New York.

NOME AND SEWARD PENINSULA, 1905

CHARLES W. WELLS

Charles W. Wells, was born in Pennsylvania July 17, 1847. Came west to California in 1867, afterwards moving to the state of Washington. In 1870 he went to British Columbia and remained until 1879 when he went to Sitka and the following year he, as stated in the Juneau narrative, settled here. He has made many trips to the Pacific coast states, where he has extensive acquaintances. He married in Juneau on December 21, 1894, Miss Loreno B. Fisher, who was a native of Vermilion county, Illinois. Mrs. Wells came of Revolutionary stock on both the father's and mother's side.

Mr. Wells built the first blacksmith shop and worked at the trade for nine years. He speaks of the dense forest that covered the entire town site at the time their party landed. Mr. Wells saw Juneau grow from a tent city to the Capital of Alaska.

ALASKA MONTHLY MAGAZINE, Oct-Nov. 1907

ELMER J. "STROLLER" WHITE

Elmer J. White was born near Cambridge, Ohio in 1860(?). He married Josephine Kays in December 1891, in Tacoma, Washington.

He began his career in the North in 1898 as a member of the staff of the SKAGWAY NEWS. Later, he went to Dawson to accept a position on the NUGGETT, and from the Stroller's Column of that newspaper he took the pseudonym by which he was known to his friends. Subsequently he moved to Whitehorse, where he purchased the STAR, which for several years he published and edited the notable success. Then he came to Douglas and bought the DOUGLAS ISLAND NEWS. He maintained it either as owner or lessor until the abandonment of mining and milling operations at Douglas, when he transferred the printing plant to this city, changing the name of the publication to STROLLER'S WEEKLY. Before coming to Alaska he was a newspaperman in Washington state and Florida.

In addition to newspaper activities, Mr.

White gave some attention to politics. He was a Democrat. Fair in partisanship, he always commanded the respect and often the support of political opponents. To the public benefit, he served from 1918 to 1921 as territorial publicity director. He was elected to the Alaska House of Representatives in 1918 and the regard of his colleagues was evidenced by his elevation to the Speakership. At the solicitation of party associates, he became a candidate for Congress in 1922, and conducted a creditable campaign.

Elmer J. "Stroller" White died in Juneau, Alaska, on September 28, 1930. He is survived by Mrs. Josephine Kays White, two sons, John Mcburney White of the United States bureau of Standards, Washington, D.C., and Albert Hamilton White, executive in a large industrial plant at Springfield, Ohio, and a daughter, Lenora White, teacher in a high school in Los Angeles, California.

DAILY ALASKA EMPIRE, September 29, 1930

JOSEPHINE WHITE

Josephine White came to Alaska with her husband, the late E.J. 'Stroller' White, well-known pioneer Alaskan journalist and their young daughter, Lenore.

They arrived at Skagway when the town was a tent city of gold-hungry stampeders. Mr. White took a job with the SKAGWAY NEWS, a weekly paper, and the Whites lived in Skagway until the autumn of 1899.

Then they went over the new White Pass Railroad to Lake Bennett. Although they did not have the $500 required before they could pass the Canadian Border, a barge owner told the Canadian officials that Mr. White was cook on the barge.

They boarded the barge in October, late in the year for a start down to Dawson, and they floated down the Yukon to within 15 miles of Dawson before the river froze.

"We went to Dawson for the mad excitement of it," Mrs. White says, "We didn't know what we would do, but Mr. White got a job with the

DAWSON NUGGET right away."

They stayed in Dawson until 1905, when they moved on to Whitehorse. Mr. White bought THE WHITEHORSE STAR, and the White family stayed in Whitehorse until 1916. Their son, Albert H.(Young Stroller) was born there.

In 1916 they came to Douglas and Mr. White bought the DOUGLAS ISLAND NEWS.

"Douglas was the big town then," she recalls. "The Treadwell Mine was going full swing."

The Whites completed construction of a new newspaper plant in time for the mine cave-in in 1917. The new plant included a cast-off press from the EMPIRE. They moved the press back to Juneau from Douglas in 1920 when STROLLER'S WEEKLY was established.

"I didn't work much on the paper," Mrs. White says. "I had two children to bring up and a little grouse-shooting to do. But when Stroller was sick I'd take over."

Mrs. White was employed as the Territorial Museum's assistant curator in 1925 by the Rev. A.P. Kashaveroff who established the museum in 1920 and was first curator.

Her husband died in 1930.

"I was the one who always talked about getting out of Alaska," she says. "How Stroller did love the Territory! You couldn't get him away."

ALASKA WEEKLY, January 13, 1950

ROBERT WHITE

Robert White was born at Boston, Mass., May 15, 1846; passed through the Boston Grammar and High schools; graduated in medicine at Harvard University in 1867; was for several months resident physician of the Royal Maternity Hospital, Edinburgh, Scotland; was six years assistant surgeon in the Massachusetts militia; was an expert in microscopical investigations, and was appointed into the marine Hospital Service August 23, 1878. During the yellow fever epidemic of 1878 he was directed by the late Surgeon General Woodworth to proceed to Cairo, Ill., Memphis, and several other towns in Tennessee, for the purpose of pursuing microscopical investigations in yellow fever cases, the results of these studies being presented by him before the Public Health Association which met at Richmond, in November, 1878. Dr. White was on duty for several months in Washington, assisting in the preparation of the BULLETIN OF PUBLIC HEALTH during a portion of the period when it was published by the Marine Hospital Service. In May, 1879, he was ordered to Alaska, at his own request, to serve as medical officer of the revenue steamer RICHARD RUSH.

Dr. White died in New York, February 24, 1879.

ALASKA APPEAL(San. Fran.), March 15, 1880

CABELL WHITEHEAD

Dr. Whitehead is a prominent banker, ditch owner, and mining operator of Seward Peninsula. He came to Nome first in the spring of 1900 as the representative of the Bureau of the Mint. At that time he was chief assayer of the United States Mint, and his primary object in visiting the northern mining camp was to make a report upon its prospects and permanency.

Believing that Northwestern Alaska offered better opportunities than a Government job for accumulating a fortune, Dr. Whitehead resigned his office in the United States Mint to devote his entire time and energies to the work to be done in the development of Seward Peninsula.

His first conspicuous identification with the development of Northwestern Alaska was in connection with the Topkuk Ditch Company. This company owns an extensive and a valuable ditch property in the topkuk region of the peninsula. As manager of the Alaska Banking and Safe Deposit Company in Nome he has aided many miners in the work of developing their properties.

Dr. Whitehead is a native of Lynchburg, Virginia. He was born October 5, 1863. He belongs to an old Colonial family, his father's people having come from England in the early part of the sixteenth century and his mother's ancestors emigrating from the same country in 1728. He was educated in the Virginia public schools, and at the age of seventeen went to Lehigh University, South Bethlehem, Pennsylvania. He was graduated from the mining and engineering department of this institution in 1885 with the degree of B.M. He subsequently attended the Columbian University at Washington, D.C., receiving from this school the degree of Ph.D.

After he was graduated from the Lehigh School he went to Boise City, Idaho, to accept the position of assayer, at the United States Assay Office at that place. In 1888, when he was only twenty-five years old, he was appointed to the position of chief assayer in the Bureau of the Mint in Washington, D.C. He held this office until 1901, resigning to take up the work he is doing in Northwestern Alaska.

In 1895 Dr. Whitehead was sent to Europe to make a report on the subject of European mints, and to secure data to be used in building a new Government mint in Philadelphia. He visited the mints of England, France, and Germany.

Among Dr. Whitehead's duties as chief assayer was the supervising, assaying, and testing of all coins issued by the mints of the United States Government. The first coins made were used for this purpose. The requirements of this work not only necessitated a comprehensive knowledge in metallurgy, but proficiency in chemistry.

He is a member of the American Institute of Mining Engineers, of the American Chemical Society and the Society of Chemical Industry of England. During his career at the mint he made a specialty of electro-metallurgy, and has contributed liberally to the literature of chemistry and metallurgy. While Dr. Whitehead was chief assay of the mint, he trained a number of young men for positions in mint and assay offices of the United States. He visited Seattle in 1898 and established the Seattle Assay Office.

Dr. Whitehead was married October 1, 1889.

Mrs. Whitehead was formerly Miss Bena Ayres, daughter of Colonel E. W. Ayres, a well-known newspaper correspondent of Washington.

NOME AND SEWARD PENINSULA, 1905

F.B. WHITING

Dr. F.B. Whiting was the chief surgeon in charge of all medical and surgical work, on the White Pass & Yukon railroad, when construction work started in that project. Dr. Whiting went North to Skagway in the early spring of 1898, to take up his duties. He remained on that job for two years, when the railroad was completed. From Skagway, which had been his headquarters, he joined the stampede in Nome, where he opened an office and practiced in that camp for a year and a half, then returning to Seattle. In 1906 Mr. Heney secured the contract for the building of the Copper River and Northwestern railroad, and again named Dr. Whiting as the chief surgeon. Dr. Whiting remained on that job for four years, or until the railroad was finished. He thereupon returned to Seattle to resume his practice.

Dr. Whiting came of pioneering stock and was born in California.

ALASKA WEEKLY, September 7, 1928

J. POTTER WHITTREN

J. Potter Whittren is a civil engineer who has done the surveying for some of the important ditch enterprises of Seward Peninsula. He is a native of Boston, Massachusetts, and was born August 3, 1872. He was graduated from Harvard in the class of 1895 with the degree of B. S. During a period of two years he was assistant engineer for the Wisconsin Central Railroad. He went to Dawson in the spring os '99 and came to Nome in 1900. He is the consulting engineer of the Council City and Solomon River Railroad Company, and was associated engineer in the survey of the Topkuk Ditch and the Gold Rum Ditch. He surveyed the ditch line of the Solomon River Ditch Company, and is the mining engineer for the Goode Quartz Company, whose locations are

on Trilby Mountain in the Solomon River region. Mr. Whittren holds the appointment of Deputy United States Mineral Surveyor.
NOME AND SEWARD PENINSULA, 1905

JAMES WICKERSHAM

James Wickersham was born at Paloca, Marion County, Illinois on August 24, 1857. His father was Alexander Wickersham, a Kentuckian, and his mother Deborah Bell of Rochester, Illinois. He was admitted to the bar in 1880, became a Probate Judge in Pierce County, Washington, in 1894 and City Attorney of Tacoma and a member of the Washington Legislature in 1898.

Judge Wickersham came to Alaska in 1900. He lived a year at Eagle, a year at Nome, two years at Valdez, and 16 at Fairbanks. Since 1921, he had been a Juneau resident, maintaining an office in the Valentine Building and appearing bright and early almost every morning, even though in retirement.

Judge Wickersham on June 6, 1900, at the age of 43 was appointed Judge of the District Court in the Third Alaska Precinct, as it was then known. At an age when most men were beginning to think about settling down for their declining years, Jim Wickersham was just beginning a public career which was to carry him far and high. He was a Judge until December 31, 1907.

As Delegate from 1909 to 1921 and from 1931 to 1933, Judge Wickersham's principal achievement was the Alaska Act, known as the Wickersham Act, giving a measure of home rule at the Territory and setting up the system of Government which still prevails.

Among the important bills he introduced and succeeded in having passed in Congress were those incorporating the City of Fairbanks, establishing the Terr. Legislature, authorizing the location and construction of a Federal Government RR from Seward to Fairbanks, providing for the granting by the Federal Government of four sections of land as a site for the Agricultural College and School of

Mines, now the University of Alaska, and for the setting aside of Section 33 in each township in the Tanana Valley for the support of the educational institution; and authorizing the erection of the Terr. and Fed. Bldg. at Juneau.

Judge Wickersham edited eight volumes of the Alaska Law Reports and is the author of "Old Yukon," a comprehensive historical work of 514 pages, published last year.

In the course of his political and judicial activities, he visited every part of the Territory.

James Wickersham belonged to the Sons of the American Revolution, and American Anthropological Association, the Asiatic Society of Japan, the Masonic Lodge, the Elks, Eagles, Moose, and Pioneers of Alaska.

His BIBLIOGRAPHY OF ALASKAN LITERATURE 1724-1924 won him lasting fame as an author and scholar. His personal library which has been kept intact in Juneau is admitted to be the finest Alaska library anywhere.

Judge James Wickersham died in Juneau, Alaska October 24, 1939. Besides the widow, Wickersham is survived by a son, Lieut. Commander Darrell P. Wickersham of San Francisco.

DAILY ALASKA EMPIRE, October 24, 1939

JENS C. WIDSTEAD

Jens C. Widstead first went into the northern territory in 1889, there to accept a position under Dr. Sheldon Jackson, then head of the U.S. Bureau of Education's Alaska service, with headquarters in Sitka, then capital of the territory. It was Dr. Jackson who took the initiative in importing reindeer into Alaska, for the benefit of the native population of the territory, and it was Mr. Widstead and his brother-in-law, William A. Kjelman, who were sent to Norway to procure the first reindeer that were shipped to the Northland. Mr. Widstead went to the Seward Peninsula, Alaska, in the service of the bureau of education, before the Nome gold fields were

discovered, making his headquarter^S in Port
Clarence. When the gold fields were
discovered, Mr. Widstead severed his connection
with the bureau of education, and followed
mining. He has made his headquarters in Nome
since that town was founded, and is a pioneer
of the Seward Peninsula. He is now the
Northwestern Alaska member of the Alaska Game
Commission.

ALASKA WEEKLY, June 1, 1928

WARREN C. WILKINS

Mr. Wilkins has had an interesting and
varied career in Alaska, beginning in the
spring of 1897. He was an architect and
builder in Philadelphia, Pa., and started for
the Klonkike in 1897 on a vacation, intending
to remain only a few months. While in Dawson
he acquired several valuable mining interests
and among other properties, 49 bench, Bonanza
Creek, which has, since he relinquished it,
produced $1,000,000. He staked this claim in
the spring of '98. He returned to the states
in the following fall and went back to Dawson
in 1899. In 1900 he made a trip to the head-
waters of the Koyukuk. He descended this
stream in a rowboat, floating down the Yukon to
St. Michael. This trip covered a period of
twenty-two days. He had grub-staked a man in
Dawson in 1899 to go to Nome, and through this
grub-stake arrangement acquired some property
on Dexter and Glacier Creeks, which he still
holds.

He went to Philadelphia and in the spring
of 1904 organized the Seward Peninsula Mining
Company in that city. This company purchased
the holdings of the Nome River and New York
Hydraulic Mining Company which owned 1,280
acres of mining ground on Nome River above the
mouth of Dexter Creek. During the summer of
1904 Mr. Wilkins prospected this ground with a
keystone drill and having satisfied himself of
the values which it contained, succeeded in
securing the necessary funds to work the
property.

Mr. Wilkins was the first man that ever

went from Haines Mission across to the Yukon with a pack train. His first trip in Alaska was made by this route. He took ten horses with him, and before reaching his destination was compelled to kill several of the animals for food for himself and companions.

W. C. Wilkins was born at Mt. Pleasant, Pa., and educated at the Mt. Pleasant Classic and Scientific Institute. He was equipped for the profession of civil engineering, and for a period of twelve years was an architect and builder in the city of Philadelphia.

NOME AND SEWARD PENINSULA, 1905

EDWARD GRAY WILL

In the early spring of 1904, Mr. E. G. Will was unanimously nominated as a candidate for the council. In the campaign he made a number of public speeches which showed he was a student of political economy, entertaining advanced ideas on the subject of socialism and believing in a government "of the people, for the people and by the people." He was elected by a majority.

The fact came to light during this campaign that Mr. Will always had taken a deep interest in politics, being led thereto by industrial tendencies, and the firmly rooted idea which he has often expressed the "the wealth producers should cease to be the slaves of the wealth absorbers." When a resident of South Dakota in 1890 he helped to organize the Independent Party, which was afterward merged into the Populist Party, and in 1896 he took the stump in behalf of Wm. J. Bryan.

Mr. Will was born in Iowa May 24, 1861. His parents were James Will and Margaret Gray Will, of Dundee, Scotland. When he was twenty-one he owned a stock ranch in Jerauld County, South Dakota, and this was his home for thirteen years. In 1895 he moved to Le Mars, Iowa, where he resided until 1898, when he went to Dawson and engaged in mining. He came to Nome in 1900, and since then has been mining and conducting a transfer and freighting business.

E. G. Will and Miss Lizzie M. Prescott were married in Preston, Minn., Dec. 24, 1884. They have five children, two sons and three daughters, all born in South Dakota. Their names are Cameron Gray, Julia Enid, Lizzie Marie, Edward Clarkson and Bessie Rowena. The family recently removed from Le Mars to a new home built for them on University Heights, Seattle.

NOME AND SEWARD PENINSULA, 1905

HENRY WILLETT

Henry Willett, in March 1888 went to Juneau, Alaska. In the same year, he went over the Chilkoot Pass on the Fortymile country. He operated there for three years, and then came outside. He went back to the Fortymile district in the spring of 1892, and operated there until the great Klondike discovery, which called him in 1896, to the new gold placer camp. Here he operated until the year 1897, when he came outside, enroute to Maine, where he was married. He went back to the Klondike in 1898, and continued operating on No. 30 above discovery on Bonanza Creek. At the same time, he owned Nos. 10, 29 and 31 below discovery on the same creek. In the year 1904, Mr. Willett went to Fairbanks, Alaska, and operated on No. 5 above discovery on Cleary Creek, where he remained for a period of seven years. In 1911, he went to the Ruby district, where he operated on Trail Creek for nearly two years. He then returned to the Klondike. Mr. Willett came outside to Seattle in 1921.

ALASKA WEEKLY, April 25, 1930

GEORGE T. WILLIAMS

George T. Williams is one of the organizers of the Northwestern Commercial Company, and is the vice-president of that corporation. He is president of the North Coast Lighterage Company, one of the leading companies engaged in the business of lighterage at Nome.

Mr. Williams was born at Philadelphia, March 14, 1872, and was educated in the public schools of Pennsylvania. He learned the trade of a machinist in Philadelphia and became an expert workman. He was employed in Cramp's ship yard for nine years and has helped to build several of the large battleships which are now a part of the Navy of the United States.

He severed his relations with the Cramps in August 1897, and started for Skagway, Alaska. He was among the first men to go over White Pass, and arrived at Lake Bennett September 17. The lakes were crossed and the Yukon de-scended in a canvas boat, and Dawson was reached October 1.

He devoted some time to mining and in 1898-'99 engaged in shipping goods from Seattle to Dawson. In 1898 he made the record trip from Lake Bennett to Dawson. This trip which never has been equaled was made in four days and seventeen hours. He was a pilot of one of the first boats on the upper Yukon.

In the fall of 1899, with others, he organized the Northwestern Commercial Company, which is now the largest commercial and transportation company operating in the Nome country. The North Coast Lighterage Company of which he is president, is composed of members of the Northwestern Commercial Company. He constructed the first aerial cable way at Nome for discharging cargoes from the sea.

Mr. Williams and Miss Amanda Harris were married in Camden, New Jersey, January 11, 1900.

NOME AND SEWARD PENINSUAL, 1905

JOHN I. WINN

Judge Winn was born at Rosnoke, Missouri, October 1, 1861, and was reared and educated in that State. He taught school for several years in the Dakota and other States. He opened a law office at Snohomish, Washington in the mid-eighties, and in 1899, at the first election of the new State of Washington, he was elected Superior Court Judge on the Democratic Ticket for the counties of Snohomish, Skagit, Whatcom and San Juan. He transferred his headquarters to Bellingham, then Whatcom, whatcom county. The Legislature divided his district and he was re-elected in 1892 Superior Judge for Whatcom and San Juan counties for the 1893-97 term. Shortly after the expiration of his term on the bench, Judge Winn came to Juneau, forming a law partnership with the late John F. Malony, under the firm name of Malony and Winn. When this partnership was dissolved, Judge Winn took into partnership R.S. Weldon, the firm being Winn and Weldon with offices at Juneau and Skagway, Judge Winn remaining at Juneau with Weldon in the Skagway office. Later Newark L. Burton was associated with Judge Winn in the firm of Winn and Burton.

Winn was associated in most of the mining litigation that centered at Juneau. In the course of the years he practiced law in Juneau, Judge Winn accumulated a comfortable fortune, most of which was invested in Los Angeles and Seattle apartment houses and residential properties.

Judge Winn was not only a busy lawyer, but he took an active interest in politics. He was President of the Juneau Democratic Club during the campaign of 1916 and 1918 and was elected a delegate to the Democratic National Convention that renominated President Wilson in 1916.

Judge John Winn died in Los Angeles, August 29, 1926. He is survived by his widow, a sister of former Senator Samuel H. Piles of Seattle, now Minister to Columbia, and two sons, Roland H. Winn and John R. Winn, Jr.

ALASKA WEEKLY, September 3, 1926
ALASKA DAILY EMPIRE, August 30, 1926

CHARLES G. WULFF

Charles G. Wulff was born in Brooklyn, N.Y., May 26, 1877. He went to Valdez, Alaska, in March, 1898; remained in that vicinity for a year and a half, and then returned to his Brooklyn home.

In the spring of 1901, Mr. Wulff again headed for Valdez, accompanied this time by Joe Bourke and Bill Wagner, now deceased. Mr. Wulff was employed in various capacities until

1912, when he became interested in the VALDEZ PROSPECTOR, assuming the position of editor and manager. In 1915 he disposed of his interests in the paper and returned to Brooklyn, to assume the position of sales manager for a large coal company, which was controlled by his uncle, two brother and himself.

In 1920 he sold his equity in the coal concern and accompanied by his family moved to San Diego, Cal. He died Tuesday, August 5, 1930, in San Francisco. He is survived by his wife, Mrs. Lillie Wulff and three children, all born in Valdez, Alaska. Miss Lillian Wulff, the eldest, a university graduate, is a high school teacher in San Diego. The second, a son, Lee Wulff, a graduate of Berkeley University, is an artist by profession, now employed on one of the New York newspapers. The youngest, Miss Andri, was recently graduated from the Southern California University.

ALASKA WEEKLY, August 8, 1930

DANIEL J. WYNKOOP

D. J. Wynkoop is a resident of Nome who possesses a general and comprehensive knowledge of economic geology, mineralogy and practical mining, having devoted a number of years of his life to the study of the technical side of these subjects, and having had a wide practical experience in the field of mining operations.

His ancestors came from Holland to America in the seventeenth century. He was born in Jefferson County, Pennsylvania, October 21, 1852. When he was twelve years old he moved with his father to the oil regions, and at the age of twenty-one he was an operator in oil. A few years later he made a trip to Colorado where he became interested in quartz mining for a short time. In 1891 he went west in search of health. He located in Tacoma, Washington, and continued to follow the business of mining. Improved health was followed by a serious injury resulting from the collision of a collier and a passenger steamer on the Willamett River. His son was killed in this collision and both himself and wife were seriously hurt. This accident occurred in September, 1892, and during the four years which were required for his recovery he farmed in the State of Washington and applied himself to the study of geology.

He came to Nome in the spring of 1900 as manager of a company. The company went to pieces and left him stranded, but being a man of resources and practical ability he found employment. He has done a great deal of "mushing" in this country, having made five trips to the Arctic slope over the ice. He served as deputy recorder under United States Commissioner Tom Noyes of the Fairhaven District, and is now connected with the United States Commissioner's office in the Nome District. Mr. Wynkoop helped to organize the Alaska Academy of Sciences. He has taken great interest in the work of this institution. He was married in 1876 to Ella E. Davis, of Edinberg, Pennsylvania. Two daughters, Edith M. and Hattie E., both of whom are married, are their only surviving children.

NOME AND SEWARD PENINSULA, 1905

GRIFF YARNELL

Griff Yarnell is one of the pioneers and successful miners of the Kougarok District. He came to Nome from Dawson in 1900, and immediately went to the Kougarok region. He arrived in Nome during the month of April, and his first trip to this great interior district was made over the snow. He staked mining property on Dahl and Quartz Creeks. In the following season, 1901, he began mining operations on Dahl Creek. In 1902 he put in a line of sluice-boxes and was able to hire a force of from five to ten men. The following year the force was augmented, and he became interested in ditch construction. And thus his business of mining has grown from its modest inception to extensive and successful operations. Two hundred dollars the pan has been taken from his Dahl Creek claim. The prospects of the gold production of his properties, with water supplied from ditches, and with the aid of modern appliances, are very encouraging.

Mr. Yarnell was born in Center County, Pennsylvania, in 1869. His early life was devoted to hard work.

NOME AND SEWARD PENINSULA, 1905

C. W. YOUNG

One of the foremost captains of industry in southeastern Alaska is C.W. Young, who from small beginnings built up a great mercantile establishment which stands at the very head of commercial affairs in this part of Alaska. Mr. Young was born in the state of Pennsylvania on March 30, 1850. He came to Alaska on the old steamer Idaho, landing at Juneau on June 4, 1885. He was expecting to return at once to the states, but he saw opportunity for a carpenter and builder. He began to construct cabins and houses. His first work, he said, was to cut down a colossal Russian billiard table to the American size. It so happened that there was a great demand for buildings of the better class in Juneau at that time, and he took numerous contracts for business and residence structures.

He soon commenced the sale of lumber for H.E. Boggs, the sawmill man. Rough lumber at that time brought $25 a thousand. The Boggs mill was at Sheep Creek. From this beginning Mr. Young finally built up a business furnishing material for the building trade. In 1893 he had a government contract and built the Japonsky Island Magazine and wharf and repaired the old Russian castle at Sitka and also the jail and court house. Soon after this he quit taking contracts and confined his attention exclusively to his mercantile business. During the years that he followed construction work he employed many men and erected nearly all the first-class buildings which were up to that time in Juneau.

His business prospered and he rapidly became one of th mercantile factors in this part of Alaska. In 1906 he sold the C.W. Young

Company to J.C. McBride, in which sale was included the large store and warehouses of the company. Mr. Young has been from the very first one of the most prominent citizens of Juneau, and when the city government was organized, he became a member of the first city government.

ALASKA MONTHLY MAGAZINE, October 1907

R. B. ZEHNER

R. B. Zehner was born at Cheyenne, Wyoming, 1870. During the gold stampede to Colorado in 1866 his parents journeyed overland by stage from New York to Denver, where they remained until the construction of the Union Pacific Railroad caused them, for business reasons, to move to Cheyenne.

Mr. Zehner's father was a goldsmith by trade and the son, after finishing his schooling in the town schools, took up the trade with his father. After spending two years as an apprentice, he entered a watch construction school in Minnesota, where he remained for one year. Soon after leaving school he became connected with a jewelry house in St. Louis.

As opportunities soon presented themselves in other localities, Mr. Zehner left St. Louis to accept a position in Chicago. Later he went to Laramie City, Wyoming, where he was placed in charge of a large retail jewelry store. Upon leaving Laramie City, Mr. Zehner traveled extensively in the Western states in the interest of the jewelry business, finally locating with W. H. Fink, the Seattle jeweler, in 1897.

The Nome gold excitement that caused the historical stampede of 1900 drew Mr. Zehner from his business and stimulated him to take passage on the steamer Centennial for the Northland. On arriving at Nome he found that the store he was to occupy had not been built, and he had to camp on the beach without even a tent for shelter. Quarters finally being secured, he opened up a jewelry store and continued in business until 1901, when he sold his stock of goods and left for his mines that he had purchased in the Kougarok country.

He found on reaching his property that a difficult undertaking confronted him, as the ground was frozen to unknown depths, and that in order to do any prospecting it would be necessary to devise some means for thawing. He set to work, and by heating rocks in fires built from the small willows to be had, succeeded in thawing several holes to bedrock, and was rewarded by locating a pay-streak, which, however, was not thick enough to merit the slow and expensive operations. After sluicing for a short time on the claim he returned to Nome.

When Mr. Zehner arrived in Nome after his summer's mining experience he reopened his jewelry store, but soon moved to the location he now occupies, in the central part of the city, opposite the Cape Nome Bank.

NOME AND SEWARD PENINSULA, 1905

Bibliography

Newspapers

ADDISON COUNTY INDEPENDENT, Middlebury, Vermont
ALASKA APPEAL, San Francisco, California
ALASKA CATHOLIC, Juneau, Alaska
ALASKA DAILY CAPITAL, Juneau, Alaska
ALASKA DAILY EMPIRE, Juneau, Alaska
ALASKA DISPATCH, Seattle, Washington
ALASKA MINING RECORD, Juneau, Alaska
ALASKA WEEKLY, Seattle, Washington
ALASKAN, Sitka, Alaska
ANCHORAGE DAILY TIMES, Anchorage, Alaska
CORDOVA DAILY TIMES, Cordova, Alaska
DAILY ALASKA EMPIRE, Juneau, Alaska
DAILY ALASKAN, Skagway, Alaska
DAWSON DAILY NEWS, Dawson, Y.T., Canada
FAIRBANKS NEWS MINER, Fairbanks, Alaska
JUNEAU EMPIRE, Juneau, Alaska
JUNEAU SUNDAY CAPITAL, Juneau, Alaska
KETCHIKAN MINING JOURNAL, Ketchikan, Alaska
MIDNIGHT SUN, Skagway, Alaska
SITKA SENTINEL, Sitka, Alaska
STROLLER'S WEEKLY, Juneau/Douglas, Alaska
THLINGET, Sitka, Alaska
VALDEZ MINER, Valdez, Alaska
VERSTOVIAN, Sitka, Alaska
WEEKLY STAR, Whitehorse, Y.T., Canada
WRANGELL SENTINEL, Wrangell, Alaska

Books

Harrison, E.A. NOME AND SEWARD PENINSULA: HISTORY, DESCRIPTION, BIOGRAPHIES, AND STORIES. Seattle: Harrison, 1905.

Periodicals

ALASKA'S MAGAZINE. Juneau, Alaska: Magazine Company, April 1905.
ALASKA MONTHLY MAGAZINE. Juneau, Alaska: Johnson-Courant, 1907.
ALASKA-YUKON MAGAZINE. Juneau-Seattle: Harrison, 1907-1909.
ALASKAN CHURCHMAN. Fairbanks: Protestant Episcopal Church, 1906--.
ALL ALASKA REVIEW. Seward: 1915-1917.
PATHFINDER. Valdez: Pathfinder Publishing Co., 1919-1926.